LITERACIES LOST
When Students Move
from a Progressive Middle School
to a Traditional High School

Published by Teachers College Press, 1234 Amsterdam Avenue, New York, NY 10027

Library of Congress Cataloging-in-Publication Data

Wells, M. Cyrene.
  Literacies lost : when students move from a progressive middle
school to a traditional high school / M. Cyrene Wells ; foreword by
JoBeth Allen.
      p. cm.
  Includes bibliographical references and index.
  ISBN 0-8077-3478-0 (cloth).—ISBN 0-8077-3477-2 (paper)
    1. Articulation (Education)—United States. 2. Literacy—United
States—Case studies. I. Title.
LB1626.W45 1995
371.2'914—dc20   95-30977

ISBN 0-8077-3477-2 (paper)
ISBN 0-8077-3478-0 (cloth)
Printed on acid-free paper
Manufactured in the United States of America
01 00 99 98 97 96 95   8 7 6 5 4 3 2 1

LITERACIES LOST
When Students Move
from a Progressive Middle School
to a Traditional High School

M. CYRENE WELLS

FOREWORD by JoBeth Allen

Teachers College, Columbia University
New York and London

To Jim

To Jim

Contents

Foreword

Teachers contemplating innovative educational strategies frequently ask, "What about next year?" They worry that even if students do well in their classes designing their own learning projects, reading real books, learning to edit their own writing, working on group projects, or participating in the evaluation of their own learning, the students will be at a disadvantage when they move to a more traditional setting of textbook assignments, excerpted or contrived texts, teacher editing, "don't look at your neighbor's paper," and 0–100 grading. What happens to students who make this transition? Will they be able to reconcile their "situated selves" with their "enduring selves"?

Cyrene Wells provides the clearest picture to date of what students do to adapt when they move from a school that honors their individuality, potential, and sense of responsibility, to another school where adults believe students need to be controlled and molded into conformity. She starts "Hanging Around with Kids" (Chapter 1). In a chapter that will undoubtedly serve as a model for other researchers, Wells situates herself as a trustworthy narrator, describing how she gained the confidence of adolescent students that allowed her to document their last year of middle school and first year of a very different kind of high school. Through the lives of the students we come to know best, Ginny, John, Nicky, Chad, and Monica, we learn what a school community can mean for learners, and what a community school can mean for a citizenry.

At Meadowbrook Community School (MCS), every student has what Penny Oldfather calls an "honored voice"; in the Meadowbrook school community, every citizen has a voice at the annual school meeting (usually over six hours long), even the anti-taxes/student choice/fun and pro-grammar/worksheets/tests contingent. The community gathers to articulate, argue, and agree on visions and values, facilities and funding. Students attend. They know their education is important to adults, important enough to spark heated debate, for, as Wells points out, "community and harmony are not synonymous."

The same ongoing discussion takes place within the school community, as educators articulate core values and base instructional decisions on shared beliefs. For example, teachers at Meadowbrook have restructured the school around the values of supportive, caring relationships among and between students and teachers. Monica calls Meadowbrook "a big family kind of school." Increasingly, educators at all levels are learning that schools that expect and foster success for all its students, not just its academic elite, are focusing on relationships. Meadowbrook Community School builds relationships among students of diverse interests and talents, and between students and teachers who "really care."

The teachers at Whitmore High School (WHS) have a different vision of effective schooling. They equate responsibility with obeying rules, put down the "freedom" of middle school, and seem to have low expectations. While MCS has a 23-page philosophy statement and no encompassing list of rules, WHS has no clearly articulated philosophy and a 68-page student handbook consisting primarily of procedures, rules, and consequences. Wells is not critical of individual teachers at Whitmore, for many of them are less than satisfied with the school culture, but she clearly demonstrates that "without a shared understanding of what teachers and administrators collectively believed to be educationally important, order won out." And she shows, intimately and painfully, how schooling based on this belief system affects Ginny, John, Nicky, Chad, and Monica.

Every reader will recognize a student, a daughter, a son, or himself or herself in these carefully drawn young people. Chad is the one who really got to me. He struggled in middle school, but never alone; he had friends who helped him, teachers who believed he could achieve meaningful growth and helped him do it. In high school, he naively trusted that if he worked hard, he would do well. He didn't understand a system that did not value him as an individual. "He didn't understand that his effort in classes would not outweigh his test results."

If you begin to feel that the answer to the question raised at the beginning of this foreword is to eschew innovation in favor of cross-grade conformity, let me shift to the impact I believe Cyrene Wells' well-told-tale can and will have on education. Wells quotes Eisner as saying that the role of storytellers is to tell about how things were, and the role of listeners is to "use what we have been told to make decisions about what will be" (1991, p. 202). After reading this book, I believe there are several ways we can use what we have learned to make critical decisions.

1. *Help students have a voice in their education.* At the end of the book, Wells asks, "What if teachers at the high school had asked students how they preferred to learn?" There is an evolving answer to that question in the longitudinal work of a group of young California researchers who began in Sally Thomas' fifth and sixth grade studying their own motivation "to be or not to be" engaged learners (Garcia, Gilmore, Rodriguez, & Thomas, in press). They have continued to research their own learning with adult researchers

and are currently exploring what role they as students have in informing and shaping their own high school learning experiences through talking with teachers about how they learn best.

2. *Articulate core values.* A small but growing number of schools all over the country are engaging in the ongoing, difficult, and enlightening process of articulating their core values, setting goals, and examining their current policies and practices in relation to their articulated values. The ones most familiar to me are the Georgia League of Professional Schools and the Atlanta League of Professional Schools. These schools not only develop collaborative statements of core values, but also they design working charters for shared decision making, work continuously on educating all students, and evaluate their effectiveness through action research.

3. *Form cross-school study groups.* I have already sent this book (in manuscript form) to an outstanding elementary principal who is working with teachers and community members to design and establish a genuine learning community in a newly built middle school. I think it would be helpful initially for teachers in her previous, innovative elementary school to read the book together with teachers at the new middle school, and to look at the students' transitions as well as to design what middle school can be. Perhaps in a year or two they will read the book again, but this time with a group of high school teachers. Then maybe those high school teachers will invite a group of professors, especially those who teach freshmen, to read and discuss this book.

Literacies Lost must not leave us with a feeling of hopelessness, in spite of the sadness for individual children. It provides us with two models of what schooling can mean to learners, and demands that we ask of ourselves and our institutions what schooling means for our students. It insists that we look through the eyes of young people, that we develop the peripheral vision of a dynamic, inclusive community rather than the tunnel vision of institutional insularity and unexamined policy. I read this book the first time for the story, and a finely crafted narrative it is. I will read it again with colleagues as a call to action. Perhaps, now that Wells has documented how things are, each of us can make better decisions about what will be.

—*JoBeth Allen*

REFERENCES

Eisner, E. (1991). *The enlightened eye: Qualitative inquiry and the enhancement of educational practice.* New York: Macmillan.

Garcia, F., Gilmore, J., Rodriguez, P., & Thomas, S. (in press). It's like having a metal detector at the door. *Theory Into Practice.* (Themed issue on "Learning from Student Voices")

Acknowledgments

I will always be grateful for the experience of having been a participant observer among Nicky, Chad, Monica, John, Ginny, Rachelle, Sharon, Jan, Carl, and their peers in eighth and ninth grades. I wish I could use their real names as I thank them for their candor, spirit, and willingness to "take in" an adult researcher. They provided me with a lens that personalizes educational theory and practices. Administrators and teachers in both fieldwork sites were hospitable and generous with their time. I often wondered if I'd have been as inviting as they, had I been in their places.

Having conducted this study as a doctoral student at the University of New Hampshire, I received thoughtful advice and careful feedback from Grant Cioffi, Ellen Corcoran, Ann Diller, Tom Newkirk, Don Graves, and John Lofty. They, along with Elizabeth Chiseri-Strater, John Carney, Burt Feintuch, Jane Hansen, Pearl Rosenberg, and Pat Sullivan helped me establish a knowledge base from which I could work. My mentor and friend, Tom Schram, carefully read and responded to various drafts, introduced me to the big ideas of educational anthropology, shared his books and papers with me, and saw to it that I went to conferences and met people who could further help me. JoBeth Allen, Penny Oldfather, Judith Preissle, Denny Taylor, Henry Trueba, and Harry Wolcott provided encouragement and specific advice. It should be evident throughout this book that my thoughts have been informed by the work of others. The social construction of knowledge continues.

Introduction

Meadowbrook Community School's graduating eighth-grade class of 1992 stood on the stage of the school's multipurpose room. The 40 students had just finished singing "With a Little Help from My Friends," and their families were applauding. Shoulder to shoulder in their nylon rented gowns and precarious tasseled mortarboards, they looked more than a little self-conscious as they grinned out at the audience. Parents flashed cameras, younger siblings fidgeted in their chairs, and soon there would be parties all over town. Yet for all the excitement and anticipation, the graduates had mixed feelings. They were happy, no doubt about it, but they also felt a little sad and somewhat uneasy about leaving so familiar a place. The no-longer-eighth-graders/soon-to-be-high-school-students stood, not only on a stage, but at an educational juncture. Their beliefs and understandings about literacy and learning, established in the context of community and holistic practices, were soon to be tested in new learning environments.

Studies of secondary schools (e.g., Boyer, 1983; Goodlad, 1984; Grant, 1988; McNeil, 1988; Newmann, 1992) indicate that high schools have been less receptive to structural and pedagogical change than their elementary and middle school counterparts. That means students leave child-centered, process-oriented, and curriculum-integrated schools to attend traditional high schools. What happens to them, their developing literacies, their learning, and their understandings? We really don't know. In colloquial terms, it seems the equivalent of dropping off children on doorsteps and hoping the people inside will take good care of them—or conversely, picking up those children and rearing them, never wondering about their past.

In order to understand the effect of such a transition, I decided to be with students in the eighth grade and then follow a group of them to high school. Although I was interested in the students' entire learning experience, I was particularly drawn to their ongoing literacy development. I found, however, that I couldn't study literate behaviors without considering a host of other issues having to do with school and classroom cultures: shared vision, cultural values, learning environments, relationships among teachers and students, and the communal nature of learning. Collaborative talk, textbook grammar exercises, or reflective writing, for example, could be valued or dismissed—depending on the context of their use. The whole of school culture, not just classroom practice, would influence what and how students learned.

LITERACY AS SOCIALLY CONSTRUCTED

Literacy is wonderfully complex. Given even the rudimentary definition of literacy as the ability to read and write, we find ourselves asking questions: What is reading? What constitutes writing? Are some kinds of reading and writing more important than others? Who decides? How does purpose affect the act of reading? How does audience influence writing? In classrooms, how do teachers' and students' expectations affect the reading and writing that take place there?

At one time scholars understood reading and writing to be solitary cognitive acts in which readers obtained meaning from texts by decoding letters and words and in which writers encoded their thoughts through manipulation of syntactic and formal structures. Reading and writing were viewed primarily as cognitive operations (Bloome, 1986). Certainly literacy involves multiple linguistic and cognitive interactions, but educational theorists and researchers (e.g., Bloome, 1986; Edelsky, 1991; Erickson, 1988; Freire, 1993; Heath, 1983; Robinson, 1988; Scribner & Cole, 1988; Szwed, 1988) have come to understand that sociocultural context plays a primary role in literacy and literacy development. Cook-Gumperz (1986) asserts that literacy is a "socially constructed phenomenon" and writes that a social perspective on literacy looks not only at cognitive and linguistic operations but also at the social and environmental conditions necessary for their acquisition, development, and demonstration.

As Scribner (1988) so succinctly puts it, literacy is a "many-meaninged thing." The meanings we attach to literacy, the expectations we hold for it, and the value we give it are largely dependent on the context in which it takes place. Even in the context of schools, literacy can be a "many-meaninged thing." Social organization and cultural patterning not only influence literacy practices and development, but those literacy practices also affect social organization and the culture of classrooms and schools. Erickson (1988) notes that knowledge and skills, taught and learned in school, are not only inseparable from the concrete circumstances of their use, but that they cannot easily be separated from the situation of their acquisition as a social form and way of life in school. "It is reasonable to expect that various kinds of literacies might represent a variety of interests and be embedded in a variety of belief systems" (p. 205).

Anyone who is familiar with schools and classrooms knows that their environments, while similar in many ways, can be remarkably different in

terms of shared vision, ethos, structure and organization, and articulated as well as nonarticulated goals. Researchers (e.g., Edelsky, 1991; Grant, 1988; McNeil, 1988; Wagner, 1994) have documented how aspects of school environment can determine what and how students learn.

COMMUNITY

Bloome (1986) suggests that the ways we interpret text and use written language depend a great deal on the group we're in. We know this to be true from our own literate experiences. How often do we pass our work along for another opinion or read something because we want to be part of a conversation? It's no different for younger learners. Given certain classroom situations, "hot" authors circulate among communities of readers, writers create stories to entertain themselves and their friends, and writing partners help one another get "unstuck." If these literate interactions are not classroom/school-sanctioned, they may go underground, or they might not occur at all. If we accept that learning and literacy are socially constructed, then we need to explore how learning environments can be structured to facilitate the social interaction that is key to children's ongoing cognitive and social development.

Sergiovanni (1994) proposes that schools envision themselves as communities where students, administrators, teachers, and supporting communities work together to learn and to develop common goals. Issues of relationship are key. Who has control? How is that control exerted? Whose voice(s) are heard and honored? How are responsibilities shared? How are decisions made? How is consensus achieved? How are difficulties worked out? Communal interactions—listening, talking, writing, reflecting, and reading—are part of community building. When these notions are translated to the classroom, they not only support literacy and learning behaviors but become conduits to building and maintaining that community. In this context, language, both written and verbal, has multiple purposes.

> The learning community is a language environment. Students undergo experiences that place demands on their understanding, and they come to grips with those experiences through language. And because language maintains its usefulness—does not become an object of study—language competence is gained while learning about the world. From this perspective learning is the result of an interplay between the learner and the "other." (Peterson, 1992, p. 75)

As Peterson further describes learning communities, competition is downplayed and approximation and peer collaboration support the process of learning. With teacher guidance, students make group and individual deci-sions about what they will learn and how they will learn it. Negotiation, through written and verbal language, is ongoing. Students take responsibil-ity for their own and others' learning. Classmates and teachers speak of car-ing for one another.

This concept of literacy development as part and parcel of a "learning community" is in contrast to the more traditional notion of teaching and learning as a "delivery system," one in which teachers "deliver" and students "pick up." In this study, community was central to the Meadowbrook stu-dents' school experience before they entered high school. Layers of commu-nity, both school and town, dynamically interacting with classroom com-munities, impacted students' learning and their understandings about how they learned and what was important to know.

ASSUMPTIONS

In order to understand these connections and contextualize students' expe-riences, I needed to take what George Spindler (1982) describes as an ethno-graphic world view—one that emphasizes what natives understand (and don't understand) about their own cultures and social behaviors. Importantly, this "world view" assumes that all behaviors (including literate practices) occur within contexts and that contexts change and people change within them.

Schools serve as agents of cultural transmission, passing from one gen-eration to the next complex sets of values, beliefs, and attitudes (Spindler, 1963). Individual schools, even classrooms, might be conceived of as cul-tures—each as a variant adaptation within the larger culture of schooling and within an inclusive world culture (Erickson, 1984; Spindler, 1982). Spe-cific areas of knowledge chosen for systematic transmission, the status of teachers and students, goals and methods of instruction, and curricular restrictions depend on the fundamental beliefs and values of those in charge of schools (Hansen, 1979). Depending on elements such as supporting com-munity, perceived mission, and leadership, schools might function to trans-mit knowledge and understandings that are particular to their local communi-ties, as well as those that are widely represented in the larger culture. Thus, while they share common interests, schools can differ markedly in terms of climate, philosophy, and leadership. Students reared in one school might have different common experiences resulting in different shared expectations than students in another school.

Culture is learned (Goodenough, 1981), and enculturation is a continu-ing process of conscious or unconscious conditioning to a given body of custom (Herskovits, 1948). It stands to reason that schools transmit not only

cultural understandings that allow children to operate outside the school (e.g., the ability to read and write) but also understandings about how knowledge is learned (e.g., that reading improves with reading or that collaboration is a viable way of studying).

Students develop beliefs and understandings about what is worthwhile knowledge, what skills are important to acquire, and in what ways they will best learn this knowledge and acquire these skills. Whether they acquire them directly through instruction (e.g., a teacher telling students that writing gets better through practice), infer them through the statements and actions of others (e.g., a letter to the editor of a local newspaper complaining about lack of grammar instruction), or gain them by watching the example of elders and peers, students develop understandings that directly affect how they will relate to instruction.

Erickson (1982) has written that in school or out, the teacher's (or competent adult's) implicit and explicit beliefs about learning are part of the student's learning environment. In other words, children develop attitudes and beliefs about learning, just as they learn the names of state capitals and how to write in cursive. And, while they may forget specific information, they'll probably remember the "feel" of a classroom/school and notions about themselves as learners. These early understandings become part of their "enduring selves," a perception of the self based on early socialization (Spindler & Spindler, 1989; Trueba, Rodriguez, Zou, & Cintrón, 1993). (The "situated-self," in contrast, is the part of ourselves that continually adapts to new settings and cultural values.) The lifelong process of adaptation and enculturation, then, is a matter of reconciling the situated self with the enduring self. Meadowbrook students would draw on prior understandings and expectations of school as they set about continuing their educations at the high school. They would, however, necessarily make adaptations that would impact their development as learners and literate people.

OVERVIEW

Conceptualizing students' transition from one school to another in terms of enculturation and adaptation suggests an ethnographic approach—a cultural description and interpretation of the social interactions among students, teachers, and school/community adults. In order to learn about the culture of Meadowbrook Community School and to understand students' beliefs about learning and literacy, I spent an academic year with all the students in the eighth grade before going to high school with nine of them. In both places, I studied general school culture as well as students' social and classroom interactions. The idea was to contextualize students' behaviors and adaptations—

in terms of both cultures and from emic and etic perspectives (the participants' points of view as well as the researcher's analytical one).

Because Meadowbrook didn't have a high school, graduating eighth-grade students selected from among five local secondary schools. Eleven of the students chose Whitmore High School (9 of the 11 had parental permission to participate in this study). The names of students, teachers, and other adults are pseudonyms, as are the names of schools and towns.

Since this kind of research is dependent on relationships, it's important to establish where I "fit" in the research relationship. Chapter 1 details the process of my "participant" observation among adolescents and extends dialogue about whether adults can truly be "participants" among children and adolescents. The next two chapters describe Meadowbrook, its school, and life in the eighth grade. The detailed description in these chapters serves as baseline data for students' later experiences. Chapter 2 contextualizes the school within its larger community, describes the connection between town and school, and then examines the Meadowbrook Community School, focusing on its philosophy and its people. Chapter 3 moves the reader inside the eighth grade community for a view of how it was organized and a sense of what was important to students and teachers. Five students, introduced at the end in the chapter, play important roles in the rest of the book. The description of the first two chapters assumes added significance as Chapters 4 and 5 unfold, detailing a very different life at Whitmore High School. Chapter 4 begins with a short history of Whitmore and the high school before it focuses on the school's unarticulated emphasis on order and control, evidenced by aspects such as policies, scheduling, textbooks, and grading. Chapter 5 shows how this emphasis played out in students' social life, classes, schoolwork, and literacy development.

While analysis is inherent in the descriptions of earlier chapters, the last three chapters focus on why there were differences in ethos between the two schools and what those differences meant in terms of students' adaptations and beliefs about literacy and learning. Chapter 6 looks at the schools in terms of ethos—the nature of community and society and the role of relationship. The second half of the chapter explores students' adaptive strategies in moving from one kind of school to the other and suggests that knowledge of the second culture allowed students to play games in order to maintain deep-seated beliefs. Chapter 7 directly compares the kinds of literacies students practiced in eighth and ninth grades. Given the results of this analysis, the high school is then reexamined in terms of its cultural expectations and teachers' intentions. Chapter 8 reflects on community in terms of the interrelatedness of relationship, control, and structure—and considers implications for cultural change.

This is a story of particular students leaving one specific elementary school to attend one specific high school. It may exemplify features and patterns found in other places, but it is the reader who will make those connections. As Eisner (1991a, p. 202) points out, "We listen to story-tellers and learn about how things were, and we use what we have been told to make decisions about what will be."

CHAPTER 1

Hanging Around with Kids: Participant Observation Among Adolescents

It is clear that the role *of the ethnographer must vary from site to site. Kinds and intensity of participation that are appropriate, sex roles, obtrusiveness (participants may be more obtrusive than passive observers), and multiplicity of demands on the ethnographer all vary greatly. There are no hard and fast rules.*

George and Louise Spindler
"Cultural Process and Ethnography:
An Anthropological Perspective," 1992, p. 64

Harry Wolcott (1994) has written, "Treating oneself, one's experiences, and one's questions about research as data are effective ways to extend our research dialogue." That is my intent as I write about my sojourn among adolescents. During two years of fieldwork, I noted that my role among students shifted as rapport developed and in reaction to various circumstances. Sometimes the shifts were instinctive responses to students' behaviors. Other times I carefully considered what roles I could or should not assume in order to be a part of the group. In either case, through reaction and interaction—not unlike a rewarding conversation—we co-constructed acceptable roles for me. Sometimes I participated fully (playing floor hockey, visiting homeless shelters, taking Spanish tests), and sometimes I just watched or listened to students explain what was going on.

When I began the study I was 43 years old, and unlike Chang's (1992) experience among high school students, there was no way that I could physically blend in with adolescents. I was the mother of college-age children; an athletic klutz; a soft touch for lunch money; and someone who always carried tissues, gum, and Life-Savers. Besides that, I had a husband and a car, and I didn't have to live with my parents. Yet in order to gain insight into students' perceptions of high school transition and school literacy, I needed to gain insider status. That required participation in the adolescent school culture.

There is some question about whether adults can achieve real participant status within a child or adolescent culture. Mandell (1988) points out that researchers have commonly adopted less than full participant roles when working with children. She cites those who have assumed detached observer roles as well as those who have taken on nonauthoritative, marginal, semiparticipatory roles (supervisor, leader, observer, and friend). She advocates a research role of complete involvement, what she terms "the least adult role" for working with young children. Mandell argues that status differences generated by age, race, class, and gender are endemic to adult–adult studies and that if researchers have been able to develop strategies to deal with those differences, they ought to be able to do the same for adult–child differences.

Others have also explored the adult–child or adult–adolescent relationship (Chang, 1992; Corsaro, 1981; Fine, 1987; Fine & Sandstrom, 1988; Glassner, 1976; Gold, 1969; Manning & Matthews, 1992; Wax, 1979). Wax (1979) writes:

> It is probable that a fieldworker's age almost always limits, to some degree, the kind of situation he or she is able to study. I doubt that persons past their mid-twenties can ever become genuine participant observers in an adolescent or teenage group. (p. 520)

Fine and Sandstrom (1988) counter that researchers can fully participate in some aspects of adolescent culture (e.g., playing Dungeons and Dragons) while maintaining outsider roles in other areas of that culture. Manning and Matthews (1992) are skeptical about researchers who claim to have achieved rapport with adolescents. Chang (1992) consciously tested the limits of her relationships with high school students as she engaged as fully as possible in their everyday lives.

These researchers draw on their own experiences in the field, and while their narratives and viewpoints heightened my awareness of the unique aspects of doing fieldwork among adolescents, I expected that my own experiences would depend on individual personalities, environments, and circumstances. In hindsight, I examine the roles I played throughout the 2-year study in order to add to the dialogue about participant observation among adolescents and share how I gained access to students' behaviors and perceptions.

EIGHTH GRADE

The nature of field study is social. When I recall my first days on site at Meadowbrook, I remember a sense of isolation; I was a stranger. Most of the students had been together for 8 years, and it was their second year with the same teachers. Their histories united them, gave them an "insider's knowledge" about everything that transpired throughout the day, whether it was academic or social. They didn't need me, and I didn't exactly fit any of the existing roles in their school community. I wasn't one of their teachers or one of their past teachers. I didn't work in the office. I wasn't a school volunteer, a friend's mother, a specialist, a visitor, a teaching intern, or an instructional aide.

If I was to be a participant observer in the eighth-grade classes, I needed to find a way to participate *with* the kids. It would have been easy to align myself with teachers and still maintain good rapport with students. They often described their teachers as caring, adult friends they could rely on for personal as well as academic advice. While alignment with teachers wouldn't have driven a wedge between students and me, I nonetheless resisted the teacher role—even as I tutored kids in math or offered to edit papers. Students also served one another in these capacities, and so my activities fit with their expectations of one another. Everyone was expected to help anyone.

As it turned out, it was my researcher role that gave me viability among students. I told them I needed to learn what it was like to be eighth-graders, and true to the nature of this particular community, they set out to help me learn—just as they helped one another and as I helped them. Kids showed me how to serve a volleyball, write papers, put together science projects, paint murals on walls, and assemble a yearbook. Girls included me in bathroom discussions and wondered—only half jokingly—if I'd ever visited the boys' bathroom. One student offered to videotape his class for me if I'd take class notes for him. Others, unsolicited, offered information about classes I'd missed or showed me their assignments. When I audiotaped group discussions, kids learned to say their names before proceeding so that I'd have an easier time transcribing the tapes. They invited me to join small working groups or enticed me with lines such as, "Get out your notebook. You're going to want to write this down." They checked my notes to see if I'd included their names or asked, "Did you write about me yet today?"

Co-Worker Status

They understood I had a research motive for being with them, and indeed, that motive warranted my presence among them. My having research to do, not unlike the students having science projects to do, provided me with co-worker status, especially in the eighth grade where they always had active long-term assignments. I could, for instance, sit in the hallway with Nicky, Jaci, and Rachelle and write about students' reactions to a newly installed study period as the girls worked on individual tasks: taking notes for a humanities project, beginning a new book, and writing in a reading journal. Having authentic work to do helped me fit in.

Teachers had emphasized writing throughout the students' 8 years, and writing was generally viewed among students as important. It seemed that a day didn't go by without someone asking how many pages of notes I'd taken or whether I was "going broke" buying yellow pads. There was much curiosity about what I'd do with my notes. How long, they wondered, would the final paper be if there were hundreds of pages of notes? Some even wanted to know about the pens I used because they wrote so fast. Kids joked about my note taking. "When you go on our class trip with us, will you take your note pad?" At basketball games, they'd ask, "Where's your note pad?" After a while I realized that my note pad was a symbol of my purpose in a school where everyone had a job to do.

Building Rapport

I could have fun with kids without being responsible in the way teachers had to be. (Teachers admitted that they were occasionally jealous of my relationships with students.) I knew I'd succeeded in avoiding the teacher role when one day I agreed to "cover" a study period while the teacher made a phone call. Kids started talking out loud, something I knew the teacher would not appreciate. "All right now," I said in a serious voice. "This is supposed to be a quiet study. Keep your voices down." Teddy looked over at me and asked, "How come you sound like that?" He was referring to my tone of voice. I explained that for the moment I was no longer their friendly researcher; I was taking the place of their teacher. Teddy answered with a grin, "We like the researcher better." Whenever possible, I avoided teacher duties.

I didn't want to be viewed solely as a researcher with a yellow pad, either. I wanted students to accept me as part of their world. I chaperoned dances, drove for fieldtrips, bought raffle tickets, took part in a "Spell-a-Thon" skit (dressed in a chicken suit), attended the annual school meeting where eighth-graders provided refreshments (taking my turn pouring coffee), worked at a bake sale, donated blood for the school's blood drive (staffed in part by eighth-graders), attended parents' meetings, learned to shoot baskets, went Christmas caroling, and visited high schools with kids (sometimes as the only adult).

I didn't take my note pad to these events, even though I later wrote about them as quickly as I conveniently could. Everyone took notes in class, and my note taking helped me fit in there, but I sensed that a note pad at a basketball game would have set me apart as an outsider. Even during school hours, there were times when I thought it best to be more casual and just go with the flow of activity. Kids wanted me to have fun with them. I sensed that if

I appeared to be working *all the time*, I'd be nothing more than a boring drudge—something that would distance me from them.

Depending on the situation or individual personalities, kids seemed to expect me to respond as a surrogate mother, a big sister, a co-conspirator, a trusted adult, or a love-adviser. Often they needed me as a friend, and our different ages were just one of many aspects of that relationship. One day, for example, Kelly, a 14-year-old 6'2" basketball player, found me in the library while I was interviewing another student. "Mrs. Wells," she said. "Do you have meetings after school, or could you talk with me?" Kelly had never asked anything like this, and I sensed that I'd better not delay our talk. We met at lunch. She explained that she'd done poorly on the math and social studies quizzes that had been returned that morning and was worried about which high school to attend. (She was also upset because she thought her new hair cut was awful.) She said she probably shouldn't go to *any* high school, given the quiz scores. "I talk to my parents about high school, and they tell me to talk to my teachers. I talk to my teachers, and they tell me to talk to my parents," she told me.

I filled a gap for kids as they straddled childhood and adulthood. Because I didn't scold them or hold them to certain expectations, I was a safe adult in their "almost" adult world—one who took their concerns seriously while simultaneously having fun with them (e.g., Kelly and I had recently partnered for badminton against two of the boys and beaten them amid much laughter and teasing). As I looked to them to understand their adolescence better, they looked to me, an approachable adult, for a glimpse of approaching adulthood. Sometimes we were kids together; sometimes we were adults together. And it was okay for me to be an adult when they were very much kids. I didn't paint my name on the underside of the sink in the girls' bathroom the way a couple of girls did, but I didn't tell about it. I didn't go on the roller coaster during the class trip to Montreal (a few of the kids also declined), but I did ride a jet boat on the St. Lawrence River and swallow fully as much water as any of the kids.

Toward the end of the year, they unanimously voted for me to participate in their graduation as the main speaker. They said I knew them better than anyone else. Graduation morning, Misty, the class president, phoned. She wondered if I was nervous; she was. We compared the length of our speeches and agreed on hand signals in case either of us talked too fast. Before the ceremony I helped pin flowers on gowns, took pictures and had my picture taken, met parents, and cried with anyone who felt like crying. When it was all over, I went to Teddy's party and jumped on an outdoor trampoline with some of the other kids. The next morning Andy informed me that my speech had gone about 5 minutes too long. The kids liked me but didn't hold me in awe.

TRANSITION IN THE RELATIONSHIP

Over the summer I stayed in touch with a number of students, including those I would be accompanying to high school. Freshman orientation was 4 days before school opened. I gave rides to two of the boys but planned to keep my distance after we were all in the school. I was well aware that most students didn't start their high school careers with a researcher in tow. The first days of school would be hard enough for them, and I wanted to give them plenty of room. If I embarrassed them, I risked losing their cooperation. As it turned out, I was more careful about our relationship than the students were. During orientation they repeatedly came to me, asking directions or what they should do next. When I told them I was as lost as they were, they began helping me find where I needed to go. They invited me to sit with them in the auditorium for the principal's address, and when anyone asked, they introduced me as, "This is Mrs. Wells. She was at our school last year."

I noticed, in some respects, that the kids were treating me more as an equal. They'd liked me in the eighth grade and included me in their conversations and activities, but I'd come into *their* community; *they* had been the hosts. It was different at the beginning of their ninth grade; we were entering foreign territory together. We were *all* outsiders, and we *all* needed to establish rapport with others in the new environment. I was an adult, and the kids expected that I'd have certain adult privileges among teachers (I probably wouldn't need hall passes), but I was just as new as they were and our relationship was not only well established but preceded those that would be established at the high school.

After the orientation, we all went back to my house for a pizza party. After the initial tour of the house and first pieces of pizza around the kitchen table, Nicky, Monica, Ginny, Chad, John, Sharon, Carl, Jan, Rachelle, and I wound up in my bedroom—all of us sitting on the king size bed. The three boys and some of the girls were still eating pizza; everyone had cans of soda. When Chad went downstairs for more pizza, he asked if anyone else wanted some. Sure enough, there were takers. Carl went down with him to help bring back more sodas. As they pounded down the stairs, I shouted, "Bring some napkins, too!" The bedspread was white, and my "researcher-adolescent-self" was barely winning out over my "homemaker-mother-self," who never would have risked getting tomato sauce on the bed.

We stayed in the bedroom for nearly 2 hours (spilling nothing), looking through photographs I'd taken during their eighth-grade year, playing cards, passing around Clancy the cat, and talking. Some of the kids lay on their bellies; others sat with legs crossed in front of them. It was a record-breaking hot day, and kids took turns going down for more sodas. We reminisced about the class trip—how we all fell asleep in the omnitheater after the freezing ride on the St. Lawrence River, how they used to get away with things in the eighth grade, and how we'd tromped through the snow to Christmas carol. And then, they began talking about things I hadn't experienced: things their parents didn't know about their get-togethers, camping in the woods, sleepovers, siblings, and friends who had moved away before I came to school. They were having fun among themselves, but I had a sense that they were also pulling me into their circle, making me one of them as we stood together at the edge of high school.

We also discussed my name. I wanted to give them the option, just as I had at the beginning of the eighth grade, to call me by my first name. I'd hoped they might switch to Cyrene for high school, but they said it didn't matter if other kids called me Cyrene; it would be "too weird" for *them* to call me anything but Mrs. Wells. (As it turned out, only one freshman from Whitmore called me by my first name.) In hindsight, I believe that retaining my name from eighth grade was more than just comfortable for the kids. There was going to be enough "new" in high school, and they wanted to keep *me* the same.

Before we went downstairs to look at videos I'd recorded at Meadowbrook, they visited my office and assessed the amount of written data I'd collected during their eighth-grade year. They'd given me all their school papers in June and were satisfied with my filing system, but they wanted to see where I kept all the yellow sheets of notes I'd taken the previous year. Nicky sat with one of the notebooks for about 10 minutes before saying she didn't think she'd read my paper (study) because it was going to be too boring.

The kids stayed until about 6:00 that evening. Chad and John had soccer practice, and after I'd returned from delivering the rest to their homes (slowing the trip by jumping on Jan's trampoline, meeting parents I hadn't met, and petting favorite pets), I began to analyze the day. At first I'd thought it odd that we'd congregated in my bedroom. Then it occurred to me. When kids visit one another, where do they go? To one another's rooms! By taking their pizza and soda cans to my bedroom, they'd paid me the compliment of treating me as one of them. By looking through my papers, books, files (along with a careful survey of the entire house), they "checked me out" as I'd "checked them out" during the previous year. When Nicky went through the house, even looking in closets and back rooms, the rest laughed and said she was always like that. She could find things in their houses that they'd forgotten they had. She was treating my house as if it were the house of one of her friend's.

During their freshman year, the kids returned to my house, individually and as a group. We even had a sleep-over that lasted 20 hours. However, it was the pizza party on high school orientation day that marked a major shift in our relationship. Reminiscing about the past, we looked to the upcoming year together. I was included in their vision.

HIGH SCHOOL

Despite my sense that the kids saw me more nearly as their equal on the eve of entering high school, I was still wary of embarrassing them or drawing undue attention to them as "subjects" of study. They were 9 students among 225 from four other towns, already uncomfortable at the prospect of making their way in a big school. I didn't want to make it more difficult for them and had promised I wouldn't say anything to the other kids about following Meadowbrook freshmen. As I went from class to class, particularly concentrating on the classes of John, Chad, Ginny, Monica, and Nicky, I explained that I was there to find out what it was like to be a high school freshman. I didn't mention Meadowbrook, and I initially didn't sit near Meadowbrook students.

My plan was to establish rapport with as many students as possible so that my attention to Meadowbrook students wouldn't be obvious. Instinctively, I also knew that it would be easier for the Meadowbrook students to associate with me if I were generally accepted among all the kids. General acceptance would also give me the opportunity to hear from a broad spectrum of kids—giving me an additional context for understanding Meadowbrook students' reactions to high school. As it happened, my popularity was serendipitously boosted when freshmen from Barton recognized me as the woman who had replaced their second-grade teacher in the last weeks of school. (I didn't recognize them and hadn't considered that they might be freshmen that year.) For them, I was a piece of their elementary experience transplanted to high school; we'd sort of "moved up" together. There were at least 20 kids from Barton who knew me. They, like the Meadowbrook students, could introduce me to others. When they did, they usually commented that I was "nice" or that I'd "taken care" of them when their second-grade teacher died—an introduction that served as a stamp of approval. My presence also gave Barton and Meadowbrook students something in common, and it may have been easier for Meadowbrook kids to claim me when others were also doing so.

Still, I was careful to let the Meadowbrook students take the lead in publicly defining our relationship. I didn't immediately eat lunch with them, even though my lunch period coincided with Nicky's, Monica's, Jan's, John's, and Chad's. On September 8, Nicky wrote me a note, "Why don't you ever come and sit with us? [for lunch] I don't think we would mind." I joined them and continued to eat with Meadowbrook students for the rest of the year. As early as September 4, Monica told a new acquaintance in English class, "We're going to be famous. She's [indicating me] writing a book about us." When after a few days, extra students had taken all the spare desks in Ginny's science class, she suggested that I pull up a chair and sit next to her.

While Nicky, Monica, and Ginny were straightforward about my presence, John and Chad were less likely to announce my purpose to their classmates. Chad, quiet and somewhat insecure about his social and academic abilities, was concentrating on his own entry—not mine. John, a minimalist of sorts, didn't view my presence as particularly noteworthy. Neither of the boys offered specific information about me until I was well accepted among the freshman class and it was general knowledge that I was following Meadowbrook students.

Not a Teacher

As I had anticipated, getting along with most of the students (even upperclassmen) was key, and in contrast to my experience in Meadowbrook, I discovered early that a close association with most teachers at the high school would distance me from students. Freshmen from other towns didn't necessarily have a history of friendship with teachers, and the pattern of teacher rapport that Meadowbrook students had experienced with their elementary teachers wasn't repeating itself with high school teachers.

The relationship between some teachers and students was subversively hostile, and sometimes students from various towns asked me directly if I liked certain teachers. I tried to respond diplomatically with comments such as, "I'm more interested in what you think" and "Sometimes he's okay." I also managed to communicate my sympathy by laughing with them about teachers or shaking my head as they reviewed teachers' behaviors. Occasionally kids' comments told me that they knew I was with them in their anger but was in a difficult position. One day Monica commented, "You can't say anything bad about him, can you?" I laughed, and without my saying so, we agreed that I couldn't. In general, I sympathized with kids about homework and delighted with them when they pulled teachers off the subjects they were studying. When they were bored in classes, they asked me if I felt the same. If I'd said "no," they'd have thought I was either stupid or lying. Most often, I said I was glad to have notes to take.

I tried not to hang around with teachers when I knew kids would be watching, but even small conversations with teachers were subject to scrutiny. Chad's math teacher, Mr. Perry, was particularly disliked among students. One morning after he'd initiated conversation and I'd chatted with him as students did seatwork, Chad mentioned that he'd heard me talking to Mr. Perry. "You were nice to him," he said, somewhat puzzled. I waited.

"But then you're nice to everyone," he answered for himself. I told him I sometimes felt sorry for Mr. Perry, something that would have made sense at Meadowbrook, and Chad seemed to understand. Nevertheless, after that I was more careful about my in-class interchanges with Mr. Perry.

Sitting among students, I heard and saw a lot that teachers didn't know about, and in the beginning I sensed that I was being tested by at least some of the students. There were the usual things of forbidden gum and copying homework from one another, but the kids in Ginny's science class seemed to push me the hardest. It was mid-September when, in the midst of sneak-eating Doritos and popcorn, one of the boys asked me if I thought he should crack open a soda. I answered, "No way are you going to get me in trouble. You'll get caught and say I said it was okay." I passed the test, and he didn't open the soda.

I didn't want to get on teachers' bad sides because I needed to maintain rapport with them as well as with students, but if I had to make a choice between students and teachers (and no one was going to get hurt), I behaved as one of the students. I was sitting behind Monica in science when she turned around with a sandwich bag of cookies—somewhat concealed in the palm of her hand. "You want a cookie?" she whispered. Eating in class was against school rules, and eating in science class was especially prohibited. "Sure," I said as I took the bag, put it between me and the front of my desk, and extracted a cookie. I was hungry and glad for the sugar lift, but even if I hadn't wanted the cookie, I'd have taken it.

It wasn't that I needed to be careful about Monica's feelings; we'd known each other long enough that my refusal would have meant nothing. Other kids were watching, though, and since I'd only recently changed my schedule to include Monica's and Nicky's science class, many of the students in the room were new to me. (Each change in schedule precipitated a mini-entry and the need to establish rapport with new students.) I sensed that if I turned the cookie down, I'd have affirmed my adult status. When you're in the ninth grade, and someone offers you a cookie, you usually take it. I then had to show that I wasn't stupid about eating in class. I took bites and chewed only when Mr. Brinkley turned away. It was tempting to giggle as I felt the boy next to me watching, but I knew better than to make a big deal out of it. I just ate the cookie—sneakily—the way I'd see it done in other classes.

At other times, I passed notes, laughed at kids' jokes about teachers, and watched as students copied homework from one another. I saw cheating and didn't report it, and once a boy in Monica's and Nicky's English class copied a wrong quiz answer from my paper. I didn't know he'd done it until he complained after class. "Because of you," he scolded, "I missed one. You're supposed to know all the answers." The other kids thought it was very funny, and the story got around quickly.

The Meadowbrook kids knew I wouldn't ever tell on them. We discussed this several times and agreed that the only exception should be for dangerous activity. (They offered smoking as an example. I had been thinking of more serious possibilities.) Monica and Jan told me how they were able to get out of class to visit with Jan's boyfriend. Chad told me how he'd purposely shown up late for a class when he didn't have his homework done. John told me about taking textbooks home that were supposed to stay in classrooms. Our trust was well established, but I looked for signs of trust among the other students.

In algebra class, one of the girls clued me in on what had happened to another student's textbook when peers were picking on him. I found a way to get the book back to the student without getting the perpetrators in trouble. When I saw a boy named Charlie in the hallway during class time with two girls, he assured them that I wouldn't hassle them for not having hall passes. "She's one of us," he told them.

Sometimes a Mother

There were times when I needed to draw the line between who I was and what the kids did. When report cards came out and Becky from Ashfield penciled a change from a 68 to an 88 for one of her grades, she asked me if I thought her mother would be able to tell. It was a deception that I didn't want to share, but I answered truthfully that I didn't think her mother could tell. I also asked if she'd like to know, from a mother's point of view, what her mother's reaction might be if she found out the truth. When Becky said she would, I told her that her mother would probably lose confidence in her. I'd managed to be truthful about the quality of the altered grade while at the same time not condoning the deception. Because I was a mother, I could speak as a kind of "universal mother," a role that allowed me to say things that a "friend" or a "friendly researcher" might not.

When John started slacking off in his classes, I didn't want it to appear that I was scolding him, but on the other hand, I didn't want to see him fail. I asked, "Does your mother have any idea you're doing this badly?"—in effect placing his mother as a buffer between him and me. Approaching it this way, I made it clear that I was concerned about his inattention to homework (something that Jan, Monica, and Nicky had also mentioned to him) without turning him off with adult advice. At the same time, I was able to remind him that his parents might not be too happy with his academic performance.

Effective as the mother role was, I used it sparingly because I didn't want to identify too strongly with parents—or worse—become "boring" by using the same line too often. I usually asked permission to voice a parent's point of view (e.g., "Would you like to hear what a mother might say about that?")

because it seemed to make us cohorts in the speculation, thus setting the scene for conversation rather than a lecture. I sensed, too, that the mother role wouldn't work with all kids and might actually hurt rapport. I usually saved it for those I especially knew or cared about and for circumstances that seemed important enough to warrant a dose of adult wisdom. The best part is that *I* didn't actually give the advice; a mother did. We all understood that I wasn't any of their mothers.

Hear No Evil, See No Evil

Whenever possible, I "didn't see" things that had no relevance to my study. I "didn't see" the upperclassmen who put a smoke bomb in a wastebasket outside the office. I "didn't notice" kids sneaking food in the library. I "didn't smell" cigarette smoke coming from a closed stall in the girls' bathroom. And I "didn't hear" about which kids pulled the fire alarm, precipitating a cold January evacuation from the building. If I suspected kids knew I'd seen or heard something that might be compromising, I said things like "I didn't hear that" or "It's a good thing I'm not a teacher."

Occasionally students explicitly protected me from knowing things that might put me in a difficult position. I was in Chad's science class, and the teacher was busy with deskwork. The students were passing a note around the room, and when it came into our area I asked if I could read it, too—not an unusual thing for me to ask; almost everybody was reading it. Chad looked hard at me and said, "I don't think you want to see this." Diana, a "tough" girl who sat in front of me, read the note and agreed with Chad. "This will upset you," she said. I had no recourse except to thank the kids and not press the issue. Chad told me later that the note was making fun of a new student in class and that the language had been pretty bad. He said he didn't want to embarrass me. I was grateful because I don't know how I might have reacted. The new student had told me that he'd been in five schools that year and that his father had just died. Seeing the note would have put me in a very uncomfortable position—one where it would have been difficult to just be one of the kids.

Sometimes the language was "explicit" between classes as kids jostled for position or tried to get lockers open quickly. At first, kids I didn't even know apologized or warned one another that I was around, but after several months, they swore in front of me as if I were one of them. I didn't respond to the language, any more than they did. I didn't swear though, and swearing was not common among Meadowbrook students. The occasional epithet went unacknowledged unless it was new phraseology (e.g., "wicked sucky"). The Meadowbrook students did assure other students that it was okay to swear in front of me, however. Sometimes I just laughed when they said this, and kids generally thought it was funny, too. It was similar to my getting in trouble with the teacher for talking in wellness (health) class. My position among adolescents was incongruous at times, and we could only laugh.

One of Them

Being one of the kids required some premeditation. I didn't carry a purse because most girls didn't, and like some of them, I was afraid of leaving it in a class. I varied the clothes I wore—sometimes wearing skirts but mostly wearing khakis and loose-fitting sweaters. Kids wore jeans more than khakis, but khakis let me straddle the world of teachers and students. Besides, I didn't want it to appear that I was trying too hard to imitate kids. Still, I was walking down the hall one day when a student from Ashfield caught up with me and said, "From the back, you look just like a student. Your gray hair only shows in the front."

Most of the freshmen had lockers in the main lobby, and I made sure to get one with them. From the beginning, it established me as a kind of hybrid adult; adults didn't have lockers. During the first weeks it served as a vehicle for introductions when students repeatedly asked what I was doing at the lockers. It also gave me a legitimate reason to spend time after school in the lobby, where a lot of kids hung out until their rides came. I could go to my locker and get caught up in conversation. More than anything, it gave me something in common with the kids. When in the spring some upperclassmen discovered my combination, individual freshmen warned me for 2 days that I needed to get a new lock.

Teachers didn't use student bathrooms, and early on I decided to use them. At first girls were surprised to see me there, and a few asked what I was doing. When I stated the obvious, we laughed. One time Monica and a few of the other girls left science class under various pretexts (an easy class to get out of). I found them in the bathroom. Christine was having boyfriend problems and was crying in one of the stalls, where she had easy access to toilet paper for blowing her nose. Before it was over, I took my turn hugging Christine. The other girls complained about how mean boys could be, and after a bit, we staggered our entries back to science class. When asked what was going on, I told the teacher that one of the girls wasn't feeling well.

Rather than using the side door to the kitchen or cutting in front of kids, I stood in line with them to get my lunch. I'd made a point of getting my picture taken for an I.D. card and presented it every day so that the kitchen worker could pass the bar code through the machine. Back at the table, I took bites of "communal" ice cream bars and bought my own to be passed around. The potato puffs were awful, and I couldn't make myself eat them as the kids so often did, but I sometimes ate packaged doughnuts for lunch or had a bag of pretzels with a carton of milk.

I didn't go to gym class often, since I was more interested in academic classes, but I sensed that going, at least a few times, would help build rapport. I also sensed that I'd have to participate, not just watch. In the first class I attended we did the bent elbow hang, and I managed to "hang in there" long enough not to embarrass myself or Monica, who was in the class. Since we didn't exercise much, we didn't have to take showers. The second time we played coed field hockey. The teacher positioned me somewhere in the middle of the field and yelled at me when I took short breaks from running. When we got back to the locker room (after more running), I observed that some girls were taking showers. I did what I thought I had to do, got undressed, and then made it into the last available shower. (I learned that it was available because there was no curtain and only a dribble of cold water came out the shower head.) While I was drying myself with my sweatshirt because I'd forgotten a towel, one of the girls held up her deodorant, and in a rather sympathetic tone, told me that I could have just borrowed her deodorant— that a lot of girls didn't take showers. After that I made sure to have deodorant, and I didn't take showers either—even when I played basketball in other sessions.

One session of field hockey, though, and word spread that I'd gone to gym. I'd shown that I was serious when I said that I wanted to know what it was like to be a freshman. One student told me that her mother never would have played field hockey. When the wrestling unit began, a number of kids wanted me to learn how to wrestle with them. I thought of my sore muscles and didn't get around to it.

Spanish caused fewer body aches, but it also put me on the line with the kids. As a condition of sitting in on Spanish class, Mrs. Larimer, the Spanish teacher, made it clear that she expected me to participate fully as a student. I liked the idea; it was a chance to personally experience homework and tests. I did my homework and I studied for tests and generally did pretty well, but students often did better than I did on individual tests and papers. At first, some of the students were surprised that I received grades but were somewhat disappointed that I wouldn't be getting a report card. "What did you get, Mrs. Wells?" was not an uncommon question, and knowledge that someone would ask the question across rows of desks was often my motivation for studying.

Classwork was somewhat daunting, especially when Mrs. Larimer corrected my pronunciation or called on me when I didn't know the answer. Once when I hadn't studied transportation vocabulary very well, she sent me to the board, along with other students, to list possible ways of arriving at school. I cheated by asking the kids in the front row for help. Mrs. Larimer

caught me and good naturedly told me, in front of the class, that I was setting a bad example. I did study, though, and the Meadowbrook students and
I often studied together, sometimes over the phone at night. Spanish directly
preceded lunch, and talk of tests or class usually dominated discussion at
some point. I could participate fully in both the food and the talk. In science, I slyly studied verb conjugations and vocabulary lists just as Monica,
Nicky, and Jan did.

In January, when I started taking a power and energy class with John
and Carl, I was really out of my element. The students, all boys, patiently
showed me how to disassemble and reassemble lawnmower engines. Sometimes they handed me parts and let me try to fit them in place. Then when
several of the boys began welding a go-cart that would eventually get a new
engine, they taught me and others in the class how to wire weld. When it
was my turn to try, one boy helped me on with gloves. Another showed me
how to use goggles that made everything black except the arc coming from
the welding torch. They shouted encouragement and advice to me as I worked
and then pointed out a spot where I'd laid down a decent bead.

Throughout the year, I was struck by the kids' familiarity with me. Once
rapport was established, they often treated me as they treated one another.
Nicky and Monica always reminded me when it was my turn to throw away
trash after lunch, and kids asked where I'd been when I missed a day of school.
One day in April, I decided to record typical incidents that indicated acceptance. In Ginny's science class, a girl I barely knew absent-mindedly played
with the back of my hair—just as she did other girls' hair. One of the boys
touched the sleeve of my shirt and wondered if it was silk. (Mine wasn't; his
was.) Later in the day when a bunch of us were sitting at the lunch table
waiting for the bell to ring, I mentioned that I was going to try to go to the
bathroom before keyboarding class. One of the boys from Whitmore, whom
I'd come to know quite well, picked up on the word "try" and started teasing me about having to try. In Monica's and Nicky's English class, Christine
asked me to check the corners of her mouth for gum.

It would be misleading to imply that I was always in the thick of adolescent high school culture. Even though I hosted the sleep-over for Meadowbrook kids and attended a lot of basketball games, no one invited me to a
sleep-over and no one invited me to ride with them to games. I didn't learn
that Jan made the varsity cheerleading squad until the Monday after the
Friday announcement, and Nicky didn't tell me that her parents had separated until nearly 2 weeks had passed. There were times when I felt that my
presence stalled social interaction between Meadowbrook kids and their
friends, and I found ways to leave the scene. There were also days when I
sensed that kids just didn't have time for me; I avoided calling at home when
I knew they had basketball practice or a lot of homework. I developed a closer

rapport with girls than with boys. One boy from Whitmore was teased for "coming on" to me at a basketball game, and he kept his distance for a while after that. And even though I sat with students through their classes, I didn't usually do homework, and I certainly didn't have to work for grades. Because I was older and married (to someone the girls assured me was cute), I didn't share their concern about boys.

I did live somewhat vicariously through the students' descriptions of dances and events I did not attend. I heard about parties, romances, and arguments. And if I didn't hear it all, I did learn enough to give me a flavor of students' lives. When the year ended, Meadowbrook kids continued to call and visit my house. Monica, Nicky, Jan, Chad, and John asked me to be their cabin leader for a week of summer camp in the White Mountains (during which time we climbed Mount Washington and did a bruising ropes course). The next fall, during one of the times when Nicky called to say hello, we talked about the beginning of basketball season. When I said I'd feel funny about going to see a game, that I didn't want to sit alone, she assured me that plenty of kids would talk to me. "Lots of them asked where you were at the beginning of the year." They'd expected me to show up for our sophomore year.

George and Louise Spindler (1992) write that participant observation is particularly difficult in school settings. One might participate as a teacher, but participation as a student is another matter. Still, during George Spindler's 1968 study of an elementary school in Schoenhausen, he did class assignments, went on hikes, climbed towers, and ate lunch with third- and fourth-grade students. He found that doing so made him less threatening and more familiar among them. For 2 years, I "found my way" as a participant observer among adolescents. In addition to building trust, it gave me access to information and insights that I would otherwise have missed. Students didn't talk about subjects such as literacy and transition on cue—or only upon solicitation. I found that I just had to be there with them.

CHAPTER 2

Meadowbrook and Its Community School

It may be that thoughtful literacy cannot be fully mobilized without a strong sense of community—without widening circles of meaning, through which individuals can understand themselves and their condition and construct coherent, purposeful lives . . . to go beyond the mere technology of education, to build and sustain coherent, vital communities in and around their schools.

Rexford Brown
Schools of Thought, 1991, p. 56

The schoolchildren of Meadowbrook knew they were valued members of a larger community. "They always find a way to get us the things we need," one seventh-grader explained about how townspeople took care of the school. She and her friends knew, too, that what they needed often cost money and that local property taxes were high. They appreciated the sacrifices adults made for them and recognized the importance of community in their classrooms, as well as widening circles of community that supported their classroom families. When they were sixth-graders, the children of this study wrote a song for the dedication of their new school building, the Meadowbrook Community School, which included the lines,

> Cooperation and volunteers,
> communities have been here for thousands of years.
> Big and little jobs, people reaching out.
> That's what community is all about.
> Community means together,
> community lasts forever,
> communities stretching across our lands,
> communities reaching out with helping hands.

They knew of the debate that surrounded the construction of their new school and the cooperation it took to get the job done. They understood there was still work to be done and that they would be a part of it.

SCHOOL AND TOWN: A BLENDING OF COMMUNITIES

Meadowbrook was one of those picturesque small New England towns where photographers stop to take pictures for calendars and postcards. Winding roads curved around eighteenth-century houses; old cemeteries dotted the countryside; and stone walls, built generations earlier, bordered expanses of rolling fields. Its clapboard town hall stood two stories high and sat across a paved road from the Baptist Church and the Community Church, two old white buildings with tall spires, one of which held a bell that was an early copy of one made by Paul Revere. A brick library and a community center that was once a church stood near the two church buildings, and with them, constituted Meadowbrook Center.

Once predominantly agricultural, the town had undergone a change in demographics and a jump in population, especially in the previous 10 years. More than 3,000 people lived within the town's 26,000 acres (64 square miles), and 425 children attended the elementary school. Tucked away from cities but within a reasonable distance to major highways, Meadowbrook had become a haven for those who were willing to commute to work and drive for services. Young families, often drawn by the elementary school's reputation for innovative teaching, either moved into existing homes or built new ones. Clusters of houses sprang up on old roads and in small developments.

Most families in town had middle-class incomes, but the economic recession that hit the entire region in the mid-1980s also hurt Meadowbrook. Property taxes were high; people complained, and some couldn't pay. More than a few families needed to rely on welfare and the town's food pantry. There were also wealthy families in town, ones who could afford to restore big old houses or build roomy modern ones. The weekly newspaper described increasing diversity of occupations by writing that residents included "business owners, doctors, lawyers, airline pilots, engineers and retired military." The number of retired professionals who had moved to the town and newcomers with high-profile professions often gave outsiders the impression that the town was wealthy. Residents disagreed and pointed to those, old and new to town, who worked extremely hard to just "get by." There was, however, a quiet sense in town that Meadowbrook was somehow "different" from surrounding towns, perhaps better.

While it would be wrong to imply that all newcomers were wealthy and college educated and that longtime residents (sometimes defined as those having parents born in town) were poor and lacked post-secondary schooling, it could be said that there was sometimes tension between groups. As more new people came to town, longtime residents sometimes felt they were losing control. In a town where everyone had once known everyone's business, some complained that they didn't know the names of even half the people at the annual town meetings.

Local politics was a source of friction in town, with two groups (each group consisting of both old-timers and newcomers) at the extremes of a conservative–liberal continuum. Members at these extremes were barely civil to one another. The majority of townspeople were publicly more moderate, even when they had strong feelings about town, church, or school issues. They believed that everyone deserved "a say" in whatever went on, and tolerance was valued—even when it was difficult to achieve.

People took pride in the town's churches, its youth groups, its baseball teams, its volunteer organizations, and its school. The lines between school, church, and town were blurred because many were involved in all three. For instance, the Meadowbrook Community Center—which provided space for the town's private kindergarten (public kindergarten was not mandated by the state), scouting meetings, senior citizens' lunches, the historical society, and events such as the Christmas craft fair—was run by volunteers and owned by the Congregational Church. When the town decided to build the new school, the old school became home to town offices and the police station, with space for a video store, a pizza shop, a bakery, and a day-care center—important conveniences to a town that had neither grocery store nor commercial downtown. In its transformation, the old school retained a central position in town.

The new school stood at the edge of a woods, alongside a pond, with trails "out back"—built by volunteers and schoolchildren for everyone's use. Much of the landscaping had been done by local committees, and talk of grass seed and a tree nursery dominated a portion of at least two annual school meetings. Town groups used classrooms and the school library for meetings, and the school's gym was used by adults for aerobics, volleyball, and basketball. Evening education sessions for adults included topics as diverse as organic vegetable gardening, CPR, and foot massage. The building was open long hours before and after children were in the building. Weekends were also booked for activities, and the annual town and school meetings were held in the gymnasium.

Again and again, groups and individuals emphasized that the school was for the *community's* use and for lifelong learning. Named after much discussion about that philosophy, Meadowbrook *Community* School was central to the town. It was built and named with the idea that it and its grounds should benefit local citizens as well as schoolchildren. During dedication ceremonies it had been noted that the building was a "facility that can truly bring citizens together." A woman who worked in the voluntary position of school–community coordinator oversaw and helped plan events that united school and community efforts.

School/Community Organizations and Events

At the intersection of where a paved road led from the state road to the elementary school, a signboard visually integrated school and town activities with announcements such as: "PRE-SCHOOL STORY HOUR—MEADOWBROOK LIBRARY—THURSDAY 1 PM," "SOLAR ELECTRIC—FREE LECTURE—FRI JUNE 26, 7–9 PM—MCS [Meadowbrook Community School]," and "MOTHERS DAY BREAKFAST—7:30–10:30 AM—MEADOWBROOK COMMUNITY CENTER." Much the same could be said for *The Communicator*, a monthly "School/Community Newsletter." Part school and part community news, it was funded by FOCUS (Forum of Citizens Uniting with the School—a group of citizens representing various aspects of the school and town whose "focus" was to provide a link between the school and the larger community). It was written by committee, printed at the school, and delivered by mail to every house in town. Three to five double-sided legal-sized pages in length, it was a hodgepodge of information: news about the town's Halloween party, a library pie sale, a schedule of sports and fitness programs offered for adults at the school, and an update from the eighth-grade "Wellness Magnet." Unlike the weekly school memo that went home with students every Friday, the newsletter was intended for the general public; organizers operated under the assumption that town residents wanted to know about both school and community, as well as details about specific events such as "Tricky Tray," the town's major fund-raiser.

Tricky Tray was a prime example of school–community cooperation. Local businesses, individuals, and classroom communities donated items such as homemade dolls, carpentry work, and baseball tickets. Trays of items were given numbers, and on Tricky Tray Night townspeople crowded the school gymnasium for multiple raffle drawings. As helium balloons floated into the rafters and adults painted kids' faces, seventh-grade students sold popcorn and drinks, eighth-graders served as runners, and young children pulled winning tickets from a rotating drum. Yearly profits funded school projects as well as community ones (e.g., a community phone book, recreational programs, a boiler for the Community Center, and "visiting authors" for the school).

In another example of cooperation, townspeople arranged for the 39th Army Engineers Battalion to bulldoze and level the construction-damaged land around the school. Townspeople fed and entertained the servicemen. In subsequent summers, they arranged for Volunteers for Peace, an international organization of young people, to do such things as build a picnic area on school property, cut and fit sod for the baseball diamond, build a nursery to hold trees and plants that were donated to the school, paint at both churches, and spruce up the town's food pantry. During all the work, local families provided food, and students and adults joined the work crews.

Just as residents served on search committees for prospective teachers, staff members worked with residents on a High School Study Committee, the Long-Range Planning Committee, and the "Big Picture" Committee (a group seeking to enunciate a vision of how school and town could work together to provide optimum learning opportunities for everyone). People didn't always agree about how things should be done, and much time was spent listening, clarifying language, and seeking consensus. Goals were often reviewed, and progress could seem slow. During one session a teacher/resident reminded a school board member, "I am the community. You're the community. Our goals are for everyone to be lifetime readers and writers. If that's not true, then we need to change the name of the school." People in Meadowbrook didn't underestimate the power of community, and they worked hard to build and maintain it.

Locus of Control

Before the Civil War there were 16 one-room schoolhouses in the town, each one controlled by the people in its neighborhood. In 1950 the Central School was built and the whole town became responsible for supporting one school. A 1966 history of the town stated, "The community can be proud of its school history and will continue to meet the needs of the students even though taxes will increase." Although the state had taken over some of the decisions that could be made in school districts, townspeople still sensed that their elementary school was locally supported and locally controlled. That relationship ended once the town's children were ready for high school. As was true with many small towns in the state, Meadowbrook had no high school. For generations, ninth-grade students had attended public high schools in towns as distant as 20 miles away. In 1991–92, 200 students attended five different high schools—at a cost to Meadowbrook of nearly $1,000,000. Meadowbrook residents had no voice in the curriculums and practices of those high schools.

The annual school meeting (sister of the annual town meeting) was a forum for all. For the 1992 meeting, school board members, authors of the petitioned warrant articles, and members of the municipal budget committee contributed information to an "advice package" that was mailed to all

townspeople. The idea was to give voters an opportunity to reflect on issues before coming to the meeting. There were 17 relatively ordinary articles (e.g., approval of a teachers' contract for a 2.6% salary increase [recommended by budget committee], $2,500 for an improved fire-water access hole [recommended by budget committee], and $7,000 for continued landscaping of the school site [not recommended by the budget committee]). The proposed school budget, including high school tuitions, was $3,621,818.

As each warrant item elicited long discussion, eighth-graders, who were manning the snack bar to raise money for their class trip, rotated out of the kitchen so they could listen to proceedings. They asked adults to review what was happening, and when they returned to work, they told their friends the news. The friends wanted to hear about particular people, ones they knew had been negative about the school. "What did they say?" "How many times did she talk?" "Did people vote against him?"

The 1992 meeting lasted less than 6 hours, the shortest one in anyone's memory. Still, there was opportunity for one political camp to harass the other. (The owner of the local weekly newspaper kept track of who talked most often and announced the outcome by name and number of times at the microphone in the next issue of the paper.) Antischool expenditure proponents garnered the highest tallies, demanding, for example, that gifts and donations to the school be made public, that a tuition cap be put on high school tuitions, and that monies collected from the teachers' room soda machine be accounted for in the budget. When, in her 11th turn at the microphone, Mildred Harrington implied that the principal misused a discretionary principal's fund and had been seen at the local convenience store buying his lunch with school money, the crowd stopped being patient and began to laugh and joke among themselves. Her motion that the principal be denied such an account was immediately defeated. The eighth-grade students, outside the kitchen to hear the complaint, cheered the vote.

Official comments and questions, as well as conversations carried on in small groups, revealed that many of those assembled were well versed in the elementary school's philosophy and operations. People seemed to want to talk about big issues, and Harrington's request for a high school tuition cap led to a philosophical discussion about choice. Even though tuition for the various schools varied by as much as $1,000, the consensus was that it was important to do what was best for individual children—despite the differences in cost. In any case, not one of the high schools could accommodate all Meadowbrook students.

Even though the school board was highly active and directly responsible to the town with regard to school operations, most people explained that the principal, Bill Peterson, was the driving force of the school. Teachers, school board members, and parents—those who were critical of the school as well as those who were highly supportive—indicated that they couldn't imagine the school as it was without the man who had served as principal since 1980. The school board chairman, retiring after 12 years on the board, remembered Peterson's second year and his own first year at the school as one in which they'd decided to give Peterson the kind of responsibility ordinarily reserved for the superintendent's office. In the early years Peterson worked with an open budget created in Meadowbrook for Meadowbrook. It allowed for flexibility that would otherwise not have been possible. Most important, they gave him the right to deal with contracts for both professional and nonprofessional staff, which meant that Peterson could seek individuals that fit his developing philosophy. The chairman explained that Peterson and the board had spent long hours talking about philosophy, about how kids learn, and about how the school should run.

As the school grew larger and Peterson's time became more constrained, the board returned some of the more tedious tasks to the superintendent's office, but by that time, the tone of the school was set. Peterson and his staff were looking critically at traditional practices such as standardized testing and reading instruction and were seeking ways to make school relevant and interesting for students. At the same time, they set about educating the community about what it was they believed was important for school children. Some of the teachers began home visits, Peterson sent weekly memos home to parents, teachers started experimenting with narrative report cards, and townspeople were included in multiple aspects of the school. Many of the teachers who came to teach moved into and became part of the community. Their own children attended the school.

Rooted in Community, the Vision Evolves

Peterson explained,

> You have a group of people within the community and some teachers on staff and an administration, all having a vision of what a school should look like—and I think it's an educational process—and the process is to get as many community people [as possible] involved so that they can understand why we're going in the direction we're moving.

Peterson was a leader. He said he worked for consensus, but some who knew him best explained that his talent lay in making people believe *they* had come up with the good ideas—ones that he had in mind all along. No matter the origin of ideas, Peterson facilitated conversation in which he and others could explore possibilities. He believed that he and others needed to educate the

community so that, with the community, they could go about educating its children. "I think the school is probably leading the community," he admitted.

From the beginning Peterson encouraged innovation. When early in his tenure a first-year teacher wanted to use "real literature" rather than basal readers, Peterson and the staff found money for her to buy books. When the state university began offering courses about writing process, Peterson and a couple of the teachers took a course. They brought back what they learned, and teachers began opening their classrooms to one another. And as they did, they looked hard at old practices. In the midst of experimenting with writing, they changed how they approached reading. Peterson admitted to it being a messy process:

> We did some really dumb things, but it caused change. . . . It got people thinking. . . . So it was a gradual process, but everybody was a part of that decision making—as we kept evaluating and looking to the next year. . . . It's a gradual thing to empower people and set up small committees and make sure that those committees have the right mix of people.

Peterson had faith in collaboration and a sense of community. "I just personally had this strong feeling," he explained, "that people need to collaborate and communicate on a regular basis." He remembered the end of his first year at Meadowbrook. "That day," he explained, "people who never [usually] spoke said some wonderful things." Eventually the format of giving everyone a chance to speak (which later developed into a "round robin") became tradition. "It was a way for everyone to be heard. And that was real important because it was the silent majority that was really going to help us set the direction for the school."

They did set direction. By the time the eighth-grade students of this study became first-graders, Meadowbrook students were writing daily and reading "real" books. Workbooks had become a thing of the past, and teachers were about to begin a multiyear word-study project that would result in a developmental approach to the teaching and learning of spelling. As Peterson was quick to point out, change did not proceed without glitches and detours. Everything took time, and nothing was ever really finished. Meanwhile, a strong philosophy about how children learn was developing, a philosophy that was based on practice and close observation and that, together with professional reading, university courses, and lots of conversations with other educators, would guide subsequent decisions about what was "best for the kids."

In 1986 community members, teachers, school board members, and Peterson wrote an official school philosophy, a document of 23 pages including philosophies for the teaching of specific subject areas. It highlighted a

developmental model in terms of both social and intellectual progress, emphasizing the importance of individual learners and lifelong learning for all.
Teachers would, for instance, help students develop their own learning
strengths and interests and assist them in making choices and decisions. Strong
relationships among students and between students and adults were viewed
as critical to learning. By 1992 the philosophy had further developed to
include schoolwide beliefs about the advantages of integrated learning (what
some might refer to as whole-language and what the Meadowbrook school
board called project learning).

Having lagged behind the early elementary grades in terms of integration, the junior high section of the school (by 1991 called the middle school)
set about restructuring its instruction—a restructuring that greatly affected
the eighth-grade students' final year at MCS. A 2-hour humanities block
replaced social studies and language arts. Math and science stayed the same,
but there was a selection of five thematic "magnets" to which students needed
to make official application and for which they would be interviewed by
magnet advisers. Art, music, physical education, advising, and electives would
be integrated within magnets, and once students received their placement,
they would meet with the same eight to ten peers and the same adult
each morning and every afternoon all year. (See the discussion of magnets
in Chapter 3.)

Middle school teachers had found a way to better fit within the written
and implied philosophy of the school. There were problems along the way,
but ongoing assessment led to improvements during the year and more per-
manent changes for the following year. (Students were involved in the planning as well as the assessment.) Nearly everyone, including parents and students, believed that magnets helped create a better sense of community among
the older students. Discipline problems were practically nonexistent, and the
magnet advisers could monitor and guide students' academic efforts—all in
keeping with the school's philosophy of respect for individual learners.

Community was integral to the developing school philosophy. Communication, connection, collaboration, and consensus helped build community,
just as they grew out of community. Adult practices of working together were
mirrored in classrooms where students built and maintained their own communities with their teachers.

Community and harmony are not synonymous, however. Individual students of all ages sometimes acted out, refused to be a part of the process, or
just had bad days. The same held true for the staff, and there were more than
a few who believed that an "outside view" of the staff as well functioning
was deceiving. They believed that growth and the size of the new school had
made community more difficult. They cited problems of communication and
trust, and yet individuals brought those very issues to staff meetings. During

one meeting a teacher explained, "I think it's that we've gotten afraid to not agree. It's easier to go back to our rooms and talk with a select group of people. I've heard that what goes on isn't always harmonious." The statement precipitated an emotional discussion, complete with tears, that was not completely satisfying but kept the issue on the front burner.

There were other difficult issues as well, some precipitated by Meadowbrook citizens. There was a push to be more explicit about expectations for student learning and for specific ways of assessing that learning. The staff grappled with those demands while at the same time identifying their own areas for work. They believed, for example, that writing instruction could and should be improved. They plunged into the work, even though all were not equally equipped to do so. They recognized that, as with the children, each of them needed various amounts of support and patience. And sometimes consensus took more time and energy than any of them thought they could afford.

Still, they nudged one another forward, and the nudging caused some to balk, to complain that it was all too much. Teachers got tired and stressed-out over writing narrative report cards and planning school events. Too often, personal time was sacrificed for the school, and there were ongoing jokes about sleeping overnight in the school or annexing houses to the school building. Jealousies and misunderstandings arose, but talk, even among teachers who felt frazzled, continued, and they looked for new connections because they cared about children.

Some of the teachers worked with the "Big Picture" Committee, a group of townspeople and school staff who were developing a document, called "Meadowbrook Vision for Learning," that would show how the school and community could more fully integrate their resources for lifelong learning. Surveys and updates were mailed to everyone in town, and as the group continued its work, they discovered questions they said they couldn't have known to ask a year earlier. And the talk, the careful listening, the reading, and the writing continued.

WHOLE-SCHOOL LITERACY

A visitor making the rounds of the hallways and peeking through open doorways would find children planning projects, collaborating over writing, reading to one another, singing songs, chanting poems written on charts, and telling stories. They were using written and oral language in the course of initiating and maintaining friendships, learning subject matter, evaluating and planning activities, and having fun. Each context made new demands of developing literacies. The teachers worked to make sure that students had a variety of contexts in which to work and that they were supported in their efforts.

Students weren't the only ones who were busy reading, writing, and talking at the school. The adults at MCS often delighted themselves with their own literate inventiveness. While, certainly, they expected their behaviors to serve as positive literate models for students, they also relished a good time. For example, every day there was a "memo" from Peterson to the staff. The memo was actually a collection of comments from any adult (and sometimes students) to all adults in the school. There were the usual notices about schedules, visitors, and requests for children's books on specific topics. Yet even the "usual" notices offered tantalizing glimpses of what was going on in classrooms: "In case anyone is wondering about my attire, I'm in costume. The 5F class is traveling to Wyoming today . . . by bicycle." There were also jokes and stories. From the maintenance department came: "Bill [the principal] is back. He's the tall one with the black thinning hair and a little gray. He has a tie on that sort of sticks out at the bottom. Guess there wasn't much time for exercise on his vacation. Please don't stare at his stomach." Some were serious: "I've seen foxes two nights in a row—blessings reminding me of how fortunate we are to share this community." One morning Peterson wrote a half-page, single-spaced story about his leaky kitchen plumbing. "I need some encouraging words," he wrote.

A Literate Environment

Elliot Eisner (1991a) has written that school buildings can be designed as egg crates or as large living rooms. "The spaces can be regular or irregular. The surfaces can be mechanical or organic. The environment can include growing plants and living animals or can be furnished to meet janitorial needs. 'What is it like to be here?' is a nontrivial question" (p. 72). There wasn't a classroom in MCS with desks arranged in rows. Instead there were tables or groups of desks to facilitate small-group learning. Teachers' desks, primarily used for storage, were messy places; many teachers operated from tables or children's work areas. Easy chairs, sofas, and big pillows shared space with more traditional school furniture, and children and teachers often sat on the carpeted floors. There were bookcases and classroom libraries, room dividers, and hanging plants. During the year, classrooms took on the characteristics of the children who inhabited them. The classrooms, however, were not small enclaves, different in nature from the school as a whole. Much of what existed beyond classroom walls reinforced and extended what happened in the smaller communities.

Inside the school's lobby was an explosion of printed information. To the left of the centrally located gym doors was a 3-foot-by-5-foot commu-

nity events calendar and a 2-month schedule for gymnasium use. Next to the calendar was the Education Information Center—a bright yellow bookcase filled with books such as Denny Taylor's *Family Literacy*, Margaret Meek's *Learning to Read*, and Jim Trelease's *The New Read Aloud Handbook*, along with books about child development, nutrition, and art. On the other side of the gym door was a large bulletin board that classrooms used to display work. With posters listing information about adult education classes, photographic chronologies of classroom activities, and student-made posters about fund-raisers and other events, there was little space wasted on lobby walls. Townspeople, coming to the school for various reasons, couldn't miss it.

Hallways were decorated with student work such as Native American research, graffiti boards about the Civil War, and student-made maps of the United States. Wall space by water fountains was popular for functional print, such as sign-up sheets for presentations and activities, but notices were everywhere. Student bathrooms had child-written reminders about cleanliness and notices of upcoming events. Adult bathrooms were lined with photocopied tables of contents from current professional journals.

The library was a large open area with a cathedral ceiling at the center. Quilted wall hangings (one made by an entry-level class and the other by a teacher) were on two walls, and student projects were often displayed on tops of book cases. Student-made papier-mâché animals and mobiles hung from the ceilings. A 16-foot cardboard totem pole made by seventh-graders, held steady by wires, stood against the front windows. Jigsaw puzzles and picture storybooks sat on tables, ready for use—even by older students. One corner was designated for story reading, and there was a small rocker for the younger children. The school's "publishing house" equipment was against one wall, and computers were available for staff and student use. Children also had quick access to back issues of magazines and newspapers. The professional library occupied one section of shelves, and teachers and the principal consciously modeled their own literacy by working next to children at library tables. The librarian's office was part of the library, entirely visible to everyone who entered. While classrooms had schedules for visiting the library, individual children could visit at any time. The librarian and library volunteers not only knew students by name but knew them well enough to gauge how much help they might need in finding information or books for personal reading.

When the students of this study were seventh-graders, their curriculum focused around nature, and they built and marked trails in the woods behind the school. Teachers took their students outside whenever they wished, and the outdoor environment often became a stimulus to reading, writing, and talk. Functional print had its place outdoors as well as inside. For instance, when a bird's nesting site was observed, the area was cordoned off and labeled with a sign that read: "Killdeers Nesting. Please Do Not Disturb."

Talking and Listening, a Communal Necessity

Talk was part of the glue that held the school together. Conversation was ongoing. Among adults, staff meetings were frequent, and there were numerous ongoing subgroups and committees such as COGS (Curriculum Oversee Groups) for each subject area and the Writing Framework Committee. Groups of teachers met mornings before the 8:00 opening, and meetings after school often extended into evening hours. Whether groups met around tables or in circles, there was a "going-around" ritual in which all participants could either pass or speak. Individuals spoke without being interrupted. Good listeners were valued, but it was also believed that everyone should have a chance to talk. Those new to the staff learned the ritual by participating in it over and over again. Groups connected with the school, such as PAC (Parents Advisory Council) and FOCUS, also met in circles and "went around." Children and teachers used this procedure in classrooms, especially during sensitive discussions or when decisions had to be made. The eighth-grade class president "went around" at the end of each officers' meeting to make sure nothing was left out. The pervasiveness of the "circle" was underscored when Nicky, another eighth-grader, suggested positions for characters in a play: "They should be sitting in a circle. When people talk, they have to sit in a circle." Talk was universally viewed as a tool of learning, and students had ample opportunities to talk to one another as they worked throughout the day in various social configurations.

Telephone and in-person meetings with parents went beyond the usual parent–teacher conferences at progress report time. Parents "stopped in," and some teachers make it a practice to visit students' homes. The principal also made occasional home visits. The telephone was an important link in a town that was geographically large. Teachers liked to "phone home" with good news as well as not-so-good news. Students phoned teachers to clear up questions about homework, sometimes even just to chat. (Once when the eighth-grade girls were seventh-graders, they frightened themselves with a Ouija board at a slumber party and called their math teacher to calm them down. They said they knew she always stayed up late. And, indeed, she was awake for the call.)

Writing and Reading, a Communal Way of Being

Adults and children wrote collaboratively and individually for personal enjoyment and communication, and adults modeled various functions of print. There were the usual forms and permissions that were sent from school to home, but there were also plenty of classroom and subject-area newsletters such as MAG News (the *Music*, *Art*, and *Gym* newsletter)—"Published now and then for parents and friends." Peterson sent parents weekly memos on subjects as diverse as a summer learning program and pizza night to benefit the playground fund. All teachers, including those in music, art, and physical education, wrote detailed narrative progress reports to parents, a task that required ongoing notation. Fifth-graders wrote a prospectus to encourage start-up investment funds when they decided to launch a calendar company. Children wrote and distributed surveys, then tabulated the results. In fact, during one year it seemed that about every committee or organization that had anything to do with the school wrote a survey. Authentic, purposeful writing was highly valued at the school and in the community. On the other hand, school administrative unit (SAU) paperwork in quintuplicate from the superintendent's office for something like a fieldtrip to the school librarian's house (no bus required) was considered to be a silly, if bureaucratically correct, task. One teacher deliberately used a light blue pen for the top page of the form and pressed lightly as she wrote—an act of quiet rebellion.

Children and adults also communicated through the school's post office. Each class had a mailbox outside its door. Postage was 1 cent, with special delivery costing a nickel and packages priced by weight. Classrooms took turns serving as postal workers, and mail received before 8:45 A.M. was delivered the same day. Improperly addressed envelopes were returned to senders. Children were encouraged to conduct surveys by mail, maintain pen pals, and correspond with children of various ages.

An in-school "publishing house," consisting of adult volunteers who typed, formatted, and bound books, had existed for almost a decade and was funded through FOCUS. Eighth-grade students had used the publishing house since first grade and had carefully saved their books, such as *The Slime Men*, *The Fast Moving Motor Machine*, and *The Lonely Spotted Bunny*. In looking at their books, they noted the different bindings and compared them in terms of durability. They also remembered the early days of elementary school when they sat with adults and translated their words and showed how much space they needed for illustrations. When they were older, they filled out official "publishing requests" indicating, among other things, the size of book, where on the page the printing should be, whether or not binding was desired, and if so, which kind of binding. Students could also submit drawings and writing to the FOCUS-sponsored *The Dragon's Pen*, the school's annual literary magazine, a copy of which was sent to each family.

Children read one another's writing, just as they read professional writers' stories and books. The reading of literature was often a social event during which students shared books with others or recommended things they'd enjoyed. Book "talk," whether written in literature journals, shown through artwork, or shared in conversation, was a daily routine. Children and adults shared the belief that people became better readers through reading.

Literacy and Play

Daily and in many small ways, children and adults found pleasure in the making and sharing of language. There were special events, though, such as the annual Spell-a-Thon, which highlighted literate play. In small groups (teams), students at all grade levels chose names for themselves and then went about selecting words they thought other teams at their grade level ought to be able to spell. Eighth-grade students, wanting to give their classmates a "fun time," read through class notes and books, choosing tricky terms from math, science, and the humanities. Just before Valentine's Day, teams assembled in stairwells, offices, and hallways to "spell-their-hearts-out." Only after team consensus did they offer their answers to the adults who judged their correctness. The highlight of the celebration, however, was the show that adults put on for students.

Prior to the Spell-a-Thon, all adults in the school were assigned to teams. As the children did, the adult teams gave themselves names (e.g., The Spellcasters, Knights of the Holy Grammar, and Elliot Gness and the Unspellables), wrote word lists for other teams, and participated in spelling for a judge. Then they performed skits they'd written that addressed themes of spelling and grammar (often in a satirical fashion, since the school had gone head-to-head with the state board of education over a number of issues and because Harrington and others had been critical of the school's grammar and spelling instruction). There were two performances, one at a party they gave for themselves and the other in the gymnasium for students. One team's skit began with a knight and squire riding onto the stage (the squire clapping blocks of wood together to simulate horses' hooves—much to the delight of the younger children). The knight began:

> My name is Sir Scott [reference to state's governor], knight of the royal board. I am on a crusade to find the elusive Holy Grammar for my Queen, Nancy [reference to chairperson of state board of education]. It is said the Holy Grammar holds many wonderments for learners. The fair people of this most noble land shall have their dreams renewed when I fulfill my quest of returning the Holy Grammar to its rightful heirs.

The adults laughed, and children laughed to hear the adults laugh. The costumes, "hammy" acting, and variety of skits kept students interested. When Mr. Peterson came onto the stage, wearing a dress and a wig, portraying Spell Right (Snow White) trying to teach her dwarfs to spell the word *Meadowbrook*, students laughed and clapped. Some of the eighth-grade students sensed that there were subtle messages in several of the skits; the educational debates had been highly publicized. But mostly, like the younger children, they got a kick out of seeing their teachers and other school adults (secretaries, instructional aides, kitchen personnel, the maintenance director, and bus drivers) dressed up in silly costumes and performing—in ways not completely dissimilar from the presentations and simulations students regularly performed in classrooms.

The Spell-a-Thon performance was not unique. Teachers dressed up as characters during the study of historical periods or in conjunction with other subject matter. One tradition was very important for children—the fourth-grade biography study, which was kicked off by adults assuming the costumes and personas of individuals they'd researched (e.g., Christopher Columbus, Beatrix Potter, Deborah Sampson [a farm wife of the prairie with four children], Georgia O'Keefe, Leonardo da Vinci, Edward R. Murrow, and Adolph Hitler's mother [telling about Hitler]). The adult performances were intended to spur curiosity about biographies and serve as models for fourth-grade research and presentations. The eighth-grade students didn't go to the library for the presentations, but they remembered 4 years earlier when Mr. Peterson had dressed up as Kareem Abdul-Jabbar. They also remembered the year he was Gandhi and walked about the school in a sheet. They remembered, too, the individual characters they'd researched and the oral presentations they'd given and how their parents had come to school. Their memories made them smile.

During 8 years, students collected many literate memories—ones created while in the spirit of play. Monica remembered first grade: "Older students came and read to us, and we read at the rug. They read us these big books and we had little ones to match." Chad remembered when their class made an ABC book that was professionally published. Others chimed in, "And we visited it [the company] to see how it got published and stuff." "Yeah. We wrote our names on these papers and we got a copy of them." "And we signed the book. And we gave them autographs." They remembered *Stone Soup*. "We read the book, did the play, and made the soup." "And we put rocks in it. And everyone who brought a rock got a second bowl, but nobody wanted it because it was so gross." They remembered a book that one of their fifth-grade teachers read. "He read to us about these people who put laxatives in these people's drinks and they had the craps for weeks. Remember? What's that book?"

BEING DIFFERENT

The sense that Meadowbrook itself was somehow different from its surrounding communities extended into the school. Students had a hard time explaining what it was that made MCS different from other schools, or, for that matter, what made *them* different for attending the school, but they did believe their education was different. One commented, "The whole town is unique, and so is the school." Another added, "We do everything different here."

Small things pointed to how students sensed their school as different. One of the eighth-grade classes was in math, and Alicia wanted to make sure she was doing a problem right. "So, we're summing?" she asked the teacher. The teacher looked back at her and responded, "You mean adding? Yes, we're adding, but whatever you do, don't say 'summing' next year [when you're in high school]." Immediately one of the kids chimed in, "Or, they'll know you're from Meadowbrook." Almost everyone laughed. Even though "summing" was not a common Meadowbrook mathematical term, it was different, and as such it fit the image that students held for themselves.

Throughout the year, the eighth-grade students mentioned qualities of their school life that they believed made it different: caring teachers, student voice, "all" the reading and writing, humanities, magnets, so few subjects (because of integration), long classes, the way the teachers taught, working in groups, the size of the school (perceived as small), the opportunity to get close to teachers, the way all the kids in the class were so close to one another, no textbooks (on a regular basis), and everyone talking to everyone else. The students also believed that they had more fun than kids in other schools and that other schools spent more time teaching spelling and grammar. Many believed they would be behind in those subjects when they went to high school and that everyone would be able to tell they were from Meadowbrook—or as one girl explained, "I'll just tell them [the teachers] that I'm from Meadowbrook and that we never covered it." A sense of being different worried some of the students, especially as they approached high school, and some parents were less supportive of the "different" environment than their children were.

Most of the 40 eighth-grade students had been raised in Meadowbrook and knew no other schools; they didn't have a reference for "different." Occasionally a new student came, and stories were shared of workbooks and spelling tests, but the sense of being different seemed to come from others—both in the school and within the larger community. As one of the boys said, "We don't really know [that it's different]. It's just what we've heard."

Bill Peterson didn't think that "different" was a very good adjective for describing the school. He did say that the staff was of a higher quality than in other schools. He preferred to think of MCS as a "better" school rather than a "different" one. A teacher who had lived in town for 25 years and

had been on the committee that hired Peterson commented that she'd never heard of a school staff that knew as much about how children learn as the teachers at MCS. At times, however, she was afraid that such knowledge was interpreted as arrogance and made people stop listening. Some people, she explained, would rather see the school run in ways that were more similar to their own school experience, not different. She said there were other good schools around that didn't rankle the community as much as MCS did.

For others, parents and community members, "different" carried a certain status. In answer to a statement such as, "It'll be different when the kids go to high school next year," a typical response was, "Anything is different from Meadowbrook." There was a certain pride in being different, a way of thinking that mirrored Yankee stoicism. It was as if people wanted to believe that the school was different, not necessarily because "different" implied better-quality education but rather that "different," in and of itself, was something of value. Even critics of the school appeared to take some perverse pleasure in thinking of the school as different—at least in terms of its being different from those in neighboring towns. It was being "different" from how education had "always been" that made some people uncomfortable. Being different from their own experience in school could carry a negative connotation.

The concept of different, whether it implied good or bad, carried extra meaning for graduating eighth-grade students. They'd heard how different their school was for as long as they could remember. They found examples to fit their idea of what "different" meant, and then they took that concept with them to high school—a daunting experience given that most adolescents would rather be anything than different. In response to a newspaper reporter who was doing a follow-up story to another article that had been triggered by critics of the school, one boy told her, "This is a different school, and we learn a different way. Here we get help. We have references, and we can talk to a teacher or another student. In high school it'll be a challenge because it won't be like that."

CONTROVERSY

Misty, the eighth-grade class president, sat in Mr. Peterson's office, holding a draft of a letter she was writing to the editor of a newspaper. At issue was a news article that began, "Just how prepared for high school are students graduating from Meadowbrook Community School? Not very, if you listen to some parents in town." Misty believed that the article unfairly validated the viewpoints of local critics of the school, and she was angry. She told Peterson why she was writing the letter:

I want people to see that the article is totally one-sided. In my opinion, it was totally one-sided. I mean, they threw in like two quotes
from you, right? To somewhat balance the article? And I just wanted
people [to know] because it's frustrating to be a student here and get
labeled [as not being prepared]. Like, we're all getting labeled because
of what [names two women] say. We're all getting labeled.

She was angry because she didn't agree with the women, and the article made
it sound as if they were speaking for a great many of the people in town. She
was angry that she and her peers were being accused of "lacking in language
skills" and of being less prepared for high school than kids from other
towns.

Misty was afraid, though, that her letter would bring more trouble. While
she was trying to paint a picture of what it was like at MCS, she realized that she
was also making some personal statements about specific individuals. She
shared the draft with Mr. Peterson, just as she'd shared drafts of other writing with peers and teachers throughout her 8 years at the school. She was
concerned about audience:

Do you think it's going to turn into this big deal? Into a big deal
where it's like—I don't know. I don't exactly know what I mean. I'm
worried that it's going to turn into something I didn't intend it to turn
into. I don't want them writing stuff back saying like, "What would
she know? She's only a kid," and stuff like that.

Misty was caught in the controversy. It wasn't unusual that a town, especially one that sent its graduating eighth-graders out of district to a number
of high schools, should be interested in academic preparation. Longtime residents, even ones who were schooled in Meadowbrook, couldn't remember a
time when there hadn't been talk about high school preparedness or about
the quality of the local curriculum. In recent years, however, the talk had
heated up—some said because Mildred Harrington moved to town in 1985.
Harrington's activism at the local and state level was well chronicled in
several newspapers. After coming to town, she co-founded Meadowbrook's
antitax group and began fighting the fiscal and curricular "liberalism" she
found at the school. She advocated a return to the basics, citing grammar
and spelling as examples of why students were not adequately prepared for
high school, while at the same time decrying the high cost of schooling. The
two-pronged message attracted antitax proponents as well as those who disagreed with the school's curriculum and policies. Individuals within the group,
some as vocal as Harrington, wrote frequent letters to editors of newspapers
and spoke often at public meetings. As a result, the debate about high school

preparedness had become highly visible. Harrington's tactics, summarized in at least two articles by different newspapers, had served to polarize camps more than the issues alone would have. The debate had at times become highly personal, what some called "nasty."

Money aside, the heart of the curricular debate seemed to be one of philosophy. Through their many contacts with community members and parents, those connected with the school had tried to clearly define the educational philosophy that anchored instruction in Meadowbrook. In doing so, however, they'd risked unsettling people by introducing foreign concepts such as individual development, student decision making, self-evaluation, choice, and approximation.

One parent who supported Harrington's activism, Nancy Wilcox, had been to all the meetings and had heard the discussions. She credited her own success in school with having "got the basic foundation down pat." For her, "creativity" was fine for first, second, and third grades, but after the early years she thought students needed to "settle into learning something." Her experience told her that creativity and learning were not natural partners. She'd heard about the importance of relationship and community in the classroom; she'd heard about "facilitating" instead of "teaching" but felt that teachers spent too much of their energies trying to get kids to like school. Magnets were a waste of time; she wanted more structure, what she described as "sitting down in the classroom and getting the information out of a textbook." Learning was work; it didn't have to be fun. At a public meeting, she voiced her concern that children get an education that would allow them to compete in high school and the world. "We want textbooks. We want testing. We want classroom learning and homework."

Her comments and her often-angry assaults alienated some people, even those who agreed with her about some issues. They didn't want to align themselves with her publicly, and because they agreed with most of what the school was doing, they remained quiet. A longtime resident and MCS staff member pointed to areas of parental concern: "Grammar and spelling represent ways parents were taught. That's comfortable for them. When kids go home with uncorrected spelling, parents don't know what's going on." Teachers continually explained about approximated spellings and children's developing understanding of sound–symbol correspondence, but there seemed to linger a parental fear that their children would never learn to spell unless they used more traditional methods. The same was true for language usage, what most people referred to as grammar. Both spelling and grammar were defined by rules, and there was something reassuring about the discipline required for learning and following rules. As Newkirk (1991b) surmised, parents became frightened when they perceived a certain permissiveness in the education of their children—a concept of permissiveness that was triggered by words such as *choice* and *fun*.

This fear seemed to grow and become more of an issue as children approached high school age. Even parents who had come to understand the school's philosophy could get a bit edgy as high school approached. At a meeting for parents of middle school students, parents wanted to make sure that their children were getting enough homework, and they wanted to know if there was a policy for missing homework. They wanted to know if the teachers had methods for making sure that students were organized. All of these concerns were rooted in discipline—making children do what they might not want to do because it was somehow good for them. Another parent felt caught between his appreciation of the affective goals of the magnet program and his sense that it wasn't rigorous enough: "This may be perfect for here, but what about getting them ready for high school?" The sentiment was echoed by another parent, one who seemed to understand what education in Meadowbrook was about. "Are high schools in tune with middle schools?" she wanted to know. No matter how sound she believed the philosophy of MCS to be, she knew the kids had to move on.

The very public debate about high school preparedness did little to quell concerns that some parents had. As both sides went at it, most parents could only trust in their children and in their children's teachers. Parents wanted the best for their children, but they became less sure of what that was as their children prepared to leave Meadowbrook for the "real world."

SUMMARY

The school was at the center of the Meadowbrook community. It was the link between the smaller learning communities of classrooms and the larger supporting community of the town. It was a hub for social activity as well as a catalyst for community effort and discussion. It was a reminder that continuing education was the goal for all community members. Talk, writing, reading, and listening were important within each of the communities and served as essential links between them. The communities didn't always run smoothly, and consensus, a highly valued goal, could at times seem unattainable. A vision of what might be, sometimes shared and sometimes fought over, forced groups to reflect on and expand their understandings of what was important. Growth during the preceding decade had strained ties, and for some, new ideas were hard to incorporate into old ways of being. The debate about schooling and what was best for children was a sign that the community took the responsibility for educating its children seriously. The school itself provided a literate environment in which both adults and children learned about the world and themselves through engagement with language and one another.

CHAPTER 3

Life in the Eighth Grade

*People learn language to participate more fully in the social life of family
and community, not for the sake of learning language. Language and
learning are both social. It is by using language to learn and to participate in
the world that understanding of language and the world develops.*

Ralph Peterson
Life in a Crowded Place, 1992, p. 76

The students in the eighth grade had a reputation for being a "good" class.
Parents, teachers, and the students themselves agreed that the class had always
worked and played well together. Former teachers remembered them with
pleasure. Parents routinely put extra plates on for dinner, and sleeping bags
were standard visiting equipment. The students knew they were loved, and
they tried to live up to their reputation. "Good" meant being kind. It meant
listening to and accepting other people. It meant behaving in ways that were
acceptable to various circles of community. It meant belonging. Monica
echoed the comments of peers when she explained of the school, "It's a big
community. A big family kind of school. Not just out for learning. It's out to
build relationships with other people and to learn how to handle situations.
It just welcomes people." Monica, who had attended MCS for 8 years, was a
hard-working student and learning was important to her, yet she instinctively
appreciated the social nature of that learning. And though she couldn't have
articulated it, reading, writing, and talk were bound up in the interaction
between cognitive and social development.

MAGNETS: SHARED AUTHORITY AND AUTHENTIC LITERACIES

When the eighth-grade students arrived at school in the fall of 1991, their
teachers had surprises for them—humanities and year-long magnets. Even
though their class president had joined the middle school committee for summer meetings and they'd heard tales of changes, the students were somewhat

skeptical. They liked the "old" elective program, and they wondered whether a 2-hour humanities block (reading, writing, social studies) was a step backward when they should be having separate teachers for separate subjects in preparation for high school. Their teachers explained their concern that students lost a sense of "belongingness" when they moved out of self-contained classrooms and into departmentalized ones. They said they hoped magnets and a 2-hour humanities block would help students build closer relationships with peers and adults.

Magnets were "themed" and, as much as possible, integrated music, art, and physical education into those themes. Magnets met every day—for 20 minutes first thing in the morning and for 45 minutes after lunch. The principal and the occupational therapist co-advised the health-themed Wellness Magnet. The special education teacher advised the Communications Magnet, which, among other activities, wrote the yearbook. The eighth-grade humanities teacher advised the information and musically themed Music and Media Magnet, and the math teacher advised the socially conscious Kids Care Magnet. At the beginning of the year, the advisers "marketed" magnets to students, who listened to the oral presentations and read written descriptions, such as:

> In this MAGNET, students will be made aware of some of the problems that face Americans today. The issues of poverty and homelessness will be discussed, as well as what students can do to make a difference in these areas. This may include organizing food drives for the Meadowbrook Food Pantry, making toys and writing books for children in homeless shelters, and involvement in a variety of outreach programs. Give of yourself, become part of "KIDS CARE," and find out what life is all about.

Then, in a process similar to job hunting, students wrote resumes, completed applications for first and second choices, obtained peer recommendations, and were interviewed by magnet advisers (examples of authentic uses of reading, writing, talk, and listening).

After the initial organization and as students and adults "settled in," each magnet developed its own personality, its own accepted behaviors, and its own goals. Each dealt with problems—ones met when reaching consensus or in sustaining energy to see projects through. (An eighth-grade Archaeology Magnet, advised by an inexperienced teacher-intern, failed after the first 6 weeks, and the other four magnets then incorporated the members into their own groups—an action that increased group size to about 10 and set the newly gelled magnets back a bit.) Because magnet advisers awarded no grades, self-assessment and assessment of communal efforts were ongoing and purposeful. Students felt responsible for how their magnets operated and took pride in their accomplishments.

Choice, Voice, and Ownership

In keeping with the school's philosophy, students had voice in determining magnet direction and activities. Sometimes advisers presented various possibilities; other times students brainstormed for ideas. Even after a general direction was set or an activity was selected, students had a say in how it actually ran. For example, after the members of the Music and Media Magnet decided they liked Mr. Carew's idea for a "radio" program, it was they who decided on the name (WMNM for W Music and Media), the format (taped segments dubbed with a music "bed" onto a master tape and reproduced for individual play in MCS's classrooms), and individual responsibilities (e.g., manager, sports and current events reporters, and birthday announcer). Mr. Carew trained them to use equipment and offered coaching, but the program always belonged to the students. When some of the students lost interest midyear, it was the students who discussed the problem.

Casual talk, as well as focused discussions, was highly valued in magnets. Much of it occurred while students worked on projects, but advisers and students understood that they could take time for chatting about things such as sports, arguments with siblings, and shaving. They didn't have to feel guilty about robbing time from the curriculum because talk was integral to it. Students, especially quiet ones, found that magnets were safe places to talk about things that mattered to them; everyone understood that personal conversations remained within groups. Advisers were conscious of not dominating student talk and tried to contribute only as much as others did. If the situation called for an adult's point of view, the adviser often prefaced remarks with comments such as, "I'm speaking as an adult now . . ." When one student dominated conversation, other students or the adviser attempted to draw those who hadn't said anything into the conversation with comments such as, "Mike hasn't said anything yet. What do you think, Mike?"

Authentic Contexts for Literacies

Reading, writing, and talk were authentic in terms of the magnets' themes and the groups' purposes. Depending on the magnet, students read theme-related novels, plays, advertising brochures, copy for the yearbook, newspapers, letters, and instructions. Students wrote dialogue journals to their advisers; thank-you notes and letters seeking information, materials, or money; newsletters; radio copy; questionnaires; articles for the local newspaper; memos; plays; musical lyrics; and promotional materials.

When the students in Kids Care decided that the local food pantry needed money in addition to their donations of food, Rachelle wrote to FOCUS (school/ community organization). "We are doing well, but there is always a need for more food. We would like to ask if FOCUS could make a donation." FOCUS sent Kids Care a $300 check for the pantry. At other times, students collaboratively wrote articles for the local weekly newspaper asking for donations to the food drive and updating citizens about their plans to help homeless shelters. They wrote, not for grades or as an assignment, but because they honestly hoped to garner assistance. They also understood that the magnet program was being closely evaluated by the public and wanted to give their magnet some good press.

Responsibility and Reflection

Student representatives met about once a month during lunch hours to evaluate how their magnets were operating. Problems, such as students' perceptions of inadequate gym time or a perceived need for magnets to occasionally "get together," were addressed as they arose. At the end of the year a committee of eighth-graders wrote a magnet assessment survey for their peers. The committee compiled the results of the survey (e.g., 85% were comfortable with their advisers and magnet peers) for the middle school committee and the school board.

Students also assessed their own and their magnets' efforts. For example, when the Wellness Magnet played a Saturday morning basketball game against a Special Olympics team, they spent time the following Monday reviewing their play and sorting out their feelings. The central issue was competitiveness. How hard should they have played the other team, and was it right to play less well than they knew they could? And if they did, could they make their play believable? As one said, "It's hard for me to slow myself down, and then it looks like I'm trying not to win." Most felt that they'd played unevenly—trying too hard to win at times. Their adviser, Mr. Peterson, asked occasional focusing questions, such as "Would it have been a good morning if we'd lost 12 to 2?" and "Why were we there?" It was the students, however, who assessed their efforts—and created new criteria for success on the basketball court.

Coming Together

Certainly students and teachers had opportunities throughout the day for interaction; magnets weren't the only factor in building community and strengthening relationships. However, teachers and students alike asserted that magnets helped everyone get along better, even outside of magnets. (Students responded to open-ended survey questions: "I learned not to prejudge people." "I can speak out more as a person." "I've learned to be more tolerant.") "Best" friends were often separated by magnets, which meant that tighter friendships developed among students whose friendships had formerly been more casual. Working closely together every day, whether it was in making rag dolls for homeless shelters, painting wall murals, learning to play the guitar, or helping during a blood drive—all the while dealing with issues of responsibility to the group and personal growth—brought students and adults together in ways that weren't always possible in classrooms. Feelings of trust and self-esteem that developed in magnets augmented what was happening in the larger community, making it stronger and more supportive of teaching and learning. And, importantly, within this supportive context, students practiced literate behaviors for a variety of real purposes and audiences.

ORGANIZATION FOR LEARNING WITHIN A COMMUNITY

One can tell a lot about people by entering their homes or work spaces. Indeed, organization, both physical and temporal, may define what takes place there. Objects, by their presence or by their absence, may indicate what is valued or even how involved occupants are in their surroundings. If the eighth-grade students of Meadowbrook Community School thought of themselves as a big family, then the school, and specifically the space that they inhabited, might be considered a type of home. As such, its organization of space and time not only characterized but facilitated what they did there.

Bells were not only unnecessary at MCS but would have been an intrusion on people who thought of time in terms of "abouts." Elementary teachers took their students to recess when it fit their flow of activity and returned with them when students had had "enough" time outside. The only nod to electronic signaling was a quiet tone at the end of the day—reminding everyone that it was time for buses. Even then, some eighth-grade students, so accustomed to going with the flow, not only didn't "hear" the tone but were surprised to learn that there was one. On the other hand, students didn't notice the absence of bells during the rest of the day. Nobody really thought about it.

Until time was carved out of the schedule in March for a short study period, class periods were in easy-to-remember 1-hour and 2-hour blocks. Teachers and students changed classes close to actual times, but no one made a fuss if a class was a bit late. The seventh- and eighth-grade classes rotated through the back doors of the connecting classrooms, with students in the last room filing out the front door, down the hall, and into the first room again—a kind of elliptical traffic flow that eliminated the bumping and shoving of two-way traffic. Whichever class finished first started the rotation by lining up and someone from that class softly knocking on the connecting door. If the next classroom wasn't finished, students waited quietly until it was and then began emptying into the next one. The whole process took only a few minutes; because most of the students had simply moved from one classroom to the next, and because individual homerooms stayed together as units, transition between classes was smooth. No bells, no tardy students, no warnings or detentions.

After morning magnets, first-period classes began when everyone was accounted for. Often, the first few minutes of a period were spent in activities that didn't demand everyone's presence, so a quick drink at the fountain or a fast trip to the bathroom didn't create a problem. If a student wasn't present after that time, it was for a good reason, and a bell wouldn't have made a difference. In many ways, the group managed time; time didn't manage it. Students and teachers took a 15-minute (or so) snack break midmorning and had all their academic classes finished by the time they ate lunch at 12:30. Only magnets remained for the afternoon.

The classrooms reflected the activities that took place in them. The humanities room was a clutter of resources and equipment—everything from a donated microfiche reader/printer and a shortwave radio to a collection of borrowed guitars and a movable bookcase filled with back issues of news magazines. Each of the rooms contained at least one hand-me-down easy chair and a bookcase filled with paperback novels. Plants in various stages of health hung from ceilings. Walls were filled with student work, lists of things to do for current projects, news clippings, and informational notices. Chalkboards were the best indicators of where the fronts of rooms were, since students sat either with desks shoved together or at tables. Teachers' desks were never at the "front" with the chalkboards but against back walls surrounded by equipment or bookcases. A homey feeling pervaded all the rooms, particularly the adjacent math and humanities rooms, the homerooms of the eighth-graders.

There was also a physical closeness among students. They often sat with elbows and knees touching, and although the easy chairs and rocking chairs were designed for single occupancy, students often tucked two of themselves (sometimes more) into the seats. They worked with partners or groups on the classroom floor and in the hallway, and with plenty of room to spread out, they sat cross-legged, knees touching, and heads together. Pairs sat against the wall with shoulders and hips touching. Students plopped on their stomachs side by side and read or wrote together. The carpeted floors were considered important work space, and teachers met their students where they frequently were—on the floor.

Gender was not a barrier to this physical closeness. Boys were just as apt to sit with one another as girls were to sit together. Girls and boys also sat together—as friends. "Couples," of which there were few, planned their seating arrangements more consciously than the others, but their physical closeness was not out of the norm.

This physical closeness was a given, something they'd been accustomed to since the first and second grades. Girls played with one another's hair—rubbed it against the backs of their hands or against their cheeks. They patted one another or rubbed one another's backs while teachers read to them or they watched films. At snack time, students shared bites from sandwiches and cookies. Students lived in their space, generally accommodating one another's personalities and needs. While, as in any family, there were those who got along better with everyone than others, comments such as "That's just Andy" signaled general acceptance of peers' behaviors. Students rarely put one another down, at least within the classroom.

CONTROLLING THEIR OWN BEHAVIORS

Eighth-grade students believed themselves to be responsible people; a heavy emphasis on rules and consequences would not only have been demeaning but might have undercut students' sense of self-control. It didn't make much sense to resist authority, because although ultimate authority lay with adults, students did have a voice in day-to-day operations and had recourse through their class officers to influence policy. When they didn't like having to stay in their homerooms for snack break, for example, the student council negotiated a compromise with teachers.

Their attitudes about rules and responsibility became abundantly clear when Mr. Carew, with all apparent sincerity (as an introduction to a unit on revolution), distributed copies of "New 7th and 8th Grade Rules":

1. Students will not be allowed to go to recess until 15 minutes after the lunch period has started. During lunch, you may talk to your neighbor only the first 5 minutes of the lunch period and the remainder of the time you must stay silent so that everyone will be able to enjoy lunch in peace and quiet.
2. Any student who is late to class and does not have a note from a teacher will automatically receive a detention.
3. During snack time you must stay in your own homeroom and also in your own seats.
4. In order to eliminate problems going to the bus at the end of the day,

each student in the 7th and 8th grade will be escorted by their home-room teacher to their appropriate bus; this will be done by homeroom.

5. A detention will automatically be given to the student who: (a) leans back in his/her chair, (b) is found wearing a coat, (c) is chewing gum, (d) is wearing a hat.

The immediate response was one of disbelief. They questioned the authority under which the rules had been formulated. Who wrote them? Kids had no input. Were parents on the committee? One of the students pointed out, "It's not official. There aren't any signatures here." They wanted to know what precipitated the new rules. Were there problems with the buses? Was there a problem at lunch? They questioned the workability of the rules: "They can't be enforced; too many kids will have detentions." Finally, students began to doubt themselves. Janelle asked, "Doesn't anyone trust us? Everyone says how good we are." Someone added, "Mr. Peterson has always made it clear that he trusted us." As students become more upset, Lenny suggested, "Could we all sit in a circle and be organized so we can hear everyone?"

Students were troubled on a number of counts, and they remained upset about the "rules" even after Carew told them they were bogus. There was a feeling that the rules would have set kids up for getting into trouble. "I'd do everything bad," Andy said. Mark added, "I wouldn't care if I got a detention for tipping in my chair. I wouldn't care. The rule is stupid."

Many of the "rules" reflected what students already did. No one, including adults, chewed gum in the school. Students did occasionally lean in chairs or wear hats, but they stopped when asked—without argument and mostly with an "I'm sorry." It was the idea of rules, ones that seemed to be set up for their own sake, that made students angry and doubt the foundation of trust they'd built over the years with adults in the school. Official rules and accompanying punishments undermined the students' sense of being trusted as responsible eighth-graders. As one asserted, "We can control ourselves. We're old enough."

During the year, fewer than a handful of students needed to be "talked to." Detentions were nonexistent. When in the spring about a month before graduation several of the eighth-grade boys began flinging stones on the playground, Mr. Peterson called the entire eighth-grade class together and asked them "as a favor" to him to behave for the rest of the year, just as they had behaved up to that point. The stone flinging stopped—either as a favor to Peterson or because students understood that it didn't make much sense. Peterson had determined that singling out the offenders might trigger more "senioritis" misconduct and, instead, had appealed to the eighth-grade community to do what they knew they should do, thus making sure that responsibility for controlling behavior remained with students.

ACADEMIC CLASSES: LEARNING AND LEARNING HOW TO LEARN

Pleasant as the social life in the eighth grade often was, the shared expectation among students and teachers was that people were there to learn. That
didn't mean that the adults were the only teachers or that students were the
only learners. ("It helps me to learn in a group because other people can help
when I need help, or I can help them.") Everyone, to some degree, was responsible for the learning of others. Whether the subject matter was barometric
pressure, common motifs in various versions of "Cinderella," the Cartesian
coordinate system, or American westward expansion, collaboration was one
of the primary means of exploring and mastering content. Social and learning communities were thus dynamically entwined.

"Doing" was also central to the learning process. When students studied the U.S. legislative system, they researched and wrote bills before presenting them in day-long "congressional" hearings. When they studied mathematical proportions, they graphed, enlarged, then distorted comic-strip
characters onto posterboard. Students especially appreciated science for its
hands-on approach. Porosity of various soil types meant little to them, for
example, until they measured amounts of water that the soils could absorb.
Follow-up activities—written reports, short essays, and discussions—were
teacher-designed to give learners a chance to reflect on and make sense of
experiences. Students also operated in more traditional modes—taking reading and class notes, doing library research, studying from textbooks, memorizing information, and answering study questions—but they did these things
within the context of wider classroom experiences.

All of the teachers had strong individual personalities and instructional
preferences, but the persona of "caring teacher," together with working in
groups and hands-on learning, mattered most to students. As Nicky explained,
caring meant not giving up on students when they couldn't figure things out
or didn't try very hard. Caring also meant being kind and teaching others to
be kind. Miss Arno, the math teacher, was very strict. "She has these eyes,
and you know when you're in trouble," but she also praised students' efforts
and served as a model to students who encouraged one another with "Way
to go!" and "There you go." When Arno wouldn't tell the lowest score on a
test, Ginny explained: "That would make somebody with the lowest grade
feel bad."

Caring meant thinking of students as kids, not just learners—listening
to their stories and empathizing with their problems. Students routinely talked
with Mrs. Taylor during lunch or after school, usually about nothing very
important, just friendly talk. As Nicky explained, "Mrs. Taylor—I like more
in a friend way because she's easy to talk to." For others, it was Mr. Carew
or Miss Arno they enjoyed talking with most. "Mr. Carew is like a second

father," Misty explained. "Miss Arno's a cupcake," Ginny offered. The feeling, however, was that each of the teachers, all of whom they'd had for both seventh and eighth grades, was approachable and sincerely interested in the students as people.

The threads of collaboration, hands-on learning, and caring teachers were woven throughout academic classes, linking them in spirit with magnets and providing predictable stability for learning. The students believed that these threads were somewhat unique to Meadowbrook. When, for instance, they wrote individual letters to eighth-graders in other states, they repeatedly highlighted their importance: "There's a lot of hands-on activities." "We constantly work in groups and textbooks are rarely opened." "We have very caring teachers. It's hard to describe them to you because even 'wonderful' is a grand understatement. They really care."

Humanities

A typical day in humanities began with Mr. Carew explaining the daily agenda he'd written on the front board. One day in late October, the agenda included: "Intro. Stuff, Content Check, Historical Novel Picks, Intro. to Roanoke, Break, Status-of-the-Class, Writing." There wasn't a slot for current events, and some of the students were disappointed; they liked talking about the news. Recently they'd discussed Clarence Thomas and sexual harassment, Gorbachev cutting back on nuclear weapons, a meeting between Haiti's Jean-Bertrand Aristide and George Bush (a topic that elicited interest because a visitor had spoken about Haiti a few weeks earlier), and the World Series.

Instead, they were working with their social studies textbooks for a few days, something they did infrequently. The students "didn't mind" them; they'd used textbooks before in other classes and grades, though never as sole sources for information. They understood that Carew was assigning the texts to help them access specific information about the colonial period but perhaps, more important, to prepare them for high school. He'd told them before, "When you get into high school, the teacher is going to say, 'Read such and such pages and answer questions one through five.' You're going to use textbooks as your main source of information. Now that's not bad, but it's not what we do."

The students had learned through experience that reading textbooks was different from other kinds of reading (as Sharon explained, "I don't learn by reading textbooks. I can tell you that much. I don't remember a single thing."), but they were willing to go along with Carew for the sake of making it easier the following year. The day before, he'd shown them a structured overview

of "Political Changes in the [American] Colonies" and explained how he'd constructed it from the boldfaced headings in the book. The students had copied the overview into their notes. Their homework assignment had been to read the chapter and flesh out the overview. Telling the students to use their notes from the night before, he assigned groups of four and five students and told each group to refer to a specific section, discuss it, and prepare a presentation for the rest of the class. Carew circulated among the groups, answering questions and providing suggestions about how they might dramatize their summaries.

One group spent as much time discussing process as planning the actual presentation. Nicky wanted to reread the text first ("We have to *hear* it"), and Lenny wanted to compare notes ("We all have the same notes, so we shouldn't have to read it"). He wanted to compose a master set of notes and read it to the rest of the class; she thought they needed to do more. By the time they'd decided they didn't have enough time to reread the text, Carew was with them, suggesting that they pick out an important part from their section and dramatize it in a vignette-like skit. With time running out, they quickly decided that they'd show King George and Parliament telling colonists that England wouldn't put a lot of restrictions on the colonists because it had too many other things to do—something that would make the colonists happy. The students assumed roles of king, colonists, a business owner, and a member of Parliament.

After the presentations, they "debriefed" the activity. Carew asked them what they'd needed to do in order to summarize for the rest of the class. Various students pointed to the importance of first sentences in paragraphs, the boldfaced print, and the "boring stuff" with dates. When no one mentioned the big picture of the structured overview, Carew reminded them of its purpose. By that time, students had stopped listening. Nicky told him that she thought the questions at the end of the chapter were "dumb." Susan added that the answers were always in the boldfaced print anyway. Carew reminded them that they didn't have to "play" textbook questions, that he hadn't assigned them. While the students had been willing to read and consider the text, they made it clear that they didn't value end-of-chapter questions—a reaction that was endorsed by Carew.

When the class returned from a quick bathroom and water-fountain break, Carew introduced six novels about the colonial period and distributed multiple copies of each. Students could choose from among them or "clear" other titles with Carew. The assignment of a historical novel meant that some would be reading more than one book at a time. For Nicky it meant three: one for magnet, one she was reading on her own, and the one for humanities. "It's okay, though," she said. "They're all different."

When Carew handed out sheets of project ideas for the books, students' hands shot up. "Can we do more than one?" "Do we get extra credit if we do?" "The books are different lengths, and we have to do this project in 20 days?" They went over the list, which included ideas for a timeline, a flow-chart for characters, a play based on the continuation of the story, a diary of one of the characters, a letter to the author, a front page of a newspaper dating to the time of the book, and a mural. Carew told them that the ideas repre-sented various levels of difficulty and that they should choose something that challenged them. If they had other ideas, they needed to talk to him. Know-ing they'd eventually have to write proposals for projects, students immedi-ately began making plans. "I'm going to write a play." "If we do posters, can we put them around the school?"

The class was full of voices, and Carew needed to get everyone's attention before proceeding to the next agenda item—Roanoke, a section in their social studies textbooks. After he told them that the story was one of his favorites, he asked them to think like social scientists who were studying the lost colony of Roanoke. They had 2 days to write a field report of a couple of pages stating the basic outline of events and restating the basic questions surround-ing the mystery of Roanoke. Then they were to write their "professional" opinions about what really happened. Students considered this a typical assignment—even if they had to read a textbook to complete it. It was simi-lar to the reflective essays they wrote after discussions or simulations.

Time was running short. Carew and the students often complained about the lack of time. They had only 20 minutes left when they gathered in the corner to do a "status-of-the-class," where the students, by turn, stated their plans for writing time. Most had writing projects under way, and one of the boys wondered if they could begin writing as soon as their names were called. He told Carew that he "wouldn't have time for anything" unless they did. Carew apologized for running late. Students found places to be alone or gathered in pairs and small groups. It took a while to settle in, and by the time kids were writing, it was time to pack up. Some grumbled. Others reacted as if they were off the hook.

Math

In spite of clustered seating, easy chairs, available trade books, and occa-sional forays into projects such as the previously described enlarging and distorting of cartoons, math instruction was traditional—at least in the con-text of the rest of eighth-grade experience. Collaboration was casual, not structured, and "hands-on" typically meant students putting pencils to paper. Without exception though, students said that Miss Arno was a good math teacher. ("She's real strict, but she makes you learn.") When asked if they wished for more hands-on math projects, some said they did but most were satisfied with the way things were.

They also understood that Miss Arno expected them to read—as well as do their math homework. At the beginning of one midwinter class, Arno distributed monthly book-club orders, pointing out that there were two novels by Paulsen, the author of *Hatchet*. Hank complained that all the books were too short, that the book company should include "fat" books in the brochures. Students talked about that and about the movies *Hook* and *Beauty and the Beast* as they read through the fliers. No one ever questioned why it was Miss Arno who was in charge of book orders or why they would use math time for talking about books and movies. It was just the way it was.

When Arno stepped to the front of the room and asked what students remembered about the Cartesian coordinate system. Lenny answered, "*x*'s and *y*'s." John added, "the axis thing." Bobby said, "a point has to have a negative and positive sign." Arno wrote an example of a point with two positive signs on the board. Jaci said, "abscissa and ordinate," and John said, "ordered pairs." All of the students' responses were directed to Arno. One of the students distributed graph paper. Arno and the students worked with the equation, "$y = x^2 - 1$," charting ordered pairs and then plotting points into the shape of a parabola on the axes they'd drawn on their papers. They charted a hyperbola, and then Arno teased, "I'm going to ruffle your feathers," before she erased some values and wrote in new ones. "I've got a problem with that," Hank challenged, referring to the graph, "you're never going to touch the axis." Engaged, students worked with Arno until she assigned homework with about 10 minutes left in the period to start it. She put on a Michael Bolton tape before circulating among groups of desks to help those who were still puzzled.

Most days were like this—presentation of material (usually via an overhead projector so that Arno could face students and watch for their reactions) with Arno's and students' questions laced into instruction. The class worked as a whole (or in small groups) to solve problems that Arno or students posed; those sitting next to one another collaborated as they worked but didn't talk when Arno was talking to the whole group. Most learned to volunteer answers when they had them so that she wouldn't call on them when they weren't prepared. (Miss Arno didn't always wait for volunteers.) They took careful notes and used them for completing homework and studying for tests, something that was especially important during the last half of the year when they studied algebra without textbooks. The class was not grouped by ability and even though students felt comfortable asking questions, Arno made a point of connecting with students who usually needed extra help. She was available during lunch recess, after school, and at home by telephone.

Science

Science class belonged to the students. The class was talkative and Mrs. Taylor sometimes had difficulty getting everyone's attention at once. Most of the instruction, however, was in small groups and often involved students' hands-on participation. Students voiced their preference for labs, especially if they went several days without them. They lit birthday candles in cylinders to measure the percentage of oxygen in the air, used computers to draw weather maps, and built barometers out of balloons and coffee cans. They voted on areas of study they wanted to pursue, wrote poems about invertebrates, wrote and produced videotapes that demonstrated knowledge of scientific phenomena, took turns teaching the rest of the class, wrote long take-home tests (even over the Christmas vacation), and more or less romped through science.

During labs, the room was full of overlapping talk. Students who hadn't listened to whole-class directions called on Mrs. Taylor to explain procedures to their groups. Other groups, tired of waiting, deliberated over written instructions: "The directions don't say anything about having to poke a hole." The students admitted that they behaved differently in science class than they did at any other time of the day, but they weren't bothered by it. Most said they liked the atmosphere, which was a nearly equal balance between social and academic pursuits, and thought their behaviors fit Mrs. Taylor's teaching style—what one student described as "kind of laid-back." Some, however, wished that Mrs. Taylor could have "controlled" the noisy ones better. Yet even as they complained about wasted time, they said they liked science and learned a lot in the class—mostly because Mrs. Taylor let them *do* things.

When students decided that they wanted to learn about astronomy and outer space, Taylor asked partners to teach the rest of the class about various space-related topics. She provided support and direction for all the "teachers" during the unit of study, which lasted nearly a month. Typical of those sessions was the day Ginny and Susan, having already taught the two previous days, asked the class to form small groups to propel rockets (straws) on strings. Susan gave them procedure sheets that listed available materials, directions, and elements to include on lab reports while Ginny distributed supplies. Amid the usual din, groups formed and set to work.

Nicky and Jaci, who often worked together, invited John to join them. The girls cut a straw in half and pushed the string through it. They blew up a balloon and held the end so that the air didn't escape. Then, with John's help, they taped the balloon to the straw. Having followed the rest of the directions, they then shot their straw along the string—five times, recording distance each time. As Jaci talked it out, Nicky began writing the report: "Purpose—The purpose was to see how a rocket flys [sic]. The balloon had a thrust that pushed it along the string just like a rocket." Then Nicky talked as Jaci wrote: "Procedure—The procedure is to take a string and put it threw [*sic*] the straw." They continued by making a table that showed the distance that the balloon traveled each time. They found a conversion table in a math book and wrote their answers in both inches and centimeters. Jaci wrote the conclusion: "We learned that the balloon flew by the air which is how the rocket flies by thrust and travels distance." Except for helping with the balloon, John didn't contribute to the process and, instead, played with a chair leg. The girls said they didn't mind and wrote his name on the report. John was their friend, and he'd probably do more next time.

Exams and Tests

Teachers explained that they gave exams to prepare students for taking midterms and finals in high school. Still, among themselves, they discussed what the exams actually accomplished, wondered if they were remnants of more traditional instruction, and considered alternatives. Carew was particularly ambivalent and told students, "I'm having a hard time with the whole midterm process. The purpose is for students and teachers to know what is being learned, but I already have an idea of that. The reason is to prepare you for high school exams." Students, nervous about what high school would mean, reviewed material with teachers and peers, took exams, and hoped that the experience would help them the following year. Misty said that her older brother, a year ahead of her in school, was glad he had taken the exams, that kids who hadn't had them in seventh and eighth grades "bombed" them their freshman year.

Consequently, eighth-grade students thought of exams as a kind of inoculation against failure in high school—necessary but not pleasant. "This is the next-to-the-worst day of the year," Brent said softly as he looked at his humanities midterm exam before adding, "Well, maybe not. Maybe I'll know more for finals. This is hard stuff." The project-oriented humanities classroom wasn't set up for the formality of a midterm exam; there were too many "things" in it. The desks, in rows for the first time all year, were crowded, so that the students' elbows nearly touched during the 2-hour exam.

There were 70 multiple-choice questions covering content and current events and 6 questions that addressed language usage in content (e.g., "Using either 'there is,' 'we are,' or 'they have' as a contraction, describe in 1 sentence and in your opinion, Gandhi's most successful moment.") Students also had to write a response to any 1 of 27 political cartoons posted around the room, an exercise that necessitated stretching their legs. Their last task was to answer 1 of 5 essay questions (e.g., "How has your opinion of revolution changed from what you thought it was entering into eighth grade? What are some places around the world that have recently experienced revolution? Use your knowledge about the differences and similarities between the Indian and American revolutions as a guide.").

During the 2-hour exam, students got up for dictionaries and to choose among cartoons. Sometimes students moved away from their desks to work as they usually did. Nicky gathered her papers, found something hard to write on, and moved her midterm to the rocking chair. A few like Misty, who generally overstudied and overworried, were near panic and could do little but hunch tightly over their desks. When exams were finished, students compared anxieties. Ann coined a word for how she felt—"staticky"—like nothing stayed where it should for long.

Regular tests and quizzes didn't have "good medicine" lore attached to them; they were part of an ongoing assessment routine that was tied closely to instruction. Quizzes helped students and teachers know where they stood before going on to new material, and tests, along with projects and papers, showed what students had learned.

Tests were also viewed by teachers as opportunities to extend classroom instruction and prior learning tasks, so they not only gave students in-class time for study but provided review sheets or outlines and planned classroom activities that would help students review. Sometimes students worked in groups to write review sheets for their peers. Other times, they were responsible for submitting questions about concepts they didn't understand or for identifying sections of class notes that were incomplete or made no sense.

Most students preferred studying together, even though they had different ways of going at it. Monica said that Nicky could be "too picky" when they reviewed together but that her questions generally helped—even though the review took forever. Nicky said that she didn't learn by answering other people's questions but only by asking questions of others. A few chose to study alone. Susan explained, "I never get to really work alone." John, definitely a social type who rarely studied at home, had his own reasons for sometimes studying alone in school. "Instead of copying it down [for later study] from everyone," he explained. "I look it up for myself and then I remember it." Different styles of studying were accepted among students and by teachers.

Students expected tests to be challenging, but they also expected classroom support for studying, just as they expected their teachers to coordinate dates so that tests didn't fall on the same days. They also knew that while test grades counted toward report card grades, teachers would recognize and reward effort as well as give them credit for doing their homework, for helping others, and for staying on-task in class. Projects counted as much or more than tests, and students understood that grades for essays and projects reflected teachers' understandings of students' individual capabilities. A poor test grade didn't "doom" a student to a poor report card grade, and students knew that teachers routinely addressed "effort" in the narrative portion of report cards.

Homework

Homework was a constant, but it wasn't meted out so much in an effort to instill self-discipline (as some parents would have wished) as it was to extend or add significance to classroom study (what teachers expressed as important). Most students, with varying degrees of thoroughness and thought, routinely did their homework; they expected it of themselves, just as their parents and teachers expected it of them.

Homework fell into three categories: standing assignments, long-term projects, and daily assignments. Standing assignments included RFP (reading for pleasure) for 20 minutes each night, personal writing (not associated with instructional material) for 15 minutes each night, and writing in a reading dialogue journal once a week. Students were also encouraged to review their class notes each evening. Students generally attended to standing assignments after other homework was finished, and everyone, including teachers, understood that.

Long-term projects, often culminating assignments to units of study, were due weeks after they were introduced and were common in science and humanities. For a "westward expansion" long-term assignment, students were given 3 weeks' notice and a list of 12 possible projects. Instructions read:

> Complete one of the following projects by Friday, February 28. A proposal listing your name, a description of the project that is more specific than the general ideas mentioned below, and a list of possible resources is due this Monday. You will also have to complete a project progress report midway through the project period. You may vary any one of these to your liking; final approval will come from Mr. Carew.

Students wrote biographies and fictional diaries. They drew detailed maps showing changes in U.S. boundaries from 1776 until the present and maps showing Pony Express routes, Indian reservations, and railroad tracks. They augmented reports with drawings and posters. And in the end, they presented their work before the class—a kind of "publication" of their efforts.

Long-term projects were frequently collaborative. For science, Monica, Jan, and Linda simulated a television news report from the site of a hurricane. "Hello. This is Linda Barrington and this is a QBDO special report. Hurricane Suzie has struck and is destroying North Carolina. The eye is in

Cape Hatteras. We will be visiting with Jan Bronson in Palm Beach." The girls wrote the 13-page script in class and at night over the telephone. They planned costumes and arranged for the guidance counselor to videotape their performance so they could broadcast their "television" news program to both eighth-grade science classes.

Daily assignments were more simple in scope: math problems, lab reports, textbook reading, and note-taking assignments. There were short writing assignments of a page or two: proposals for work to be done, reflections on class activities, explorations of ideas that were yet to be discussed, assessments of class progress, self-assessment of work completed or in progress, and extensions of class discussions, such as the following excerpt from one of Chad's assignments:

> I don't think dropping an atomic bomb is the right thing to do to end a war. I don't think killing 130,000 people who were innocent is the right way to end a war. President Truman couldn't think of any other ideas. He had to end it by killing people who weren't even fighting. What a *jerk*. . . . It wasn't the Japanese citizens [*sic*] fault. It was the governments [*sic*] fault.

TYPES AND FUNCTIONS OF CLASSROOM LITERACIES

Talking and listening, reading, and writing were all influenced by social environment. The community of Meadowbrook, its school community, and individual classroom communities supported literacies that, in turn, built and defined them. Literacy became a means of engaging with community, and through this engagement and with careful guidance, students' individual literacies developed.

Talking and Listening

Most of the eighth-grade students had been at the school for at least 6 years. Only 2 of the 40 had arrived after the beginning of sixth grade. Their experience as eighth-graders and their understandings of how literacy functioned were certainly influenced by prior interactions within and beyond the classroom communities. When they came to eighth grade—to classes and magnets—they expected to have opportunities for talk. They expected that someone would listen. In part this was because they were accustomed to working in a combination of social configurations (with a partner, within a small group, as part of a whole class, alone, individually with the teacher, or as part of a group with the teacher) that allowed for different audiences and different kinds of talk.

While some students talked in all groupings, others rarely talked in whole-group settings. In spite of the supportive environment, they just didn't feel comfortable. Monica explained, "I don't talk in the big groups. I don't know why. I just don't." She did, however, talk plenty in small-group discussions and said that she learned more in small groups than when the class was all together. Jan explained why: "Because more people are involved usually in smaller groups." Depending on the group, even the quiet ones assumed leadership. Chad said, "There's one or two leaders who really mostly explain what's happening and stuff. . . . It depends on the group you're in. Different kids become leaders." The students recognized that they learned through talking and listening to peers, and it was hard for them to imagine classroom situations in which they might not have various formats and audiences for content-related talk. Without small groups, there were those who would have been voiceless.

Jaci was one of those students who didn't say much in a whole group, explaining that some of the more assertive boys intimidated her. She preferred small-group work. So, when Mrs. Taylor grouped her with Sharon and John to create a computer-generated weather map, she was happy. She liked the challenge of getting John to work and found it easy to work with Sharon, who participated in all groupings. John took the first turn at the keyboard, and the girls sat on either side of him. Jaci held Mrs. Taylor's instruction sheet, which outlined the weather phenomena they needed to chart. They'd already figured out which direction frontal systems' symbols should be faced, but they were confused about the differences between warm and cold fronts.

JACI: But is it called a cold front, or is it a warm front?

SHARON: Okay. (*waiting for Jaci to continue*)

JOHN: So, it's going to go straight across—where? Right here? (*impatient and pointing at the screen, ready to type something in*)

SHARON: It's going to go whaa! (*seeing the problem about whether it was a cold or warm front*) Right here?

JACI: But you guys, wait a minute. (*noticing John type in a cold front*)

SHARON: We don't know if it's warm or cold yet.

JACI: John. (*Jaci stops John from going further*) If it's blowing from the southwest, it's going to be warmer.

JOHN: So, which way do I put it? (*wanting to position the cold front icon*)

JACI: It's not a cold front.

JOHN: So, I'll tack it on here. (*adds symbol to a cold front they've already made*)

SHARON AND JACI: Yeah.

JACI: Good. Yeah. That's perfect. All right, we did that. Wouldn't it be (*interrupted by John*)

JOHN: So it's a cold front?

JACI: No. Wouldn't it be a warm front? If the wind is blowing from the southwest, and it's warm here? Wouldn't it be a warm front?

JOHN: Does it say warm or cold? (*referring to Mrs. Taylor's instruction sheet*)

JACI: It doesn't say either.

JOHN: Then get Mrs. Taylor then.

JACI: No. You guys. Think about this. It's warm here, and it's coming from the southwest, and it's warm all on the coast, and it's going this way—which means it's going to cause a warm front.

JOHN: Yeah. So, then it would be this one? (*pointing to cold front icon*)

JACI: No, that's cold.

SHARON: That's cold.

JOHN: I'm sorry.

JACI: You should be. (*joking*)

JOHN: So rotate it? (*going back to the problem of which way to aim the icon, now that they know it's a warm front*)

SHARON: Facing that way.

The talk about the weather map was focused yet served a number of purposes. In a short time, Jaci solved a problem in the process of explaining it to others. Sharon helped Jaci define the problem and then confirmed Jaci's speculations. John didn't actively participate in the problem solving but did serve as an audience for Jaci. At other times in the exercise the girls took charge of the keyboard and John offered advice, "Put it in. . . . Over more. . . . Put it on top of that *L*." It was likely that without his partners, John might have "blown off" the exercise. Talk, in this case, served different functions for individuals. For Jaci and Sharon, it was a way of thinking. For John, it helped involve him in a process.

There were times in all the classes when only the teacher talked. If teacher-talk was too prolonged, students complained of being bored (e.g., "Science [today] was all Mrs. T's talk. Nothing else. It was very boring."). There was, ordinarily, ample opportunity for student talk: presentations, simulations, debates, whole- and small-group discussions, plays/role playing, and students teaching peers. Students gave directions, asked questions, offered suggestions, speculated, tried out opinions, provided answers, confirmed ideas, and argued with teachers and peers.

Reading

Until the introduction of humanities and magnets and the accompanying schedule change, students had always had regularly scheduled times for reading. In seventh grade they'd read in their homerooms and corresponded in reading dialogue journals about their books with their homeroom teachers. In eighth grade, they read at home, sometimes read in humanities, and carried their books with them to other classes in case there was time to read. They corresponded weekly about their books with Mr. Carew. Teachers intended this reading to be enjoyable for students, and for some it was. For others, its main purpose was to fulfill teachers' expectations. This was the official reading of eighth grade, but other kinds of reading subtly wove their way through the eighth-grade experience.

Teachers, particularly Carew, read to students. When they were studying the Civil War, he read *A Nation Torn* by Delia Ray in daily installments, and when they were studying World War II, he read them the picture-story book *The Lily Cupboard* by Shulamith Levey Oppenheim. At times like these, students gathered on the floor in the corner of the room. Carew's stated purpose was to introduce concepts and initiate discussion, but the oral readings were also a continuation of a practice that students had known from first grade— a very comfortable feeling for some or, depending on the day and the book, a somewhat less engaging process for others. Still, students asked questions or made comments during the reading, and as they sat, they were apt to rub one another's backs or lean against one another's shoulders. In this sense, reading aloud also functioned as an occasion for social relaxation.

Students had never used basal readers and had written in reading dialogue journals since the fourth grade. They'd never been ability-grouped for reading instruction but understood that people had different rates of reading and that reading textbooks was different from reading novels. They expected to make personal connections with what they read and often wrote about those connections in their journals. (For example, Monica wrote, "I am still reading *Full Circle*. When I read this book it makes me think about my future. I always wonder if the things that happen in the book are going to happen to me. It reminds me of high school and how nervous I'll be.") Students were not tested for reading comprehension, nor were they encouraged to remember every detail of what they read. Friends recommended books to friends, and often books passed from one reader to another to yet another. They believed that reading should be enjoyable, even though some of them didn't always find it so and chose not to read if given the option.

Students felt comfortable doing independent research in the library and understood that the encyclopedia was not the ultimate research resource. They used the microfiche machine for reading a special students' version of the *New York Times* index and followed up by reading articles that came with the index. They read newspapers, newsletters, teachers' and peers' writing, magazines, picture-story books, textbooks, letters, brochures/mail-aways, working drafts, directions, fiction, and nonfiction. They read for pleasure, information, to be part of a social group, to engage in correspondence, to fulfill teachers' requirements, and to learn about themselves and others.

Writing

For the students who said they enjoyed writing, humanities was fine, but they didn't have as much time for what they called "real" writing as they did when they had regular English classes. For them, real writing was not content writing or writing that was incidental to classroom or magnet activities. Real writing involved stories or poetry—pieces they initiated and could choose to finish or abandon. Even when reports were written as fiction or poetry, students ultimately viewed them as reports or projects—not as real writing. Nicky made the distinction, "I am not a good writer, but my reports are okay," and dismissed a fictional diary she wrote about a woman traveling west in a covered wagon as "something I did for the westward expansion unit." As a humanities assignment, she wrote the "last chapter" of a Louis L'Amour story and called it "homework," not a piece of writing, even though she thought it sounded good:

> "I saw are [sic] new land. It was so wonderful. All green and pretty. Pa would have loved it here."
> Ma said, "I hope no souix [sic] live here."
> Tyron replied in a strong studied voice, "If they do live here, then we will fight for the land."

Nicky was class secretary and took careful notes at all meetings. She also kept thorough class notes and, like her peers, engaged in a variety of types of writing, such as memos, posters and signs, plans, lists, essays, reading dialogue journals, reports, poetry, surveys, letters, lab reports, proposals, progress updates, reflections, articles for newsletters and the newspaper, and speeches. Students often took much of this writing, done in the context of accomplishing other tasks, for granted. The products varied widely in quality, but in the process of writing, students discovered ideas, synthesized and extended thinking, organized information, communicated ideas, and planned future work—if only to be part of the action that surrounded them.

THE GREAT UNKNOWN: EDGING EVER CLOSER

Throughout the year students and teachers made comments that reminded them that high school was on the horizon. When Andy complained that it was hard to keep up with the class, Lenny replied, "Wait until next year,

buddy." When Carew asked the class why he might have given them bogus rules (see the earlier section in this chapter, "Controlling Their Own Behaviors"), one of the students answered, "To prepare us for the big stuff and stricter rules in high school." When Miss Arno told the students that some of them had made out pretty well with partial credit on their math quizzes, Bobby asked, "Do they do that [give partial credit] in high school?" Reviewing for the science midterm, Jerry asked, "In high school do they have whole-year exams?" When Jaci was upset with someone in science and went to the girls' bathroom to calm down, she worried out loud, "I'm scared about high school. I can't just leave the room like this." Students tried to anticipate what high school might mean. They talked about common apprehensions (getting lost, not knowing anyone, and having to sit alone at lunch) as adults engaged in debate about their preparedness for high school.

Making Beliefs Explicit

There was more than the usual public controversy about high school preparedness during the class's eighth-grade year (see the section of Chapter 2, "Controversy"). The attending publicity affected students in three ways: They felt somewhat unsettled, they sensed a need to defend their school and teachers, and their defense impelled them to make explicit some of their tacit understandings about education and learning.

When an article appeared in a statewide newspaper questioning their preparedness, the students took it personally and talk among parents, teachers, and peers escalated. About a week later, the author of the article came to the school, and all 40 students met with her in the humanities classroom. One of the boys spoke directly to the issue of preparedness: "We get individual attention here, and we're not going to get it in high school. We won't get it in high school, but maybe we won't need it by then because we've had it now." Another took a slightly different approach: "Teachers are like a second set of parents, and if you have problems, you can go to them. So in high school we'll know how to go to our teachers for help." One of the girls explained what the school was like: "Instead of sitting and copying out of books, we get in groups. We work with everyone and get to know one another better so we can help each other." A friend added another example: "Earlier this year we got all these strict rules in humanities. We found out the rules weren't true, and that led us to unfair laws in the colonies and a debate. It made learning fun." That theme was extended with comments such as: "We have simulations and organized groups for debates," "We have mock trials," and "I don't remember so much when the teachers write it down on the board as when we're doing things like that."

The reporter didn't write the follow-up story she promised, and the students were left feeling even more angry and vulnerable than before. In addi-

tion to the letter Misty drafted to the newspaper editor, Jack wrote and broadcast a piece about the reporter's visit on WMNM, ending with "I've been reading [the name of the newspaper] for days, and I haven't found a follow-up
story yet!"

All the controversy, arguments that they'd heard for years about grammar and spelling, plus the most recent publicity about high school preparedness, forced them to think more critically about education than they might
have otherwise. It made them aware of what they valued (e.g., collaboration, hands-on learning, and caring teachers), just as it planted seeds of doubt
about how they'd compare to other high school freshmen.

Choosing a High School

In addition to the students' normal concerns about going to high school and
their awareness of local controversy, they had to choose which of five high
schools they'd attend—a decision that might separate them from friends and
perhaps determine future school success. Some would simply go where their
siblings or parents went. For others, it wasn't so simple. One school had a
good basketball program. Another was so large that making a team would
be impossible. One had a large selection of classes. Another was very small
but relatively close in distance. One was known for taking students with
special needs. Another had a reputation for "eating up" small-town kids.
From January on, there was talk of high schools. WMNM did a series of broad-
casts on choices and expectations. Groups of students, as well as individual
parents and students, visited high schools, and representatives from all the
schools visited MCS.

All of the presentations focused on schedules, listing requirements, and
citing numbers of credits necessary for graduation. The representative from
Whitmore High School told students to take enough credits to allow them
to fail one class and still have enough credits to be classified as sophomores
the following year. A guidance counselor from Midtown High School warned
students to avoid foreign languages if they were getting D's in English, telling them repeatedly, "You're going to get killed. You're going to die." The
message was clear: Success in high school was predicated on earning a certain number of credits; "not failing" was a credible goal. As the guidance
counselor from Midtown pointed out, 25% of the students in his school
dropped out.

Students took the presentations in stride, even though most of the schools
sounded very different from what they were used to. The principal of Midtown warned students against theft, didn't know if there was a freshman
football team, and bragged that their guidance counselors had an average
caseload of *only* 250 students. "Every counselor knows you and your

dreams," he told them. Afterwards, one of the students remarked that she knew which counselor she'd get because her name was at the end of the alphabet and they assigned counselors that way. She didn't expect personal attention, even though she'd loved being a part of Kids Care advisory group.

The students, however, responded positively to the principal of the smallest high school, who told them, "The critical factor in whether you get a good education is what you put into it. We help you do that. . . . It's a goal of ours to help students really get involved." No one could say exactly why, but more students than ever before decided to attend this school the following year. Mr. Peterson did recommend that some students attend the school, even though he understood the curriculum to be quite limited and traditional. He told them that the school had a strong community and that kids would get more personal attention from teachers. As it turned out, nearly equal numbers of students attended three of the schools, with fewer attending the other two. Only a handful chose Midtown. Many of the students would have preferred not to choose at all or wished that high school could be just like Meadowbrook Community School. During one of the presentations a student whispered, "I'm not going to high school. I'm staying here."

FIVE STUDENTS CLOSE-UP

The end of the school year was a whirlwind. Students completed final exams, took a 3-day class trip to Montreal, graduated, and were taking a postgraduate last-day-of-school trip to the ocean. On the bus they were happy and talkative and full of themselves. Some of the boys ate the entire way—pretzels, Milky Way bars, bags of chips. Kevin's root beer can had a hole in it, so the kids passed it around, squeezing it and sucking soda out of the hole. They sang songs they'd learned while growing up together and played handclapping games that got faster and faster and more complicated as they went. "Couples" who had formed in the waning weeks of school sat together on the bus's bench seats, holding hands and talking more to their friends than to each other. As it turned out, it would be the last time the class was assembled as a group.

The students had shared a collective life at the school, but it would be wrong to assume that they were cookie-cutter copies of one another. They were individuals with unique personalities, interests, and abilities. Indeed, acceptance of differences among individuals had allowed them to spend energies positively—building common understandings.

As in any group of students, some cared more about learning than others. John, for example, who'd been in Meadowbrook since first grade, admitted to doing "just enough to get by." He knew he could be a good student, but he didn't want to work very hard. He didn't read much, and he rarely finished pieces of writing other than reports and assignments. "I'm just lazy. I always have been." He appreciated the work others did, though, and his social interests motivated him to do work for others that he wouldn't do for himself. He visited a friend's house after school to help her with her homework, even though his own wasn't finished. If he was part of a group that was ambitious, he'd let them do the work. If he was with someone who was less motivated than he (there were a couple in the class), he'd take the lead. He worked well with Nicky and several other girls because they told him what to do without being too pushy.

Monica was a good writer; she couldn't remember not being a good writer. Unlike John, she wrote voluminously and saved everything. Her bedroom was packed tightly with boxes and bags of papers. She wrote at home to entertain herself or to think things over. During odd moments in school she was likely to list random thoughts that might later become poems. She was a good reader but didn't have the hours of uninterrupted time she said she needed to do it. She liked being with her friends and would take the lead when working in small groups. "Talking" cemented things in her mind, but she didn't talk in whole-group situations. She explained that she had a reputation for being a good student, something that "carried" her through eighth grade, a year in which she claimed to have done less work than usual. Yet, even in the eighth grade, she did all her homework, worked diligently on projects, and studied carefully for tests. Teachers' written comments on progress reports complimented Monica's work habits, and her grades were mostly A's.

Nicky had nearly "stayed back" in the second grade because she was so small. Even in the eighth grade, she wore size-2 shoes and was four feet, eight inches tall. She equated reading and writing with pleasure, even though she didn't think she had enough imagination to be a good writer. She hated to be pressured to get things done, so she began projects early and worked on them regularly, usually finishing before deadlines. Doing group projects could be frustrating when she was partnered with someone who didn't like to work. She said she knew how to make John work, though. Nicky believed that she was not as smart as a lot of kids in the class, that she had to work harder than most, but said she didn't "really mind." She spent time with friends, took care of her animals, did housework, and got her homework done—with time left for reading long hours in the bathtub.

Like the others, Chad had been in Meadowbrook since first grade, but because he repeated the second grade, he was a year older than they were. He liked to write fiction, and he read and wrote at home for entertainment. He thought he'd like to be a journalist but worried about his grades and getting into college. Chad had problems with oral comprehension; there was a delay between hearing words and comprehending them, a disability that made school difficult. His reading comprehension was also slow, and he didn't do well when rushed. Still, his grades were mostly B's and C's, and his teachers praised his effort in the narrative portions of his report card. Like Nicky and Monica, Chad took school seriously. He almost always completed his homework, but tests were difficult—even when he had help from the special education teacher. His teachers understood that he was easily confused and checked with him often.

Ginny was one of the last additions to the class; she didn't come to Meadowbrook until the middle of fifth grade. Like Chad, she repeated an early grade and was a year older than most. She sometimes thought she appreciated MCS more than the others because she'd been somewhere else. She remembered learning how to read via workbook and having a hard time of it. She still considered herself to be a slow reader but enjoyed it more since moving to MCS. Ginny was more confident about her writing, and with a home life that was somewhat unstable, poetry was an emotional outlet. Her poems resembled paragraphs with lines ending at the edges of pages; poetic conventions were unimportant. Ginny recognized that she wasn't very organized. Beginnings of poems were scattered through her notebooks. She started notebooks for classes and then lost them. She started homework and forgot to finish it or did homework and forgot to turn it in. Ginny received Chapter 1 tutoring but was not identified as learning-disabled. Schoolwork was difficult for her. She asked for and got help from the special education teacher.

For a variety of reasons John, Monica, Nicky, Chad, Ginny, and six other students chose to attend Whitmore High School. Almost all of them had siblings who were attending or had attended the school. Parents liked to keep families together, and students expected that their older brothers and sisters might help them out at the beginning. The sports program, especially basketball, was good. The school accepted students with special needs—something that not all the schools did. Whitmore High School wasn't as threatening as big-city Midtown, yet it was bigger and offered more courses than two of the other schools.

SUMMARY

Despite individual differences in personality, motivation, and interests, the graduating eighth-grade students carried with them the imprint of Meadowbrook Community School. They valued caring teachers, interesting work, a variety of approaches for learning content, some choice in what they did, and a friendly classroom atmosphere. They believed that community was integral to learning, that they learned as much from one another in groups as they did from teachers, and that it was possible to mix social and academic goals. They generally found it easier to talk in small groups than in whole-group situations. They were accustomed to evaluating their own work and believed that grades were only one indication of how they were doing in school. They appreciated hands-on learning opportunities and knew that not everyone learned the same way. In addition to thinking of reading and writing as integral to learning, they thought reading should be enjoyable and believed that writing was the most important part of English. They expected high school classes to be more demanding than those at Meadowbrook, and they were ready to work hard.

CHAPTER 4

Whitmore High School

A high school, to be effective, must have a clear and vital mission. Educators must have a shared vision of what, together, they are trying to accomplish. That vision should go beyond keeping students in school and out of trouble, and be more significant than adding up the Carnegie course units the student has completed.

Ernest L. Boyer
High School, 1983, p. 301

It was a 40-minute school bus ride from Meadowbrook to Whitmore. Less than an hour and students were transported to a town they may have only "passed through" prior to enrolling at the high school. They and students from Barton, Ashfield, and Wayhill joined students from Whitmore to form the class of 1996. Nearly two-thirds of the 220 member class lived outside Whitmore.

A BRIEF HISTORY OF WHITMORE AND ITS HIGH SCHOOL

Once a thriving mill town, Whitmore had seen periods of economic boom and decline. Its most recent boom was one of people. Between 1980 and 1990, the population grew by 35% to nearly 7,000 people. Located between major cities and within reasonable commuting distance to growing cities in the southern tier of the state, it became home to those who desired a semirural environment and easy access to jobs and shopping. The downtown area ("the village") with its shops, tenements, and old brick factories was mostly forgotten in the population influx. Former mill workers, their descendants, longtime residents, and transients looking for inexpensive housing lived there, but its fate became more sealed with every shopping strip and mall that was built in the area. The growth of the town was most evident in its housing developments and apartment complexes, neighborhoods of their own, separated in distance and tone from the village. For some residents, Whitmore was a place to establish roots and raise families; for others, it was a quick stop on the road to somewhere else. Transiency was a growing phenomenon, especially during times of economic uncertainty.

Population growth severely strained the capacities of the schools. An elementary school built in the 1980s was nearly too small by the time it was finished. A new middle school was completed in the spring of 1992, and by the fall of that year the old building had been renovated for use by grades K–3, which meant the town supported four schools. Periodically town officials warned surrounding towns that they could not guarantee future acceptance of high school students. Building projects plus escalating operating costs associated with larger numbers of students helped drive up property taxes, and in 1990 citizens began rejecting school board–approved teacher raises and demanding sizable school budget reductions. Spending was curtailed, and by 1992 the cost per student at the high school was $1,000 below the state average, ranking the school at 63rd in per-capita spending out of 77 reporting districts.

Meanwhile, citizens reminded school board members that severe cuts at the high school might persuade sending towns to look elsewhere for secondary education. Without out-of-town tuition money, the scope of the high school would be drastically reduced. It seemed that Whitmore needed out-of-town students (and the towns' tuition money that came with them) as much as the students needed the high school—at least until the school ran out of space. As the principal told teachers at a 1993 faculty meeting, "Every bugger [out-of-town-student] that walks through that door is worth another $5,000." During the 1992–93 year, about 500 of a total of 800 enrolled students were from out of town.

Although surrounding towns, in large part, financially supported Whitmore High School (WHS), they had no control over its operating budget, curriculum, programs, or staffing. That responsibility lay entirely with the Whitmore school board and the town's citizenry—an artifact of when the high school was operated privately. Established in 1819 through private donations and a bequest (the school was twice destroyed by fire and rebuilt on the same site; additions and renovations were ongoing), it was like many New England secondary schools of its time—private. It wasn't until the 1960s that Whitmore officially brought the school's operation under the auspices of its own elected school board, thus ending management by private board. By this action, Whitmore obtained direct control over the school's policies and curriculum. With the exception of Meadowbrook, neighboring towns signed exclusive contracts with Whitmore High School, and tuition dollars were paid to the town rather than to a private board.

Meadowbrook was the only community of the four sending towns that did not border Whitmore and the only one that sent students to schools other

than Whitmore High School. Additionally, although Meadowbrook was in the same SAU as the other schools, it did not share the long association with the high school that the other towns did. (All the towns but Meadowbrook had once been connected by rail; students from Barton, Ashfield, and Wayhill had commuted by train to Whitmore.) There were periods of time when no Meadowbrook students attended WHS, and Meadowbrook was the only town, practically speaking, that had viable alternatives and could "opt out" of sending students to Whitmore. All the towns operated their own elementary/middle schools, and while Whitmore High administrators and teachers sometimes talked of attempting better communication between the feeder schools (including their own middle school) and the high school, actual communication was mostly limited to issues of scheduling/course selection and identification of at-risk students.

INSIDE WHITMORE HIGH SCHOOL

The floor plan depicted the many years the school had been there. The oldest section, built after the 1936 fire, had three stories, including the basement where the kitchen and cafeteria were housed. The two-story 1962 addition connected to the basement and the first floor of the old section, with classes on both floors. A large single-story 1972 addition connected to the first floors of the other two sections. If students were in the study hall at one corner of the newest section of the building and had to make it to Spanish class on the third floor of the 1936 building in the allowed 4-minute passing time between classes, they could choose from a number of routes, but it was a dash no matter which way they chose. Some students' schedules required them to alternate between old sections and new with each bell, making bathroom and locker stops next to impossible. Since the old section didn't have elevators, students temporarily on crutches had to hobble upstairs and down unless they contacted the office and sessions were moved to accessible rooms.

The building was well cared for and clean. There was very little graffiti, and when it did occasionally show up in bathrooms or on students' desks, it disappeared within a few days. Hallway floors were free of litter, and hallway walls were usually unadorned by decoration or student work. The infrequent appearance of something like student drawings outside the art room was notable because it was so out of the ordinary. Photocopied notices of dances and special events were posted in hallways and, as mandated in the student handbook, were removed promptly when no longer timely. College recruitment posters lined the hallway wall outside the auditorium, and there were several student-painted wall murals throughout the building. A large bulletin board–sized monthly events calendar was mounted behind

Plexiglas, as was a student display about the dangers of drugs and alcohol. A list of honor roll students and the sports schedule were similarly housed behind Plexiglas. Trophy cases decorated the main lobby outside the gymnasium. Throughout the year, a letter-board sign in the vestibule read, "WELCOME TO WHITMORE HIGH SCHOOL STUDENTS AND STAFF—HAVE A GREAT YEAR." The overall appearance of common areas was neat and orderly.

Interiors of classrooms ranged from stark to eclectic; the majority were largely unadorned and relatively interchangeable. A number of teachers, in fact, taught in more than one room, carting what they needed with them. Some of the rooms did reflect the instruction that took place in them. Foreign-language rooms were cluttered with charts, props, maps, and posters of foreign countries; unlike other rooms, they spilled their literacy into the hallway—"Aquí se habla español." The science rooms tended to collect the most "stuff," much of it irrelevant to the students who occupied the rooms. One science room, however, displayed students' work, housed tanks of fish and various plants, and had cartoons on ceiling tiles. The English rooms generally lacked the content-related artifacts or decor of the foreign-language classes; anthologies, textbooks, and class sets of novels were kept in cupboards. With the exception of labs and the art room, classrooms were arranged with students' desks in rows facing chalkboards, creating a kind of uniformity among rooms. All had U.S. flags, and many of them had lecterns at the front. When empty, few of the rooms showed evidence of students' having been there.

ABOVE ALL, ORDER

Just prior to the opening day of school, about 75 staff members sat in rows in the back corner of the school's auditorium for the first staff meeting of the year. The principal, Thomas Webster, stood before them and briefed them about pencils, handbooks, and parking stickers (none of which had yet arrived) and explained the new attendance policy. Toward the end of the meeting, one of the teachers raised his hand and asked if anything could be done right then, in the fall, to prevent a recurrence of the previous spring's problem of nongraduating seniors—students the teacher referred to as "kids on the brink." It was the first mention of students, other than in the context of the attendance policy. Webster answered quickly that all the students had been warned, some as early as the previous January. If the students failed, it wouldn't be because they hadn't been warned. Everything was in order.

The meeting itself was orderly. Like students in an overcrowded classroom, staff members sat, looking at the backs of one another's heads. When any of them had questions or comments, they raised their hands and waited to be called on. Webster managed the meeting with comments such as, "I believe your hand was up first." Teachers tended to direct their words to Webster, so that the meeting was a series of interchanges between the principal and individual teachers. Nontalkers listened quietly. Monthly staff meetings (with fewer in attendance) continued in this manner (on the first Wednesday of each month throughout the remainder of the year), satisfying a need for dissemination of information.

Order, as evidenced in staff meetings, was generally valued. As one teacher put it, "I wouldn't want to teach in a school that was disorderly." Order, however, emerged as a paramount objective at Whitmore High School—in part because there appeared in the words and actions of teachers and administrators to be no other common driving philosophical vision. There were rules and penalties designed to keep students in school, but there was no articulated philosophy about what to do with students once they were seated, beyond another orderly process—what one administrator described as making students "responsible for getting passing grades so that they can earn credits toward graduation."

There were teachers who could articulate personal philosophies for their own teaching, but no one expressed confidence in his or her ability to explain a school philosophy. Many voiced the belief that there was none or that it was the administration's job to tell them what the philosophy was. There was confusion about "the" philosophy written in the student handbook and "a" philosophy, tacit or stated, that would serve as a foundation for decision making. A few referred to the student handbook or said that a committee was working on a philosophy statement for reaccreditation. Several teachers who had been at the school for 20 years responded frankly: "I don't recall what it is." "If there is [a philosophy], they're keeping it a big secret." "Do they have a philosophy? Yes. Does anybody know what it is? Hell no!" School philosophy was thought of as a "thing," something for someone else to figure out, something quite disconnected from everyday practice. One of the four administrators under Webster, Jeff Emory, explained it this way:

> I think we're fairly fragmented in terms of our perspective about education—and people have their individual philosophies—and I think there's a sense somehow that we need to put the best interests of the students as the focus, but I'm not sure that that actually occurs. ... We don't communicate a lot about it. We don't interact and discuss those issues.

The administrative team met only rarely for any kind of discussion. "There isn't time," Webster said.

Teachers tended to speak of order in terms of students and disciplinary controls, not in terms of themsevles or their practices. Emory saw it as more endemic to the entire system. "Order and control is the issue here," he said, "whether it's at the administrative level, or teacher level, or even student level." He said that order was more important than innovation and explained how the culture worked:

> There are some [teachers] who try to do some things like group activities, cooperative learning—more interaction among the students—and unless it's formally a lab class, they're usually perceived to be out of control by the majority of the teachers. . . . The whole culture here, and this includes teachers, is one in which they demand order. . . . There's almost an obsession with it.

Some teachers saw their own overt participation in maintaining an "orderly, safe place" as overdone. One teacher routinely skipped his hall duty in order to plan curriculum. Another veteran of the school explained:

> Just look at it. It's like a Gestapo. We have everything monitored. We have just a huge amount of manpower just absolutely wasted. What is our primary duty? Our primary duty is to educate the youth of these communities and to do the best job possible. . . . We should be spending that energy on coming up with a system that works, coming up with new classes, trying to promote new teaching techniques.

Yet without a clear mandate from the administration to do so, teachers seldom met with one another. The English Department met twice from September through April. They discussed scheduling and the following year's budget. The teachers couldn't remember when they'd last met for discussions about academic expectations or curriculum. They routinely ordered replacement sets of class novels rather than trying new ones because, as one teacher explained, new books or materials would have disrupted the continuity of classes. Teachers needed to know what was "covered" at each level in each grade. Thus order appeared to be purchased at the cost of innovation, even in small ways.

So, without a shared understanding of what teachers and administrators collectively believed to be educationally important, order won out. Emphasis was placed on the accumulation of credits toward graduation. (The graduation rate was nearly 80%.) Educational practices such as the heavy reliance on textbooks (with accompanying study guides, questions, or worksheets) made sense in terms of order, as did tracking and a "no-exceptions" adherence to the discipline policy. Policies, actions, and practices at Whitmore High School were not only rooted in a need to establish and maintain order but found meaning and validation in that order.

SCHOOL ORDER: EXTERNAL CONTROLS AND INTERNAL SYSTEMS

It was Winter Carnival, a time for parades and snow sculptures and silly games, a welcome relief from winter and the monotony of the school year. Surveillance was tight as the freshmen walked quickly from lunch in the cafeteria back to the gym, where they would play a series of games. Taking the route past the teachers' room and auditorium, through the double doors, past English classrooms and the office, students were monitored by teacher-sentinels, posted about every 30 feet in doorways and along walls. Most students paid little attention to the unusually heavy watch, but one student explained, "They're afraid one of us is going to sneak into a bathroom or go to our locker." Under ordinary circumstances, control measures were much more subtle, but external control, no matter how it was wielded, was a part of students' everyday lives at Whitmore High School.

Order was established and maintained at the whole-school level by a web of policies and rules that were strictly adhered to and consistently applied. Through discipline and attendance policies and internal systems of leveling of classes (tracking), scheduling, and time enforcement, school officials hoped to direct and monitor students' academic progress as well as circumscribe students' behavior. Order and control were mutually supportive.

The New Attendance Policy

It took 8 pages of the 68-page student handbook to explain the rationale for and procedures of the new attendance policy. (Five pages were allotted to student activities.) If students missed a class 12 times in a semester, they lost credit for the course, or, as expressed by teachers and students, "13thed-out." If they missed more than 12 times in one semester for a year-long course, they lost credit for the entire year even if they had perfect attendance during the other semester. Having lost credit, students were not excused from attendance in classes and were still expected to do the work, even though they could receive no credit for it. If they successfully completed the work and received a passing grade for the course, the noncredit grade would be averaged into their grade point averages and would allow them to take the next sequentially ordered class, for example, sophomore English after passing freshman English.

Four "tardies" of less than 15 minutes to any one class counted as an absence for that class, as did in-school counseling sessions, in-school suspensions, out-of-school suspensions, and the first 3 days of any hospitalization. There were limited exemptions for absences: long-term illness, court appearances, athletic events, and deaths in the family. A parent's note allowed students to make up work but did not exempt the absence. An appeals board was rumored to be "tough."

By mid-December, three boys had 13thed-out of their level-2 (general studies) algebra class, and if they hadn't lost credit in their other classes, they were close. Since they would receive no credit for the year, they stopped working and began socializing with anyone who was interested. Carl, a freshman from Meadowbrook, sat near them, and by the end of the year, he'd joined them in horseplay and nonwork, even though he hadn't 13thed-out.

By January 12, half the students in a first-period level-2 English class were on noncredit status. Attendance dropped further after students realized they'd be receiving no credit. There was no point in coming, as far as they were concerned, except to see their friends. On a typical day, there were 11 students in the class (out of about 20); the rest were in ISS (in-school suspension), suspended out of school, or were plain absent. When students did attend class, it was unlikely that they'd done homework.

In another English class, Mr. Frost distributed a test to Mark, a freshman from Wayhill who'd 13thed-out weeks before. As others worked on the test, Mark, who went from class to class with no books, sat quietly. When everyone finished, Mr. Frost picked up the tests, wrote Mark's name on his, and stacked it with the others. Frost and Mark said nothing to each other. If Mark had been rude, he'd have been sent to the discipline office and then would have been punished by detentions or suspensions (many of his absences had been the result of suspensions). As it was, he'd mentally dropped the class, but as long as he was quiet about it, his nonparticipatory behavior was deemed acceptable.

By the end of the year, 60 freshmen (27% of the class) had failed (received less than 23 of the 100 credits they'd eventually need for graduation). Students and faculty alike attributed at least some of the failure to the absentee policy. Yet every day, in a very orderly fashion, absences were tallied and attendance sheets were distributed. Students received in-house and out-of-school suspensions that counted as absences for offenses that snowballed from behaviors as mundane as being repeatedly late to study hall. Students were warned, and teachers watched as their students stopped earning credits for the classes they were attending. By failing, students paid the consequences for their behaviors, and that was part of the policy. Everything was in order, just as it was when Mr. Frost picked up blank tests and recorded zeros in his rank book.

The Discipline Policy

Nine pages of the student handbook were devoted to the discipline code. Infractions were grouped into four levels of seriousness and listed with possible consequences; detailed lists outlined rules for detentions and suspensions. The aim, according to one administrator, was consistency. Students needed to know what consequences to expect. So a girl who impulsively punched another girl in the cheek after weeks of being teased ("I didn't know I was going to do it until I did it") received the same 5-day out-of-school suspension as the two boys who prearranged a fist fight in the lobby after school.

One new aspect of the policy was that individual administrators were assigned to specific classes; one administrator, Mrs. Porter, dealt only with freshmen. Each morning, she made her rounds: calling students from classes, explaining their situations to them, and assigning prescribed punishments. Since level-2 students tended to get in more trouble than level-1 students, their classes were interrupted more frequently than level-1 classes.

Mrs. Porter became a common sight at classroom doors, especially during early morning classes. One morning Ginny's wellness (health) teacher was lecturing about the causes of stress when Mrs. Porter came to the door to call Ginny out. (Ginny's English teacher allowed only one tardy before recommending detentions, and she'd been late a second time.) As Ginny returned to her seat, the wellness teacher continued to talk about "stressors," such as parents' long commutes to work. Dave was called out, then Ray. Afterwards, while students began an assignment listing personal "stressors" of the previous 48 hours, Dave wrote a note to explain what had happened with Mrs. Porter:

> Mrs. Porter got a notice from good old Mr. Frost. It stated that I reached my 6th tardy in his study hall, supposedly last Friday. I'm sure I wasn't tardy and told Mrs. Porter that. She said I'd have ISS [in-school suspension] for something I didn't do! This happened before. I was in class but not in my seat.

Discipline call-outs had become so routine that the wellness teacher said she hadn't thought to connect stress with Mrs. Porter being at the door. Call-outs were just part of the operation. Assuredly, students received detentions and suspensions for reasons other than tardiness, but tardiness was a prime factor in filling the detention room after school. And if for any reason students couldn't serve a detention, they received an additional three detentions—giving them a total of four for the original offense. Sometimes there were more students than seats in detention and another room had to be used for the overflow. The school imposed control from the top, and when students refused to cooperate they received more punishments. Some students, backlogged for weeks of detentions, served them daily as if they were part of their schedules. Occasionally Mrs. Porter converted multiple detentions into suspensions (policy limited the number of in-house suspensions), and toward the end of the year even small infractions could mean out-of-school suspension for some students. Suspension was a way of controlling the environment, if not individual students. Students could do whatever they wanted when they were kicked out of school, and the school would operate more smoothly without them.

Tracking, Scheduling, and Time

English, math, science, social studies, and wellness (health) were "leveled" to match student abilities and motivation. Since levels 3 and 4 were mostly for special-needs students, others chose either level 1, often referred to as "college prep," or level 2 for "average" students. Areas of study such as business, home economics, art, technology (industrial arts), and foreign languages did not have levels, but while there was some crossover, "college prep" students were less likely than level-2 students to take technology classes and more likely to take something like French.

The rationale for such leveling was that grouping students of similar abilities for instruction appropriate to those abilities would better meet the needs of students. Innate ability, then, was no excuse for failure, because the school provided levels at which all students might achieve. If that rationale was important for required classes, it was not applied to nonrequired ones. Students chose the latter based on knowledge of their own abilities and interests. Gatekeepers to more advanced classes in their departments, classes such as foundation art (which relied on a difficult concept-laden textbook) and introduction to business (which emphasized book work and memorization of vocabulary), were open to all students. When Ginny failed foundation art, it was said that she and others like her had chosen the wrong class, that freshmen had been warned that it was a difficult class. It was as if she, and the others in the class who failed, had managed to slip into what would have been level-1 domain—even though most of the students in that class also took level-2 classes.

Level-1 classes were more homogeneous than level-2 classes. Level 2 served as a catchall for students who were not clearly "college material" and who were not identified as learning disabled, even though there were also "coded kids" such as Chad in level-2 classes. While the theory was to match instruction to ability, in practice level-2 classes were often hotbeds of indifference and misbehavior. There were students of above-average abilities who had long ago decided that school was not for them, students who were constantly called out of class for disciplinary reasons, and students who sincerely wanted and needed the extra support that level-2 classes were supposed to afford them. In level-2 classes, Chad not only received watered-down assignments (he explained that level-1 students had more homework) and less instruction than he needed (he relied heavily on an out-of-class tutor), but he had to sit daily with students who lacked his desire to learn and get good grades. Still rooted in the Meadowbrook culture, he was perplexed by their behavior and repeatedly asked questions such as, "Why don't they try?" and "Why don't they just do their homework?" According to school guidelines, Chad was appropriately placed.

Scheduling was done by computer; although it was efficient and reasonably accurate, it was an arbitrary system that was limited by 50-minute time blocks, 25-minute lunch periods, and gym classes that met 2 or 3 days a week. John had 25 minutes of business class, then lunch, then the last 25 minutes of business class. Nicky's, Monica's, and Ginny's study periods were similarly split by lunch. (Ginny later found an advocate who'd been hired to deal with at-risk freshmen and had her schedule changed so that she had a full study period.) Chad had 25 minutes of tutoring, 25 minutes of study in another room, 25 minutes of lunch, and then returned to the second half of his tutoring session for another 25 minutes. During their first semester, Monica and Nicky had the equivalent of 12 50-minute study halls a week, including three each on Tuesdays and Thursdays. During their second semester, they had only three study halls all week.

When Chad, who had done well in eighth-grade math, was having difficulty in his level-1 algebra class at the beginning of the year, his only recourse was to move down a level. Scheduling policy determined that students could change classes within a given period at the beginning of a semester, but they could not move across levels to other teachers; they could only move up or down for placement purposes. The rationale behind the policy was to avoid the potential problem of students moving willy-nilly from teacher to teacher. In any case, Chad's original math teacher was a fast talker, and given his learning disability, Chad couldn't keep up with instruction. While there were slower-talking teachers who conducted level-1 algebra classes, Chad was moved to level-2, where he found the work unchallenging and where, with little effort and almost no homework, he received high grades. When scheduling his classes for his sophomore year, he learned that he could only take the continuation of the level-2 algebra class, which with his freshman year of algebra would be the equivalent of 1 year of level-1 algebra. When he asked if he could just take level-1 algebra his sophomore year, his request was denied because he'd already covered half the material.

With a series of 25-minute blocks around lunch time, students also had twice as many 4-minute between-class "passing times" as they would have had with the normal 50-minute blocks. A 5-minute homeroom was sandwiched between 4-minute "passing times" as well. That meant that someone like Chad spent 40 minutes each day getting from one class to another—about 10% of the school's 6-hour-and-50-minute day. Being late to a class or study hall was a serious offense. Three tardies to one class meant one after-school detention; the fourth time meant three after-school detentions. "Tardies" were cumulative over the semester, and a fifth tardy to study hall meant in-school suspension; a sixth meant out-of-school suspension. By comparison, if students didn't do their homework, they might lose credit but wouldn't be kept after school. If students fell asleep in class, they were generally allowed to sleep. If students were caught passing notes or forgot their books, they were scolded by their teachers but not sent to detention.

Being on time was considered a virtue. As one teacher put it: "Probably the most important thing we can teach them [students] as far as life skills is punctuality and that there is a consequence for not being on time." Timeliness was so important that teachers were strongly discouraged from giving students late passes to their next classes, so if students needed to talk privately to a teacher, even for a minute, they risked being late to their next class, especially if the teacher was already talking to someone else. Even when the teacher initiated the between-class chat ("See me after class!"), it was the students' problem if they were late. The result was that most students did get to class on time, but few stayed to talk privately with their teachers. Buses picked up students within a few minutes of the dismissal bell, so after-school talk was impossible for many, including those from Meadowbrook. In the morning, students were confined to the lobby until 7:20, giving them only 10 minutes to get to their lockers and find teachers before school started at 7:30.

Tracking, scheduling, and strict adherence to time—all helped to create and enforce orderly daily operations at the school. They also served, with other factors, to influence academic and social development.

CLASSROOM ORDER: MAINTAINING CONTROL

Classroom order was generally a microcosm of school order; its importance, long cherished in traditional education, found written precedence in a nineteenth-century Whitmore Superintending Committee report: "The most important work of a teacher is to keep good order. . . . The first work of the child as he enters school is to obey." Teachers didn't know about this report, but their classrooms often reflected its essence. While there were teachers, such as the Spanish teacher or the power and energy teacher, who relied on students' good sense and desire to learn as agents for students' self-control, others took no chances.

Mr. Frost's English class was perhaps the most outwardly controlling of freshmen students' behaviors. However, other teachers indicated that Mr. Frost was fair and consistent, that his students knew what to expect. (Ginny, John, Monica, and Nicky were in his classes.) On the first day of school, he distributed pages of classroom procedures that outlined everything from how he would confiscate uncovered English textbooks to ways in which students should write headings at the tops of their papers and volunteer answers to his questions. The bathroom procedure was representative of tone and specificity:

> If you wish to make use of the lavatory facilities, you must ask me BEFORE THE START OF CLASS. If you are allowed to do so, you must sign out, take the WHITE PADDLE and go to the NEAREST lavatory. You should be able to return within a few minutes. When you come back, you must sign in and return the paddle. THIS PRIVILEGE WILL BE GIVEN TO AN INDIVIDUAL STUDENT ONLY ONCE PER WEEK (EXCEPT IN CASE OF EMERGENCY). PLEASE DO NOT ASK MORE FREQUENTLY THAN ONCE PER WEEK IN MY CLASS. ABUSE OF THIS PRIVILEGE WILL RESULT IN YOUR LOSS OF THE PRIVILEGE. This privilege will only be granted prior to the bell that starts class and possibly at the end of class—if class work is done.

In addition to written rules, Frost frequently added verbal ones: "I didn't tell you this. When we're going around like this [checking answers on a quiz], give the answer you think is correct, not the answer that is there." Students were expected to sit with shoulders squared to the front, no feet in the aisles, even when a student in the back of the room was giving an answer and those in front wanted to hear. If students didn't ask permission first, they were sometimes reprimanded for getting up to get a tissue or lending a pencil to a peer. Students were not allowed to talk while doing seatwork: "Do not talk. If you want to talk, you have to ask my permission."

Frost would, in his own words, "throw out" students who didn't follow his rules, and it was his experience that students stopped giving him trouble by Christmas. They might not work, but they'd be silent. He ignored individual students who began sleeping through his class during the second semester. Sleeping caused no disruptions.

Teachers had individual policies about accepting late homework, allowing students to go to their lockers or the bathroom, gum chewing, and maintenance of class notebooks. Students might chew gum when they had English in one of the science rooms but not chew gum when they had science in the same room at another time in the day (because of possible contamination through contact with chemicals—even though they used no chemicals in their science classes). Some teachers threatened detentions for uncovered textbooks, while others didn't notice uncovered books. Some demanded silence during seatwork, while others tolerated various levels of talk. Students who were "stone silent" in Frost's classes, Mr. Wright's science class, or Mrs. Anderson's wellness class could be loud and rude in Mr. Perry's algebra class. Since control was external to students most of the time, their behavior was in direct response to which teacher was in control.

Textbooks and Worksheets: Controlling the Curriculum

Ginny once said, "Sometimes teachers think that just because they get books for the course that they have to use them. They could think of other things." Many of her teachers relied largely or even exclusively on textbooks and accompanying worksheets and tests. And to the degree that they did, a phantom "they" controlled the curriculum. "Trust me, folks," one science teacher said about an upcoming "book" test, "*they* have a lot of this on the test." When problems in the algebra book seemed scattered in focus, the teacher explained, "I suppose *they're* trying to do their little bit about not letting you get into a rut." Another time, one of the girls asked if students could "just go ahead and solve the equations." The teacher answered, "*They* don't ask you to." Teachers, in a sense, turned authority over to textbooks.

Some classes were almost completely driven by textbooks and worksheets. During class time, students typically did one of three things: They either did book work (completed worksheets, answered textbook questions, and outlined text), checked answers, or took tests. One day Mr. Francis handed out science tests that took 13 minutes for students to complete. Students spent the rest of the 50-minute period filling out worksheets 8-1, 8-2, and 8-3. "Water can be broken down into two gases, _____ and _____." Later, some of those same students went to business class and answered a publisher's unit test, then spent the rest of the period completing study guides to Chapter 40 and writing definitions to vocabulary listed at the end of the chapter. The next day in both classes, they "went over" the worksheets they'd completed after the tests.

Instruction via worksheet translated to prodigious amounts of time at the copy machine. At one staff meeting, Webster announced that they were making 10,000 copies on the Rizograph duplicator every three days and 1,200 copies on the regular copy machine every day—a daily average of about 4,500 copies in a school for 800 students. While these numbers included copies of things other than worksheets, worksheets dominated. (Instructional reliance on worksheets had one unheralded benefit: Substitute teachers could distribute worksheets without disrupting the ordinary flow of classes.)

Students in Mr. Frost's level-2 English class read nothing that was outside their anthologies. With each selection they defined terms and answered comprehension questions. They "covered" library skills by doing exercises in their grammar books and learned about figurative language and inference by completing exercises in the back of their anthologies. Level-1 students learned how to "discover and explore ideas" and draft descriptive paragraphs through exercises in the "writing process" portion of their English texts. They wrote very little.

Some teachers saw texts as somewhat constraining but felt that they provided needed structure for student learning. As one of the business teachers explained, "I like them [textbooks] in a way, to kind of keep things structured and ordered. . . . Students need something to go by." Students didn't always see it that way and blamed teachers for being unimaginative. Art, a freshman from Barton, complained, "Teachers don't have enough 'oomph.' They just do what's in the book."

Publisher-composed tests further robbed teachers of authority because students learned that teachers talked about things that weren't on the tests—and therefore were of little relevance to getting good grades. Nicky explained about her science teacher, "I don't listen to him anymore. When he goes on and on, I just read the [text]book." The wellness teacher told her class that no matter what they talked about in class, their tests would be mostly based on textbook information. A senior who'd been at the school for 4 years summed up how the process worked schoolwide: "All they [students] do is read the material, do the worksheets, and take the tests."

Teachers who limited themselves to the book not only limited subject matter but limited ways in which students might go about learning material. A controlled curriculum also had implications for controlling student behaviors.

Questions and Seatwork: Controlling Behaviors

Teachers said they assigned questions from textbooks and worksheets to make sure students read assignments. They asked questions in class to check whether students had actually done the work. Yet they agreed that students didn't actually have to read texts in order to answer questions (e.g., "They have a textbook, and I expect them to read the chapter and a lot of times they don't; they just look through and find the answers"). In essence, teachers assigned questions so that students would search the text for answers. When teachers asked questions from homework in class, students looked to their papers to again find the answers—sometimes reading them verbatim, just as they'd copied them from their books.

If assigning questions for homework didn't guarantee that students read the text (confirmed by students), then students' written answers did indicate that they'd put in some time "going over" the reading—which satisfied teachers. Written answers, collected as homework, served as criteria for grades and could be recorded in rank books—the reason students most often cited for doing homework. Questions also had another practical function, however, one that was not cited by teachers or students. Asking and answering questions helped pass class time and kept that time orderly.

Quiet or silent seatwork was another way of making orderly use of class time. Sometimes half a period of seatwork followed half a period of checking the previous day's seatwork. Sometimes entire periods were given over to students' working quietly at their desks. In a level-2 English class the assignment was to read and work the exercises on pages 527–534 of their anthologies. "Don't be talking with anyone. Do your work," Frost told them before he began correcting tests the students had taken the previous Friday. Within 15 minutes everyone had finished except for a boy whose uncovered textbook had been confiscated and was therefore unable to do the work. The room was silent. In the remaining 35 minutes, Frost continued to check tests, occasionally sipping from a mug on his desk. Ginny and several others wrote letters to friends. Louie started a word-find from a puzzle book he always carried. A number of boys put their heads down on their desks and closed their eyes. From experience students had learned that Frost would say nothing about what they were doing as long as they were silent and didn't draw attention to themselves. When Jay whispered to Eddie, Frost told him to be quiet. With 6 minutes to go in the class, Frost told students they had permission to talk. As he had throughout the period, he continued to work at his desk. No students had asked for help, and at no time did Frost circulate among them. A few days earlier, Frost had explained why he assigned seatwork:

> I think it's very important because it gives the kids a chance to have a time when they're with me, when I know what they're doing— because when they're not with me, I don't know what they're doing. I can be sure that they're applying themselves while they're in my room. And I give seatwork fairly often, particularly with the level-2 classes—more than with the college prep classes because they need more direction, I feel. But all of them have seat work. . . . If they're not keeping their mind on their job, I'll speak to them about that, keep them on-task, as the term goes, and give them an environment that they may not have other places because I know a study hall may not be the best environment for studying in school.

Frost's purpose seemed to be one of providing a quiet work environment for students, a kind of study hall with available support. Implicit in his

explanation was a desire to instill good work habits through experience in a controlled work environment. Exercises themselves became a vehicle in that cause. Issues of control were also at stake.

Frost and others could make students be quiet by giving them a specific assignment and instructions to work independently. A couple of students said that Mr. Frost, in the previous example, had given them exercises so that he could have time to check tests; they explained that teachers gave seatwork when teachers needed to get work done. At other times students accused teachers of assigning seatwork when they were "too lazy" to teach. For most students, seatwork was a tolerable activity, better than having homework or, in some cases, listening to the teacher. Their acquiescence meant that seatwork usually made for quiet, orderly classrooms.

Grades and Failure as Consequences

There was a sense among teachers that students needed to be brought up short, toughened up, and made responsible for their academic behaviors. Some complained that students had been "coddled" in elementary school and passed along on "social promotions" until they reached high school. If students had "failed the way they should have" in elementary school, they'd have been more responsible and wouldn't need to be failed in high school. Students needed to know the consequences of their academic efforts, just as they needed to learn the consequences of breaking school rules. A few teachers also let students in on their beliefs. Mr. Frost told students:

> There are some of you here because they [the elementary schools] wanted to get you out of the eighth grade. If that happens here [students not working], you won't be in the tenth grade next year. I know right now that there are about five of you in here who will not do the work and will not pass this year.

The word *consequence* implied a certain orderliness, a kind of logical outcome to students' efforts. It placed responsibility for success or failure directly on students' shoulders. Test results and grades, numerical and precise, were viewed as *the* "consequence," and not failing became a valid goal. The use of the word *consequences* linked with grades—in a school that also used *consequences* in conjunction with disciplinary punishment—left little doubt that grades could be viewed as academic punishments. The punitive tone was upheld when, near the end of the first quarter, Webster wanted to know if students had thought of "the consequences" (grades) before reaching the end of the marking period. While teachers talked about student responsibility, Meadowbrook students' experience was that learning and teaching were shared responsibilities.

Report card grades were given in percentages, and with few exceptions teachers used percentages rather than letter grades in their classrooms. Percentages were given for classes' quarterly grades; midterm and final exams; and for semester, current-year, and cumulative averages. The report cards had no conversion chart for percentages to equivalent letter grades (equivalents were located in the handbook), and honors were awarded by percentages—down to the hundredth decimal point (e.g., 92.99). Percentages allowed for a precision that was unattainable with letter grades and lent an air of objectivity and authority to the grading process. It was hard for students to argue with a percentage as long as the math was correct.

One math teacher believed that percentages made students too conscious of grades. She awarded straight letter grades (no +'s or −'s) on quizzes and tests, and only at the end of the quarter did students convert their letter grades to percentages that would go on report cards. Other teachers felt that making students continually aware of grades would motivate them to work. Some periodically averaged grades and reported them when they returned tests. Some, using a number system of identification, posted averages in their rooms. One teacher required that students keep a running tally of their own percentages, recording and averaging everything that was graded. Grades were precise—so many points for homework, quizzes and tests, and notebook checks. Class participation and effort were rarely counted. Teachers explained that effort would show up in completed homework and scores on tests.

At times more emphasis was placed on grades and passing than on understanding material. When one math teacher began an easy unit on algebraic expressions (work that students had previously done) after a difficult unit on word problems, he told students, "Hopefully this will be an easy section for you. It ought to bring up your grades." Later in the class students made comments such as, "This ought to help my grade." It didn't appear to matter to them that they were learning nothing new. Grades mattered. When a student was suspended for 5 days for fighting, a teacher and an administrator in separate conversations mentioned that the suspension (and not being allowed to make up work) wouldn't hurt the student because his grades were good and he wasn't in danger of failing.

Students' grades were also perceived as rewards, especially in the level-1 classes. A science teacher told his level-1 students at the beginning of the third quarter, "It's now a question of what grade you want, and then go get it!" Whether perceived as positive or negative, grades kept students in line (unless they were failing and had given up). With few exceptions, students knew their current averages in most classes.

OUT OF THE FLOW: THE EXCEPTIONS

Like the math teacher who tried to downplay the importance of grades by awarding only letter grades until the end of the term and who told her students, "Strive for understanding, and the grades will come," there were individual teachers and even a department (Industrial Arts) that didn't fit the established patterns of the high school. Within these enclaves, freshmen from Meadowbrook found situations that were somewhat more familiar to their school experience.

Industrial Arts

The industrial arts classes were physically and philosophically separated from the rest of the school. They were located at one end of the 1972 addition, and the three teachers in the department commented that other teachers didn't have much to do with them—something that didn't appear to bother them very much. They enjoyed eating their lunches together in one of their rooms, and they talked philosophy without ever labeling it as such.

Mr. Walters, in his second year of teaching, was the youngest of the three and closest to Mr. Hansen, who'd been at the school for 18 years. He was a woodworker, and he loved teaching woodworking:

> I guess what I teach year to year, quarter to quarter, week to week, whatever—depends on what's needed. I mean if nobody needs to know how to taper a leg, I might skip it. Maybe not. I guess I don't think everybody should have to learn the same skill. If you had everyone do the same project, you could teach six skills, cut the wood joints, line them up, generate a lot less scrap, a lot less beating on the machines because you'd have a lot more control.

Inherent to his statement and others that the men made was recognition that students had individual needs, that instruction should be relevant, and that external control (while needing to be flexible, depending on tasks and situations) was bought at a price. They stressed how important it was for students to learn to work together. Hansen explained:

> I encourage them to get out and help another individual because with 20 people in the classroom, you'd need roller skates to get around here. If I'm working here with one student, and somebody needs a question answered, and one of the kids can show them how it should look, well then, that's fine. That's what we want to see.

Their classes were congenial places. Students took food and cans of soda to drafting class. "We let them. It doesn't hurt anybody. The place is kept clean. The thing is, it isn't such a big deal because you know, if these people work as draftsmen, they're going to have a cup of coffee beside their desks." Students helped one another in drafting classes as well as power and energy class and woodworking. Short lessons in woodworking were conducted with students sitting in chairs pulled into a circle. Students dropped by before and after school (there was no gate from the lobby to these rooms), and former students sometimes came by to visit.

Individual Teachers

Although Mrs. Larimer had taught Spanish for 17 years, she was new to Whitmore High School, brought in after school had started the previous year to replace a teacher on sabbatical. She didn't eat her lunch in the teachers' room, where she said things were too negative for her, and pretty much stayed on the top floor of the 1936 building where foreign language classes met. Mrs. Larimer loved teaching Spanish and expected everyone in the class to learn. When a transfer student wanted to quit after a week, Larimer encouraged her to stay, asking her to give it an additional 3 weeks. "I'm a very good teacher," she told the girl, "and I'll be glad to help you catch up." (The girl stayed the year.)

On the first day of school Mrs. Larimer set the tone for the year. Rather than distribute rules or lecture students about requirements, she set them to learning one another's names. Using almost no English and a lot of mime, she taught them to say, "What is your name? My name is . . ." in Spanish. Within minutes the room was buzzing with "¿Cómo te llamas tú?" and "Me llamo . . ." Students repeatedly changed partners until everyone had a chance to speak with everyone else and hear everyone's names.

When she sensed that some of the students were becoming frustrated trying to understand her Spanish directions, she told them in English, "I want you to guess. When you were real little, you guessed all the time. We're going to have to make mistakes. You're going to have to do some babbling, some gesturing. . . . It's okay to laugh at yourself." Students were not permitted to laugh at one another, however—the one rule she spoke of that day.

Throughout the year, students worked in class with one another: presenting skits, writing dialogues, studying for tests and quizzes, working exercises, checking one another's work, and practicing new vocabulary. When they learned numbers, they played a math multiplication game that had them running to the chalkboard, calculating figures, and then, in great good humor, announcing answers in Spanish. When they learned vocabulary for sports and pastimes, they conducted class surveys to determine which activities were most important. When they learned colors, Mrs. Larimer presented the class with sheets to color and one crayon each. If they wanted other colors, they had to ask one another for them. During most 50-minute classes, students had opportunities to read, write, speak, and listen to Spanish. There was some kind of partner/small-group work every day, even if it lasted only a few minutes.

Students' desks were arranged in rows, and they used workbooks that accompanied the text; Mrs. Larimer said that in many ways she was quite traditional. She saw herself as evolving, however, and believed that the biggest change in her teaching was learning to concentrate on what kids were doing well rather than on mistakes. She seldom "counted off" for small spelling or grammar errors and provided plenty of extra-credit questions on tests. She talked of making opportunities for students to be "successful without being perfect." She expected that they would learn best by *using* Spanish, and since she was just one person, they would have to help one another learn. Spanish class may have been more conducive than other classes to interactive practices, but nonetheless these practices established a communal atmosphere for teaching and learning. There was a lot of laughter in the class.

Students from Meadowbrook said that Mrs. Larimer reminded them of someone who might have taught elementary school. It wasn't that she read a Spanish translation of Keats's picture-story book, *The Snowy Day*, to the class when they studied weather vocabulary or even that she played games with them. Nicky said that it was because she seemed to care for students, that she didn't give up on anyone—even when they didn't try very hard. By spring the students from Meadowbrook said they thought she'd fit well at Meadowbrook Community School.

Mrs. Martin, who taught wellness, was another teacher who thought students needed to work together—at least as a part of their instruction. She explained, "I think that we need to have a mixture of cooperative and individual activity. And I think that to go either direction exclusively is a disservice to everybody." Although she used a textbook and accompanying worksheets and spent days "giving notes" to students, she also planned instruction around videotapes, filmstrips, and interactive video laser. She experimented with having small groups of students teach the rest of the class about aspects of drug abuse, and she routinely assigned more writing than some of the English teachers did. Meadowbrook students said they felt comfortable with the writing assignments and group work.

There were also individuals in the science department who were experimenting with cooperative learning and group projects—even though group action sometimes meant filling in worksheets. A keyboarding (typing) teacher didn't grade students' daily work because she wanted students to concentrate on learning to type rather than on percentages. There were teachers who seemed to like students and maintained a good rapport with them, even though their teaching was mostly "right out of the book."

POTENTIAL CONTEXTS FOR DEVELOPING LITERACIES

Some programs had the potential for affecting all students in positive ways. While all were not fully utilized, they did exist. To the degree that they were inclusive, they provided authentic contexts for students' developing literacies.

The library was well equipped, with computer access to larger libraries. There were periodicals and daily newspapers, a section for popular fiction, encyclopedias and other bound reference materials, an updated collection of nonfiction books, and materials that could augment textbooks used in classrooms. Equipment was available for computer searches, and the librarian and her assistant were available to help students.

The library was not always busy, however. Some teachers were reluctant to give library passes, and even if students obtained them, they could be canceled by study hall teachers. Some freshmen, depending on which teachers they had for study hall and classes, found it impossible to go to the library. Students could choose to go to the library instead of eating but could not split the lunch period between the cafeteria and the library. "I don't know how to get around that," the librarian explained. "I don't know how else to control kids wandering around the halls." Sometimes teachers arranged for their classes to meet in the library, but as the librarian explained, not many teachers used the library as well as they could have. "This is what really frustrates me—that the teachers—some of them . . . they see this as a little attachment to the curriculum, not something that is integral." Few asked the librarian to order specific books, something the librarian said she welcomed. The school's professional library, two shelves of books and several incomplete sets of journals, was housed in the discipline office.

More students started borrowing books from the library when a "reading break" was established in March. For 25 minutes each week (rotated among days and periods), students and teachers were supposed to read. Some students welcomed the chance and reminded themselves of how much they'd enjoyed reading in the past—something they'd given up for homework and sports. Others, not allowed to write or do homework during the reading break, sat bored or thumbed through their textbooks. Teachers were also supposed to read; some did, and some corrected papers.

The writing center was open to all students, but few freshmen used its services. Staffed by on-duty teachers who were available to help students, the center was in the same large room that was used for tutoring. Most freshmen thought they could obtain passes only from their English teachers, and since they were assigned little writing, they saw no purpose in going to the writing center. Louie, a freshman who transferred to the school in the second semester, simply walked into the center and asked for a pass for periods when he had study halls. Others, in attendance from the beginning of the year, had never considered such a move and were surprised to learn that Louie could obtain passes so easily. The procedure was not highly advertised.

The school provided other opportunities for students to read, write, and talk outside classes. Teachers nominated students to act as peer-tutors during their study halls. Other students, having requested tutoring assistance through the guidance office, could then work with peer-tutors in the tutoring center. Clubs provided opportunities for authentic reading and writing (e.g., Spanish Club members writing to local merchants asking for donations to their Christmas festival). The yearbook and school newspaper also provided opportunities for authentic literacy. Freshmen did not generally become involved in these activities, however.

FACULTY MORALE

Whitmore teachers had worked 3 years without a contract, and when taxpayers and teachers finally came to an agreement in June 1993, the teachers received a contract for the following year and small raises. "You know," Rose Martin said:

> I think that when people have had as much dissatisfaction as they've had for the number of years they've had—I think once you stop working hard and look at your job as a job rather than as a career, it becomes difficult to regain that. It'll be slow, and some people will go back to being the way they were. But it'll be a long time.

A number of teachers didn't think the contract difficulties had affected instruction, but reactions were mixed. Some argued that lazy teachers were using the contract as an excuse. Others had a different opinion: "Oh yeah. I'm sure it [the contract] has [affected instruction]. A lot of teachers will deny just kissing things off, but a lot of teachers have backed off. 'Read Chapter One. Here are the words. Test on Tuesday. Shut up. Sit down.' That's it."

The 1992–93 school year was a tough one. For most of the year, teachers "worked to the contract." They entered the building at 7:20, 10 minutes before the first class, and left the building at 2:35, 15 minutes after the end of the last class. Teachers from all the schools, but primarily from the high school, picketed in front of the high school before and after school hours. When their contract was turned down in March, one-third of the high school teachers (teachers from the other three Whitmore schools voted not to participate) staged a one-day sickout, and the high school closed. The main bulletin board in the teachers' room was covered with news clippings about picketing and town meetings, and teachers' room talk often revolved around the issue—at least until "some" individuals entered the room.

Not everyone belonged to the union, and even among those who did, there were some who were philosophically opposed to "working to the contract" or to picketing. There was reluctant participation as well as non-participation in union activities. All this made for increasing distrust and hard feelings among faculty. One group, perceived by the others as being particularly "negative" or "militant," occupied the teachers' room at certain times of the day, making those who were not part of their group feel uncomfortable. As a result, some teachers didn't use the teachers' room much. At least one teacher was physically threatened because he stayed in the school instead of taking his turn among the picketers. Others who didn't immediately vacate the building after school said they sometimes felt intimidated, that the dirty looks and silences were not pleasant. There were even a few teachers who wouldn't talk to one another.

Everyone agreed that faculty morale was low. When questioned about whether "working to the contract" had affected their teaching, most said that it had not—even those who chose to take no work home when they left at 2:35. Some explained that they used their planning time more effectively than they had in the past. A union member who reluctantly picketed but stayed after school when he had work, explained:

> Those who didn't do anything before [the job action] aren't doing anything now, and if the contract was settled last year, they still wouldn't be doing anything [this year], and they're going to complain the most. . . . And those who don't take it [work] home because they are working to the clock wouldn't have taken anything home anyway. In fact, some people, because we have to stay until 2:35—end up staying 15 minutes longer than they usually do.

As serious as the contract issue was, no one believed that it was the sole reason for low faculty morale. Some cited administrative changes, primarily that of removing department heads and replacing them with one of four administrators. In a March letter to the editor of the local newspaper, the president of the union outlined shortcomings of the restructuring, citing cost at a time when the school had no money to waste. He echoed the complaints of other teachers when he wrote that communication within departments had suffered and that professional evaluation had become less meaningful. While some teachers were supportive of the new structure, others were angry that their complaints of the year before had gone unanswered. One former department head was particularly upset:

> I could sit in on any teacher's class, and if they were giving the kids bum information, I knew it. In fact, I caught it on a number of times. The one [administrator] we've got now, he could sit in on a class—he hasn't the slightest idea whether the information the teacher is giving to the kids is valid or invalid.

Webster expected teachers to take on responsibilities formerly assumed by department heads: budgeting and curriculum. He expected teachers to tell him what they needed; he thought they didn't require department heads to do so. Depending on the department—each made up of various personalities—teachers felt either autonomous or simply leaderless. Practically speaking, teachers had little to decide on; curriculum was dependent on textbooks, and there wasn't money for new texts.

In addition to organizational changes, teachers confronted tight budgets and a sense that the community was not supportive of education. One of the science teachers said that the contract issue was most visible but that the main problem was community priorities—that education wasn't valued in the community the way it should be:

> In the last 4 years we've seen an absolute depletion of all resources dealing with education—right here in Whitmore, right here at the high school . . . say in the science department. A 67% cut in the science funding. It's ridiculous. You know, we're spending less on a student basis here than you spend for cat litter for your cat, and that is so sad.

It didn't help morale that some of the budget problems had been precipitated by a $300,000 administrative "mix-up" a year earlier. All Whitmore schools were affected, and the high school department budgets were frozen. Teachers who hadn't already spent their funds found themselves with nothing to spend. The red ink carried into 1992–93, forcing further cuts in department spending. Teachers blamed the administration and felt that they were paying for administrative and school board oversights. Webster saw the budget woes as a "slow erosion." Even though the budget grew each year, it was "eaten away" by uncontrollable costs such as health insurance, utility bills, and payments on loans. Administration and faculty did not discuss these issues, and frustrations grew.

Contract issues, administrative reorganization, and lack of sufficient funding were problems that not only weakened morale but diverted attention from issues of instruction. Poor morale made communication difficult, and without opportunities for talking things out, morale continued to spiral downward. Faculty met as a group only once a month, generally for less than an hour, in a format that was not conducive to conversation. Departments met rarely. In fact, meetings of any kind were uncommon, something that had been true even in years prior to 1992–93.

There were a few friendly organizers among the faculty—individuals who planned the Christmas party, organized the "Sunshine Fund" (a fund for get-well cards and flowers, etc.), or tried to gather people together for after-school activities. But in spite of their efforts, gloom persisted, and more than a few teachers commented that Whitmore High was not a happy place to work.

SUMMARY

Whitmore High School served students from five communities, four of which had no "say" in the school's operations. The school was well cared for and clean, with little or no graffiti and litter. While there appeared to be no articulated shared educational philosophy, order was highly valued and carefully maintained through various measures: school and classroom rules and procedures; discipline and attendance policies; hallway and library passes; textbook and worksheet activities; classroom procedures such as teacher questions, seatwork, and imposed silence; computer scheduling; homogeneous grouping; and grades. Faculty members generally felt unsupported by the town and found little sense of community among themselves; morale was low for a variety of reasons. Teachers and students routinely did their work, and school life went smoothly.

CHAPTER 5

Becoming High School Students

Secondary school students' engagement and achievement are affected profoundly by experiences that cannot be identified simply by listing what is prescribed in the formal curriculum, what students do in their classes, and what is being tested. Instead, the effects of any specific school activity are best understood as cultural phenomena; that is, as outcomes that evolve through complex webs of institutionally sanctioned meanings, values, and incentives or disincentives for particular kinds of behavior.

Fred M. Newmann
Student Engagement and Achievement in American Secondary Schools,
1992, p. 182

Essence of aftershave wafted above bodies crowded together in the school lobby as students waited for the 7:20 bell and for the doors to be unlocked to the rest of the building. Cuddling against lockers, couples continued their phone conversations from the night before. Seeking last-minute caffeine and sugar highs, students sipped from soda cans, trying not to spill any as their elbows were bumped by other students seeking to make their way through the throng. A din of voices punctuated by occasional outbursts required that everyone shout in order to be heard. One teacher, whose year-long duty was to circulate among the crowd, patrolled the periphery and zeroed in on particularly rowdy behaviors.

In the midst of this early morning whirl, not too far from the entrance doors, the freshmen from Meadowbrook, not unlike a foreign tour group at an unfamiliar airport, were circled around a communal pile of bags and belongings. Retaining their places in the circle, Nicky and Monica sat on the tiled floor oblivious to the fact that no one else in the lobby circled as they did or used the floor as a place to rest.

Although there were other groups in the lobby, even some that formed sort-of circles, the MCS freshmen stood out as being different from the others. Perhaps it was the center pile of books and bags; perhaps it was the size of the circle or its routine formation in the same spot at the same time each morning. When students from other towns became friends, they sometimes mentioned being allowed to join the "Meadowbrook circle." During the year, Meadowbrook students left and reentered the circle. Sharon, who had had a steady Whitmore boyfriend prior to the beginning of the year, never joined it. Ginny only rarely joined. Others brought their boy/girlfriends to the circle, where the boys sometimes stood directly behind the girls with their hands on the girls' shoulders. By the end of March the circle had broken; too many had found other places to be. For most of the year, though, the circle held fast; Nicky, Jan, Chad, John, Monica, Rachelle, and Carl were the anchors.

The students didn't see any significance to the circle and didn't explicitly compare it to circles they'd formed while at MCS; it was, they said, just a way to stand in the morning and give them a place to put their stuff. The circle accomplished two other things, however. It provided a safe haven for any Meadowbrook students who joined it, and it served to segregate them from the rest of the students in the lobby. Only those who were friends of at least one Meadowbrook student stood with them. The circle was exclusive as well as inclusive, and Meadowbrook students were in control.

ORIENTATION AND REORIENTATION

The early days were a rush of rules and information—rules for gym, study hall, English, and lunch room—locker assignments, identification numbers, updated academic schedules, sports schedules, finding rides after field hockey practice, learning names, taking down phone numbers, remembering where to go for math, and finding people to sit with at lunch. "You can't buy lunch without an ID card." "Can I borrow your socks for phys. ed.?" "What [class] do you have next?" "Some girl came up to me and asked if I knew Chad. She thinks he's cute and wants to know if he has a girlfriend." "I get up at 5:30. I wish I could sleep on the bus." "I've had to pee wicked bad since first thing this morning, and I haven't been able to go." "Do you have any money? Can I borrow a quarter?" "Do you have any gum?" "This is so boring."

Several days before the official opening of school, freshmen had attended a morning's orientation, and the principal had addressed them in the auditorium. He told them about Mrs. Porter and her role as freshman "disciplinarian." He told them that in elementary school they'd been pushed along; in high school they would fail if they didn't earn 23 credits. "When I looked at a list of freshmen not becoming sophomores," he continued, "more than 50% of them didn't go on to graduate. That's why your freshman year is tough." He also introduced a theme that would be repeated by teachers—that in elementary school they'd not been responsible. "The responsibility this year really shifts. Where responsibility wasn't really placed on your shoulders before, the biggest change and expectation is that the responsibility is with you [now]." He told them they'd be punished for breaking rules. He stressed that visitors always remarked on how clean and tidy the school was and that there would be no "trashing" of the building.

The Meadowbrook students had sat together in one long row, not saying a word as Webster spoke. Later Nicky said that she'd listened to what Mr. Webster had said but made no further comment. The others said that the talk didn't mean much to them, that they weren't going to do "those things" anyway. Their response was similar to one they'd had on their eighth-grade class trip to Montreal, when, before entering a museum, a tour guide had warned them they'd be thrown out if they misbehaved. They'd been somewhat surprised by the warning. "She doesn't know us," one of them had said at the time.

Early Concerns

In the early days students had so much to absorb quickly that they didn't have the energy to reflect on what was happening to them. Chad's science teacher told the class, "I'll be expecting quite a lot of you, which will probably be a change from last year." Chad later indicated that he hadn't understood that his new science teacher was "putting down" his former school or science teacher. Ginny's and John's English teacher told them, "Taking responsibility for yourself is the biggest change between eighth grade and ninth grade." Ginny said that meant English would be harder, and John said he hadn't paid attention to that part. When the same teacher told Monica's, Nicky's, and Sharon's class that "the writing process" was a series of seven steps starting with "think," they copied the list into their notes. They didn't argue, even though, in their experience, writing didn't go in steps that way. In the first days, students were most concerned about "getting along"—finding the bus at the end of the day, getting to classes on time, remembering their gym clothes on the right days, and not making any mistakes that would cause them to stand out in their classes.

When Monica, who thought of herself as a good writer, had difficulty with an English assignment to complete the first four steps (think, list, organize, and first draft) of the writing process in describing her first days at Whitmore High School, she panicked: "You know how I like to write, right? Well, I couldn't do it last night. I don't know what's the matter, but I couldn't write. I got so mad. I kept wadding it up and throwing it away." She questioned her own abilities rather than the assignment. Nicky agreed with her. She didn't know why she was having so much difficulty with a simple assignment. Neither of the girls recognized that being told to follow steps in a writing process might inhibit them, that writing without collaboration was new to them, or that writing under the threat of failure if there were too many errors might freeze them. They were just trying to do what they were told.

John and Ginny, as well as Monica, Nicky, and Sharon, wrote the assignment. Their short essays reflected their early concerns. In part, Monica wrote:

> I was also nervous about having all new teachers. I had the same teachers for two years and grew to understand them and know their teaching techniques. . . . They also took the time to help us when extra attention was needed. I had never met any of the WHS teachers before and didn't know what to expect from them. Before school started I had heard a lot of rumors about how hard some of the teachers were. Those rumors made me start to worry about grades. I'm afraid I won't be as good in school as I was before. I'm also afraid that students from other schools will know more than me.

Because Monica had met new friends through field-hockey practice prior to the opening of school, her main concern was one of academics. Ginny, on the other hand, made it her business to connect socially in the first days of school. Teachers were only a secondary concern. Her essay included:

> Getting around new friends and fitting in was easier than I had thought. I was so excited that I had made so many new friends, guys included. They are so nice. I am glad I found good friends and got in the good crowd. I also found out that not all the teachers were as bad as I had thought. I've not yet found a favorite teacher, but I hope I do. My fear of sitting alone at lunch was cured. I now sit with a bunch of pretty cool friends.

"Doing Meadowbrook"

Meadowbrook freshmen had long anticipated those first days of high school. Primed by stories from older siblings and friends and reminded throughout their eighth-grade year that "this" was on the horizon, students were full of nervous excitement—an excitement that sustained them early on. They took in everything at face value. If their new teachers told them the work would be hard, they believed them. Sharon was the first to articulate a difference between expectations and what she was experiencing. Referring to classes after the first week, she commented, "I thought it would be much harder." She pulled business worksheets from her bag and said, "This is what we do." John, who figured high school would make him work harder than elementary school had, discovered after a few weeks that he could do less than he had at Meadowbrook and "get by." It took longer for the excitement to wear off for Chad. Only in the spring could he look back to the first weeks. "At the beginning of the year, I didn't really miss it [MCS] because I wanted to move on. Then I found out high school wasn't as exciting as I thought it would be."

In the beginning, students' expectations colored their experiences. They behaved as if school would be "exciting" and "challenging." Ginny, accustomed to taking class notes, tried to take them in her level-2 science class, even though the teacher wrote nothing on the board and other students didn't pretend to note what he said. When she asked him how she might get more than a "check" on her worksheets, he told her that a "check" was for doing what he asked and that it was impossible to do more than what he asked on a worksheet. At one point, the boys around her joked that she was a "schooler." She was "doing Meadowbrook" at the high school, trying to be a conscientious student. Similarly, as she had at Meadowbrook, she tried to make small talk with teachers. She assumed when she turned in her initial writing assignment that it would be the first of many. She liked writing and smiled as she handed it over to the teacher.

"Doing Meadowbrook" particularly stood out in level-2 classes. Ginny and Rachelle, who in eighth-grade had needed to take algebra notes because they didn't have algebra textbooks to refer to, wrote down everything their level-2 math teacher wrote on the board. They were the only ones in their class to routinely do so. Chad's level-2 science teacher expected students to keep notebooks of sequentially ordered chapter outlines and worksheets. Chad, along with a few others in the class, did what he was told. The rest, most of them from a school where they'd become accustomed to being grouped with low-achieving students in seventh and eighth grades, often didn't bother to do the assigned homework and so couldn't put together notebooks.

"Doing Meadowbrook" in level-1 classes was less obvious, although nonacademic behaviors sometimes set students apart. When their Spanish teacher showed a short video and Nicky couldn't see from her corner seat, she got up, moved over to where Jan was sitting, and shared her chair (a not uncommon practice at Meadowbrook). At lunch Monica told them that "everyone looked" at them when they did that, implying that it didn't look right at WHS.

Accustomed to teachers they'd called "caring," students were surprised by their perceptions of the high school teachers' attitudes and practices. Two weeks into school, Monica was puzzled that her math teacher didn't seem to know her name. A week later, she complained about her science teacher, "He just doesn't care. He doesn't care if we know it or not. . . . I don't even think he knows me. He knows Jan, but he doesn't know me." She expected more attention from her teachers.

Disillusionment showed in other ways. Their math teachers didn't teach the way Miss Arno had. They didn't get to "do anything" (experiments or labs) in science. The writing assignments were "stupid" (meaning contrived) and had given way to grammar instruction. After the first month or two—with the exception of Chad, who never completely understood what was happening to him—it was as if the Meadowbrook freshmen were standing in the Kingdom of Oz saying, "We have a feeling we're not in Meadowbrook anymore."

Reorienting

Nicky and Monica consciously decided to do what they had to in order to get good grades. Nicky explained, "I don't think it makes much difference [where you go to high school] because you adapt to where you are. And you learn how to do stuff." So if Mr. Frost told her to learn to spell all the characters' names in the condensed version of *David Copperfield*, she didn't argue; she just did it. When she realized that she was getting better grades in science by outlining chapters just the way her teacher wanted her to, she decided to continue "just because I want to get good grades."

Ginny's reaction was to balk. When she had trouble answering worksheet questions she gave up on them. She didn't sense that her teachers would help, so she didn't bother turning in what she had. She "talked back" to her math teacher, began arriving late to class, and finally began taking things into her own hands: rearranging her schedule, dropping a level to get "a science teacher who would teach," and emphasizing social connections almost to the exclusion of academic ones.

John was more passive, and since grades weren't as important to him as they were to Monica and Nicky, as he so often explained, he did "just enough to get by." He didn't think he was learning much in most of his classes or that increased effort would make much difference. He knew that if he'd tried, he could have received an A in English but he said, "We don't learn anything in that class. Nothing. I mean it. Nothing." To John it wasn't worth the effort. The material wasn't interesting, and there was nothing about his teacher's approach that was personally motivating. "I mean, he [the teacher] doesn't laugh or anything."

While the others generally recognized the different expectations of the two schools, Chad, trusting and sincere by nature, didn't understand that his effort in classes would not outweigh his test results. He didn't understand that worksheets were just worksheets and that he could put down "almost anything" the way others did in his classes and get by with it. Instead, he wrote small to fit in long answers and spent hours on homework that other students dispatched quickly. There were flashes of insight, such as when he decided not to finish a science "word-find" because it didn't seem as important as his other homework. For the most part, however, he doggedly plugged away—blaming himself when he didn't do well. His biggest puzzlement was that students in his classes didn't try very hard. "If they just did their homework, they'd pass," he said. "Why don't they do it?" He really wanted to know.

LEARNING HOW TO GET ALONG

Getting along in high school meant having friends, staying out of trouble, and doing okay with grades. Each of these criteria was relative to individuals and to the groups to which they belonged, and within each criterion, there was a range of acceptable behavior. Finding friends and maintaining friendships was probably most important to students and could affect the other two areas. As Chad explained, "My grades always go down when I have a girlfriend." Having a girlfriend also meant that he was more apt to be late to class, which resulted in after-school detentions. Getting along meant finding a suitable balance among the three criteria. If students were happy with the balance, they felt that they were getting along "all right."

Social Life

It was hard to talk to one another in classes where teachers made students be quiet and do seatwork most of the period. Even when they were responding to teachers' oral prompts, they couldn't chat with one another. Dances and sports programs were the best opportunities to meet and talk with a variety of kids. As Chad explained, the only real time they had in school for such socializing was in the locker room during gym or at lunch.

Attending classes where there were no other Meadowbrook students was particularly difficult, especially for those who were shy or quiet like Rachelle. Three of her academic classes were without Meadowbrook peers, and gym was the only class in which she had a Meadowbrook friend whom she saw regularly outside school hours. She wasn't involved in sports, and since she usually couldn't chat in class, there was no way of becoming friends with classmates. Even though she retained her Meadowbrook friends, she was lonely most of the day. By December, she wanted to change high schools.

Ginny lived near the Wayhill town line, geographically closer to those students than many of her Meadowbrook peers. Through her twin brother, who was one grade ahead of her, she'd met a few Wayhill kids during the preceding summer. When school started, she had readymade contacts to help make new friends—a number of whom had histories of getting into trouble at their elementary school.

Before school started, Chad and John had joined the soccer team, and
Monica, Nicky, and Jan had joined the field-hockey team. Despite the long
commute for practices and games, all of them said they were glad they'd
joined the teams—if for no other reason than that it introduced them to some
kids before school started. Additionally, when Jan was elected to the student council and made the varsity cheerleading squad, she became a highly
visible link between Meadowbrook students and those from other towns.
The cheerleading coach made Nicky manager, so Nicky also assumed a
prominent role. John and Monica made the freshmen and junior varsity
basketball teams, respectively, and continued to cement relationships formed
during fall sports.

Romance was another avenue for making friends. When Nicky started
going out with a boy from Barton, she and her Meadowbrook peers also got
to know the boy's friends. John and Jan went together for most of the year,
so their relationship didn't directly introduce them to kids from other towns,
but it did make them one of "the" couples in their class. John liked having
female friends, and since he was going with Jan, other girls felt comfortable
around him. He once explained that if his girl "friends" left him, he wouldn't
have many friends at all.

Ginny had a series of boyfriends who widened her circle of friends, but
since her breakups were usually less than amiable, romance was also an alien-
ating factor. She sometimes lost friends when she broke up with boyfriends.
Although Ginny remained on friendly terms with the rest of the Meadowbrook freshmen, her friends did not become their friends. Unlike the others,
when Ginny joined the morning circle in the lobby, she didn't bring her new
friends to it—at least not until it was breaking up in the spring.

Underground Literacy

Distances between towns made it difficult to visit one another's houses. Picking up (or dropping off) a carload of kids could consume the better part of
a parent's evening. Even the telephone posed a problem, since it was a long
distance call from Meadowbrook to Ashfield, the town where a number of
the girls' new friends lived. In-school communication became critical to social
life.

Students sent messages through one another. "If you have lunch eighth
period, say hello to Ryan for me." They also delivered letters or notes for
one another. "Give this to Tami. Tell her she better write back." Most easily
written in study hall where writers couldn't get into trouble for producing
them, notes and letters were also written in classes. "The bell rang, so now
I'm writing in science. We're suppost [sic] to being taking notes or doing these
stupid worksheets. I don't feel like it."

Some students wrote letters all day long. Ginny said she averaged five to six letters a day, some of which she revised and recopied. Others wrote rarely or not at all. Nicky seldom wrote letters. More students read and wrote letters in level-2 classes than in level-1 classes, in part because they tended to have more seatwork and oral checking of homework, which afforded them more convenient opportunities for correspondence. Girls wrote to girls, and boys and girls wrote to one another—even writing poetry—but boys seldom wrote to boys.

Letters were generally written to be delivered between classes or after school; quick notes, intended to be immediately entertaining or informative, were passed in class. ("Call me tonight! I can't explain everything right now. OKAY?! GOOD.") Usually students just passed them by hand when the teacher wasn't looking, but they also found more inventive ways to pass them, for example, in cosmetic compacts, along with other papers, tucked into calculator cases, inside the shoe or sock of an outstretched leg, with a book, or by accidentally dropping them to the floor to be courteously picked up by other students. Sometimes a single sheet of paper, passed back and forth, became the format for written conversations: "Steve. Did you ever wonder who made words, numbers or words for other objects? W/B [write back]." "Ginny. No. I can't say I really thought about that. Sincerely yours, Steve." "Steve, I have no idea why. The thought just popped into my head. W/B Ginny." "Ginny, That's OK. It's good to ask questions, just try to avoid those kind of questions. Steve." "Why?"

Students' intense need to socialize, thwarted by the nature of schedules and classes, manifested itself in a kind of underground literacy. The reading and writing of notes and letters not only helped maintain friendships and pass time; it also provided an authentic context (audience and purpose) for reading and writing that did not exist in most classes. In volume alone, letter writing far outweighed any writing that students such as Ginny did for academic classes. And for many students, those who didn't speak up in class or who were less than garrulous among groups of friends, note and letter writing offered voice.

Detentions, Rules, and Responsibility

A lot of students never received detentions, and for those who did, like Chad, they were not something to be proud of. After getting three nights of detention for being late to homeroom a fourth time, he told himself, "I can't do this," and tried a lot harder to get from his science class in the 1972 addition to his homeroom on the third floor of the 1936 building on time. He made sure to have his books closed when the bell rang at the end of class and stopped going to his locker. He complained that it didn't seem fair that a few seconds could

mean a detention. He knew that homeroom was usually just listening to the
PA announcements and that classes didn't usually start on time. Still, by
the end of the year he'd collected a number of detentions, and sensitive as he
was, he wondered if the detentions meant that he was "bad." After all, a
detention for him was a bad thing because it meant missing the bus and having
to arrange for a ride.

For others, detentions and tardiness became almost a game. Ginny told
of having 10 detentions lined up, mostly for being late to classes. (During
the year some students were in arrears by 30 or more detentions, collected
for a variety of reasons.) "It's fun," she explained. Ginny didn't ride the bus
and waited at least an hour for her mother every day after school, whether
she had detentions or not. There was a certain camaraderie in serving detentions with friends, and she didn't see any harm in it. Ginny also refused to
sign in after she'd been absent until "they" called her to the office to do so.
There was no penalty, and she liked causing "them" trouble.

Teachers generally saw rules in terms of the discipline policy, but students viewed rules in a broader sense. It didn't matter if rules stemmed from
the attendance policy, discipline policy, classroom requirements, sports participation, or the various sections of the student handbook (rules for the
library, for study hall, for the cafeteria, for attending dances, for posting
materials on school walls, dress code rules, etc.). It didn't matter if not following the rules resulted in detentions or in being ejected from the library.
Rules were rules, and there were a lot of them. Chad thought of the $10
participant fee for playing on a school sports team as a kind of rule. Nicky,
who received no detentions and was absent very little, complained that the
rules were too strict and too numerous and was particularly concerned about
the absentee policy being an unfair rule. Sharon implied that rules were a
sign of distrust. "You have to have a pass to go anywhere. It's stupid. We
never had that in MCS. They're afraid that you may take the longest route
back to the room." Sharon and her Meadowbrook peers hadn't needed rules
in order to feel responsible in the eighth grade. In fact, when they believed
that rules were being mandated without their input, they felt insulted and
angry, as if they were no longer trusted (see the section in Chapter 3, "Controlling Their Own Behaviors").

Student responsibility, so often cited by adults as important, was really
a matter of compliance *or* acceptance of penalties. As the teachers so often
repeated, it was all "spelled out in the handbook"—rules and penalties.
Webster's written introduction in the handbook stated, "We expect that
everyone will cooperate with the stated rules and new attendance policies or
will accept the consequences." In this sense, Ginny's "fun" with detentions
was responsible behavior because she "accepted the consequences."

Misbehaving wasn't an issue for most freshmen. They weren't rude to teachers, didn't set off smoke bombs in the hallway, and didn't sneak smokes in the bathroom; the rules were superfluous to their normal behaviors. However, the aura of rules made the issue of responsibility confusing to Meadowbrook students, who were accustomed to having enough leeway in expectations to exercise some responsibility. Monica didn't know what teachers were talking about when they said that students would have to be responsible in high school. "Responsible for what?" she wanted to know. "Responsible for your schedule? Like where you're supposed to be and when?" That was "spelled out" too.

Grades

Students did understand that they were "responsible" for maintaining passing grades. Nicky saw her responsibility as something more than that, however. She wanted to go to college, and she explained she needed to "get through high school" with good grades. Chad, who was less able than Nicky academically, was even more aware of grades and getting into what he called a "decent college." "I really want to get good grades," he explained. "I have this feeling that when I become a junior, things are really going to get hard for me. And the SATs and everything. I'm a little worried about that." Monica, who had a B average, and John, who expected to try harder when he needed to, assumed that their grades would be good enough to get them into college; they didn't think much about it. Ginny talked about going to Boston University (where she'd heard they had a good law enforcement program) without understanding that her failing and near-failing grades would preclude that possibility.

To a degree, students could determine the grades they would receive. They could do the work their teachers assigned, or they could choose not to do it. Still, not all students were equally able or motivated. For most of the year, Ginny didn't understand that not turning in homework seriously damaged her average. She felt that it was good enough to turn in homework most of the time. She didn't understand that zeros counted more than 100's when 70 was passing. She didn't turn in homework that was only partially finished because she promised herself that she would finish it that evening and turn it in late. She usually forgot. Many of the business, art, and science worksheets were difficult for her, and when she "got stuck," she put them away. Every day her teachers recorded her output, and it didn't matter that she didn't understand the assignment, took the wrong book home, or just forgot to do it. It didn't matter that she was bored by the steady stream of worksheets or thought the homework was dull: "Read the stupid boring stories and answer the damn questions." Her grades, in large part, were dependent on home-work. Days piled on days, and in the end, she failed business (57%) and a semester-long art course (42%). If it hadn't been for the 2.5 credits she received for passing driver's training, she'd have earned less than 23 credits and been a "repeat freshman" the following year. Her cumulative average was 67%. Seventy percent was passing, but cumulative averages didn't count.

Chad's diligence didn't always translate to passing grades; he had a hard time with tests and was often discouraged. Because of his learning disability, he had a tutor for 50 minutes each day (in two sessions of 25 minutes each). There, he got help with his most confusing homework and reviewed for science tests. Not doing his homework for science would have meant automatic failure, but doing his homework didn't raise his test average much. All year his science grades were close to failing. In the end he had a D+ average, not what he needed to get into a "decent college." He did well in algebra because he already knew how to do the work, but his year-end overall grade point average was 80.679%, a C.

John's year-end grade point average was also a C, but he acknowledged that he rarely studied for tests and did just enough homework to get by. He started out with B's and worked down from there, for instance, dropping from a first-quarter English grade of 84 to a 57 in the last quarter. He put in a flurry of effort only if it looked like his grades were in serious trouble.

Monica and Nicky worked consistently throughout the year, turning in homework and studying for tests. Monica could generally do better on tests with somewhat less studying than Nicky required. Monica also recognized the effort for what it was: "You look at your work, you fill out the sheets, and you take a test. Half of the time you don't even take notes." Monica did not equate good grades with learning (she did well in science but said she learned nothing: "I don't know one thing that I learned."), but both she and Nicky understood what they needed to do in order to get good grades, and they had the ability and motivation to do what they had to do.

Grades worked differently in high school than they had in most elementary schools. If students failed subjects in elementary school but did all right in other areas, they passed to the next grade, perhaps getting extra help when they needed it. In high school, failure of required classes meant repetition of those classes. A passing overall grade point average didn't propel students into the next grade. In March Ginny thought she'd pass (be a sophomore the following year) because she was doing all right in some of her classes. She also thought that individual teachers would pass her, even though the percentages didn't add up, if they saw that she was working. Until the end she believed she could pass her introduction to business course, even though her average after three quarters was well below failing.

Grades were relative. An adequate grade for one student was not an adequate grade for another. In the end, Ginny's 23.25 credits allowed her to feel okay about her freshman year. John "got by." He failed nothing and once again signed up for mostly level-1 classes the following year. Chad also passed everything, although he was surprised that his effort hadn't paid off with better grades. Monica and Nicky went from A's at Meadowbrook to B's at Whitmore and were grateful for them. Except for Spanish, neither felt that they'd learned as much as they had in previous years. "They aren't prepared for our individual personalities, what we want to learn. People come, people graduate. You know, who cares," Monica explained.

Students who succeeded were the ones who found motivation for satisfying teachers' expectations, and the emphasis on grades masked what students accomplished or didn't accomplish in the process of earning those grades. Nicky explained during the summer following her freshman year: "I think that at the end of the year that all they look at is your grades for classes. They don't look at how you acted and the way you've worked. . . . It's your grades that counted."

SCHOOLWORK

There was unspoken complicity between teachers and students. Once routines were set early in the fall, most teachers asked students to do little beyond textbook-related work or similarly controlled assignments, and students perfunctorily went about doing what was asked of them. Even though they complained to one another of boredom, students rarely confronted teachers about the nature of schoolwork—as long as teachers were genial and didn't ask them to do more than what was customary. Those who didn't do the work were quiet about it, provided teachers didn't press too hard. A sameness overcame class days. Substitute teachers, fire drills, early dismissals for sports, misbehaving students, lunch, and gym broke things up. Weeks evaporated as one assignment followed another.

Introduction to business was nonleveled and a prerequisite for other business classes. Its routine operation was typical of this unspoken complicity between students and teachers. John was in one section, Ginny in another, and Chad and Sharon in a third. John took the class because his mother was a banker and because he thought he'd need to know something about business after he got out of school. (He might have taken Spanish with Nicky, Monica, and Jan, but because he was in level-2 English, he was required to wait until his sophomore year to take a foreign language.) After the first few days he realized that it was going to be a lot of book work. He liked the teacher but thought the class was boring. He said lunch, which separated the class into two 25-minute periods, made the time go faster.

It was the same routine almost every day. "Get your worksheets out," Mr. Roux, the business teacher, told the class one morning. There was some mumbling as students figured out which worksheet Mr. Roux meant. They'd checked part of it the day before, so Roux said, "We're on number 11," and the checking began. Roux read from his worksheet, "How does your worker role support your consumer role?" After a small digression about standard of living, Ginger asked, "So, what's the answer to the question?" When Roux noticed that some of the students weren't paying attention, he told them they had work to do. He asked the next question, and the students were once again quiet.

John leaned back in his chair and stopped following along with the worksheet. After several questions, he raised his hand as others had done and answered, "vote," a 1-word answer to the 42-word question: "Your taxes help to pay for common services. Since tax dollars cannot supply all that people want, you can do something as part of your role as a citizen to help make decisions on how taxes are spent. What should you do?" Roux explained why John's "vote" was right, and the class finished up the worksheet. With five minutes left in the 25-minute period, Roux assigned "Understanding Your Reading" (referred to in the class as "UYR"), questions that followed every chapter. John asked if the answers were due the next day. They were, but the class would have the 25 minutes after lunch to work on them. The format of checking and doing homework was consistent throughout the year. Tests altered the daily routine. Students reviewed for them by dividing into two teams and playing a basketball-type quiz game. After they finished their tests, students took out their books and completed study guide worksheets for the next chapter. And so it went.

Writing Right

One Monday in October Nicky, Monica, and Sharon received the last of their three official writing assignments in their year-long English class. The written directions were, "Imagine you are one inch tall. What are some of the things you would do that you cannot do now? Put these thoughts down in the form of a paragraph or two." Frost's seven steps (THINK, LIST, ORGANIZE, WRITE first draft, REREAD first draft, PROOFREAD, Complete FINAL DRAFT) of "The Writing Process" were also listed, with explanations such as "ORGANIZE your list of ideas into some kind of order that seems good to you. Add details to each of the ideas you want to talk about. Throw out ideas you don't like. Don't write sentences yet."

The assignment was worth two "quiz grades." (Students had frequent quizzes, but all graded work was weighted in terms of quiz grades. A test

grade counted as much as nine quiz grades.) Students who didn't have completed first drafts on Thursday would be penalized 25%. Final copies were
due the following day. Incorrect use of apostrophes or FMWs (from a list of
"*frequently misspelled words*" such as *past/passed* and *writting*) meant that
students had to recopy final drafts before they would be graded. In addition,
10% would be deducted for each of these errors. Five percent would be
deducted for each incorrect capitalization, run-on sentence, fragment, lack
of subject–verb agreement, and non-FMW spelling error, but no recopying
would be required.

Sharon figured out that it didn't matter what she wrote as long as she
didn't make any errors. She composed a 100-word essay and received 100%.
Monica was still trying to make meaning of the assignment. She thought of
things like diving off faucets into bathroom sinks and wrote a 250-word essay
that included the FMW error *alot*. She had to recopy her final copy before Frost
gave it a 90%. Nicky wrote more than 500 words, lost 20% in her final draft,
and had to recopy the essay because she left out an apostrophe. Recopying it
cost her another 20% because she made new errors, such as leaving off the
final *e* in *there*, an FMW worth 10%. (Even though she committed an FMW
error, she didn't have to recopy her recopied final copy again.) Nicky's
required list (step 2) was detailed, and her first draft (step 4) was a hodgepodge of arrows, deletions, and additions. In total, she wrote six pages of
tiny script for which she received a 60%, a failing mark worth two quiz
grades.

Unlike Sharon, Nicky didn't understand that "writing short" gave her a
better chance of getting a higher score. Even at the end of the year, she saw
the purpose of the assignment as creativity. A lover of nature, she'd written
about playing with insects and exploring worm holes. She explained that if
Mr. Frost had counted content, she probably would have received a better
grade, but since she couldn't do anything about how Mr. Frost graded, she
wasn't going to let it bother her: "Oh, well. Who cares?" Nonetheless, when
Frost returned the failing paper to her, she quickly tucked it into her notebook and didn't tell anyone except Monica what she'd received.

Apart from the grades, Monica and Nicky thought the assignment was
"dumb." Monica said they'd never had to do anything like it during their
8 years at Meadowbrook. She was never going to be 1-inch tall, and there
wasn't any point to the subject matter. Mr. Frost had let students talk with
one another during part of Thursday's class in order to "edit" one another's
pieces, but he hadn't allowed it 2 days earlier when he gave them time to
write. This, too, seemed somewhat odd to their Meadowbrook experience,
but it didn't bother them as much as having to recopy the work for small
errors. Even though more than half the class had to recopy their essays, doing
it for a missed apostrophe seemed especially silly to the students in the class.

Paul, one of the more spirited boys, said loudly enough for those around him to hear that he couldn't believe what Nicky had to do. "I'd kill myself," he said. Nicky smiled at the support but recopied it for the next day, just as the others did, in order to avoid a zero on the essay.

John and Ginny had similar encounters with essay writing in Mr. Frost's level-2 class. John, who didn't like to write and wrote as little as he could, got better grades than Ginny did, even though Ginny looked forward to writing and wrote at length.

Chad's experience with writing assignments was markedly different. For one thing, he had somewhat more opportunity for writing in Mrs. Evert's class than students did in Mr. Frost's classes. He didn't know that, however, and since he did less writing than he'd expected, he assumed that he was being penalized for being in a level-2 English class. Second, grading procedures were less specifically outlined, and Mrs. Evert's comments suggested that she considered content as well as usage/conventions in her assessment.

The tone for writing was set with the first assignment. Evert wrote a list of names on the board (Horace McAvoy, Ellen O'Brien, Alex Smith [male or female], Phyllis, Ethel [a dog]) and asked students to write a description for each name. "You don't have to write a story yet, but you'll be using these descriptions in a story." The next day Evert read the students' descriptions aloud to the class, telling them that they were "all really good." She next told students to use the characters and descriptions in stories. "All characters must be in the story." (Chad's characters included a comedian, a singer, a baseball player, and a truck driver. The dog became a cat, Garfield's sister.) She explained that she gave them several major characters so it wouldn't get boring. Then she told them they could work together as long as their stories didn't sound too much alike (even though characters' names were identical).

Chad said that writing with assigned characters wasn't a problem, but he sat alone, writing nothing for nearly 10 minutes before he hunched down and began the lead. A first draft was due the next day, and by the end of the period, he'd finished the opening paragraph: "I went to this talent show in Hollywood, and I met this famous comedian named Horace McAvoy. He was so funny on stage, but in person he was so different. I found out his step-sister was Ellen O'Brien, another famous person. She was a singer."

Over a period of several days, with class time divided between writing and defining lists of word pairs such as *its/it's* and *you're/your*, students completed the assignment. After finishing the first draft, Chad commented that his story was "stupid," that it didn't have any meaning. Evert read the first draft and wrote, "Good start, Chad. *Excellent* descriptions, but no actual *plot* yet. More action or dialogue would add to this." Chad didn't know how to go about accommodating Mrs. Evert's suggestions. Later he explained:

I couldn't make a new ending plot. I couldn't know what to write for it.
It seemed harder because we didn't have like our own names. We
couldn't make up our own names. If I could have made up my own
names, then it would have probably been easier. And less characters. I
wanted less characters. . . . Maybe if she told us this was going to be a
story I could have made it better because I made those characters, like, I
made them because I didn't think they were going to be in a story.

Evert had said only once that students would be writing a story based
on the characters she named, and Chad hadn't processed that information.
And once he described the characters, he carefully followed directions and
didn't change his initial character descriptions to fit a developing plot, as
some of his peers did. As a result, he was stuck; his final draft was very similar to the first. Evert noted that there was still no dialogue or details and
gave him a 70%. Chad was shaken. It was the first D– he'd ever received for
his writing. When he asked Evert why he'd done so poorly, she told him she'd
commented on his paper. When he prodded further, she told him he hadn't
made changes between his first and final drafts.

Throughout the year, Chad wrote a number of assignments, all more or
less structured by Evert. Although his grades improved, he was never sure
why. His pieces were usually longer than other students' pieces, and he was
generally rushed to get in assignments when they were due. He lost points
several times for turning in writing 1 day late. In his last assignment, a murder mystery, he was able to engage in the fiction he loved, but he'd also learned
to do whatever Evert told him to do. "Mrs. Evert did the editing and suggested the ending line. I did what she said." He copied her last line exactly:
"unless the homeless man with the glass eye decides to come forward." He
would have earned a 97% but lost 7% because it was a day late. Mrs. Evert
wrote on his paper that he had a knack for telling stories, which pleased him
greatly. The murder mystery, assigned in June, was the first extended piece
of fiction he'd written since the initial assignment of the year.

Chad talked about the writing he did during the year: "I didn't get too
much help. When Mrs. Evert looked at them [my papers], she made correc-
tions. We never really went over them." In September, students wrote English
goals for Evert to read. Chad's goal had been to write stories. "I like to write
fiction stories," he wrote. After school was finished in June, he said, "I wish
we did more writing."

Instead of Writing

What students wrote was often very different from the kinds of writing
they'd experienced at Meadowbrook. In Mr. Frost's class Ginny and John

studied how to write paragraphs by completing exercises in their grammar books, what a fellow student from Barton described as "teaching you how to write but not letting you write." They chose among sentences to indicate best topic sentences and completed multiple-choice exercises to show which sentences didn't fit paragraphs. They wrote lists of examples for developing paragraphs and finally chose from a list of items including sour milk, the fire extinguisher, and the making of an iceberg in order to write a cause-and-effect paragraph.

After completing the exercises, they took a publisher's chapter test which began with six multiple-choice questions that resembled those in their grammar books and counted for 60% of the test. The next section was a step-by-step process culminating in the writing of an actual paragraph. They chose from five topics, including "honesty is the best policy" and "the nicest park in my community" or selected their own topics. They then chose a method of development, such as time order or cause and effect. They wrote a topic sentence for the next question and then listed four details to include in their paragraphs. Finally they wrote drafts of the paragraphs, following directions to use: their topic sentences, the details from their lists, and the methods of development they'd indicated on a previous question. Frost added that they needed to turn the page to the back side to write a first draft before writing the final copy on the lines provided on the front side of the paper.

The paragraph test counted for four quiz grades (in comparison to the two quiz grades given for each of their two writing assignments), and students lost one percentage point for each FMW committed in the writing. (Each quarter the errors counted more heavily on tests until the fourth quarter, when each cost 4%.)

Ginny lost 20% and John lost 25% on the multiple-choice section that preceded the writing portion of the test. Ginny chose "B" from the list of topics, "How colors affect my mood," and decided to organize it through cause-and-effect development. She drafted and wrote the final version as instructed, neglecting to copy *affect* from one side of the paper to the other in the opening sentence, "Colors *affect* my moods in a lot of ways," which resulted in a 1% penalty for a sentence fragment. Her final copy of the paragraph resounded with Ginny's voice and personality:

> Colors [affect] my mood in a lot of ways. Say I wear all black. I'm in a oh oh mood, or if I wear a wild shirt with alot [sic] of colors, it means I'm in a really good mood or I am outrageously hyper. Also if I wear just a green sweatshirt with black jeans and a black turtleneck, I feel down, or my moods are jumping around. So most of the time it depends on what I am wearing and the colors of my outfit.

She lost four points for the paragraph (run-ons, fragment, and FMW) and three points for not having a fourth item on her list of details. Frost's written comment was, "Your writing shows a lack of thought and organization. Also, get to the point with as few words as possible." She lost no points for lack of thought and organization, but Ginny was upset just the same. "He doesn't have to insult me. I didn't have much time." She was more irritated, however, by her perception that he picked on her during the exercises on prepositional phrases that followed the return of her test. "I gave him a dirty look, and he finally went to someone else."

John chose to write in what he recognized as the simplest organization, that of time order. He also opted to ignore the topic list and write about his normal school day. (He later said that the choices were dumb.) The paragraph started with John getting up at 5:00 A.M., eating breakfast, taking a shower, and so forth. The "bed-to-bed" type piece was basically a long list of events that satisfied the requirements of the question without presenting organizational or stylistic complications. He wrote more than he had in any writing assignment and ran out of time before completely recopying his first draft onto the other side of his test paper. He asked Frost if he could have more time, a request that would have been accommodated at Meadowbrook. Frost told him that he'd grade it from the draft. John overlooked a period at the end of a sentence and lost one point, but other than that received no deductions. Except for the length, John had played it safe and been rewarded.

Level-1 students had different grammar books that focused more on writing. They did a series of brainstorming exercises such as thinking of 10 words associated with words such as *bulb*, *waterfall*, *sand*, and *eyeball*. They completed numerous writing exercises. "Select a common object, such as a comb or an umbrella. What is it made of? What size is it? What color? What texture?" Nicky complained that she had no idea what the exercises had to do with English or with writing. One student made a game out of coming up with ridiculous answers that would entertain the class. After days of such exercises, even he complained that he couldn't use his imagination to make the exercises interesting. The class did the textbook exercises on prewriting, sentence structure, and mechanics but skipped sections on drafting, revising, and publishing.

Students in both Frost's classes asked when they were going to "get to write." After finishing with the grammar book and moving to literature anthologies in late October, one of the boys in Monica's and Nicky's class wanted to know if they'd be doing any writing. Frost answered that they'd be doing a lot of writing in response to the anthology's questions and that there was a composition section. More than a few students groaned. Monica and Nicky said that they weren't surprised by Frost's response. After reading stories in their anthologies for about a month, another boy asked, "Are we going to be able to write stories like this [as in the anthology] sometime in the year?" Frost told the students that if they wanted to write they could, but he wouldn't assign it. "There's not enough time," he offered by way of explanation. In Ginny's and John's class, another student, Art, asked if they'd ever get to write. Frost answered that in some years there was time. John didn't care, but Ginny wished they could "stop with the stories" and write.

The Dreaded Grammar

The first time Frost mentioned parts of speech, Nicky looked around nervously. Well aware of the stories about Meadowbrook students' lack of grammar preparation and nervous about its onset, she relaxed when Frost went on to other subjects. When grammar exercises did begin, Monica and the others talked about it in their morning circle. They were convinced that they were the only ones who would have difficulty. "Meadowbrook kids don't know that stuff," Monica said.

The day before, Frost had assigned all his freshman classes worksheets on subject–verb agreement. In order to choose the correct verbs in sentences such as, "Kathy's pet rat, along with her hamsters and guinea pig, (was, were) moved into a larger pen last night," students had to identify prepositional phrases and read the sentences aloud without them. In 10th-period English, Frost called on Nicky to first read the prepositional phrase and then to read the sentence without it, inserting the correct verb. After several failed attempts at getting the phrase right, she was flustered when she read, "Kathy's pet rat *were* moved into a larger pen last night." Frost asked her if that sounded right, and she answered sincerely, "It's not as good as when it had the prepositional phrase." Some of the other students laughed, and Frost asked everyone who knew the right answer to raise his or her hand. Monica didn't raise her hand, and Frost called on her. She told him she didn't know. Frost went back to Nicky and coached her until she chose the right verb and read the sentence correctly.

Of the 20 sentences on the worksheet, Nicky had missed only 2; Monica and Sharon had each missed 1. Sharon didn't comment on the incident, but both Monica and Nicky were shaken. In the morning circle Monica said that she'd *thought* she'd known the answer but hadn't answered because she was afraid of "making a fool" of herself. She and the others thought only of their own embarrassment and didn't remember that other students had admitted to not knowing things in the previous day's class, for instance, that Christine had answered, "Probably not," when Frost asked her if she could name the eight parts of speech or that Ryan had answered, "Confuse us," when Frost asked him what prepositions do.

At the end of another class in which students corrected worksheets on antecedent–pronoun agreement, Monica told the boy who sat behind her that she didn't have English in eighth grade, that they'd had two hours of social studies instead—this in response to his comment that he'd had "this stuff" since first grade. Meadowbrook students didn't necessarily know less about grammar than the others, but they thought they were behind, and that made the work even more difficult. The torment of grammar exercises ended on October 21 when Frost told students to take the grammar books home "for safekeeping" until the end of the year. Ginny, John, Nicky, and Monica didn't need to refer to them again.

Mrs. Evert didn't give grammar books to Chad's class but relied on usage/grammar worksheets: *who's/whose, past/passed, their/they're*, homonyms, synonyms, antonyms, adverbs and the words they modified, adjectives and the words they modified, sentence combining, possessives, and apostrophes. Over a period of several months, students completed grammar/usage worksheets as they read from their literature anthologies. Grammar tests were frequent: "You've had a couple of worksheets on the adverb, so hopefully it's stuck in your brain," Evert told them in advance of one of the tests. Even though grammar instruction ended in late autumn, Chad still felt disheartened at the end of the year. (He'd failed a test that required him to underline adverbs and identify the verbs they modified.) "I didn't understand adverbs at all." Yet, when he thought about it, he said he probably didn't need to know about them. "You need punctuation. That's something you need to learn. But I don't know about adverbs. Unless you want to become a teacher or something, then you might want to learn more about that. I want to become a writer, but I don't think I need to know a lot about adverbs or anything."

For all the students, grammar instruction was a series of exercises and tests unrelated to writing or reading. Even though they understood that their parents and townspeople thought they needed to know grammar, and even though they had a "feeling" that it must be important, they also wondered why they had to do it. Jan's English teacher told her level-1 class that students needed to learn grammar so that they wouldn't embarrass themselves in college.

Writing Outside of English Class

Writing, for many classes and teachers, consisted of filling out worksheets, defining vocabulary, outlining chapters, answering textbook questions, and writing the occasional short answer for a test. Extended pieces of writing and essay-type tests were rare exceptions; Nicky's and Monica's science class wrote one report during the year. Some of the science and business classes relied solely on worksheets and textbook materials that required recall of discrete pieces of information. Chad, who had difficulty with fill-in-the-blank tests, said he'd have done better with essay tests that let him *think out* answers. Almost all writing that students did for classes was graded.

Meadowbrook freshmen did miss out on one opportunity for functional writing. When students were sent to the discipline office, they filled out forms declaring their version of why they were expelled from class (to mitigate impending punishment). Most wrote something like, "Fooling around too much, I guess," but others used it as an opportunity for self-expression, and the tone of the writing represented the playfulness and creativity often found in notes that peers passed to one another:

> Well I was just sittin [*sic*] there minding my own business, doing my work (quite well I might add) and I was sharing a pencil with the girl in my group. It was a group activity. She was using it when Mrs. Anderson comes over with this real fiery look in her eyes like she's possessed or somethin. [*sic*]
>
> "Where's your pencil young man?"
>
> "Well, it's not on me but I'm sharing with her," I say.
>
> "No pencil, if theres [*sic*] any thing [*sic*] I hate in this world its [*sic*] some one [*sic*] without a pencil," she says with that real mean look in her eye's [*sic*].
>
> "I'm sorry. I can borrow one from." My sentence is cut short.
>
> "Get out!" she roars.

Students were also asked to write occasionally (albeit with less literary flair) in Spanish, keyboarding, and wellness. In Spanish, Monica, Nicky, and Jan wrote one- to two-paragraph essays using newly acquired vocabulary and grammatical constructions, skits to be performed in class, and dialogues—often collaborating over the writing. In the keyboarding classes, Chad, Monica, and Nicky wrote several letters, at least one of which was deliverable to a friend. (Students wrote the letters to practice composing on a keyboard and were not graded.) Although they didn't deliver them, they also wrote letters to the principal. Nicky's was a letter of complaint about the grading system, the attendance policy, and the teachers' contract.

The wellness teacher and her teaching intern made a conscious effort to mix writing activities with worksheets, class notes, and group activities in the semester-long class. Students collaborated with others to research and share information with the rest of the class, and they wrote several opinion pieces. Monica likened the following opinion piece to the kind of writing she did at Meadowbrook:

> I think that it is just as common with guys saying no to sex as with girls. I really don't see the difference, or why people make a big deal

out of guys saying no. Many people think guys don't care and they only want sex, but that's not true. Many guys are sensitive and caring and want to have sex with the right person at the right time. A lot of them think of having sex as a serious decision. Like in the movie Scott didn't want to have sex with Paula because he wanted his first time to be special with someone he really loves. He made the decision not to and to wait until he was with the right person. I think saying no when you don't want to have sex is being mature. It shows you care about the issue and you have respect for yourself and your partner.

The purpose of this writing was to extend thinking generated by a movie the class had watched together. The nongraded assignment gave students a chance to reflect on a sensitive issue and offered an outlet to those who didn't usually speak during whole-group discussion. Monica, Nicky, and Chad were at home with reflective writing, but it was unique to their ninth-grade experience. Even in wellness, it was a far less frequent assignment than completing publisher- and teacher-made worksheets.

English Class Reading, or "All That Stuff"

Most of the Meadowbrook freshmen read on their own during the year. Ginny sometimes read novels and subscribed to *Sassy* magazine, which she brought to school. She and her friends traded magazines among themselves. John didn't usually read books or bring magazines to school, but he did read magazines such as *Seventeen* that his girl "friends" provided for him. Sometimes he read them when he was supposed to be outlining chapters or filling out worksheets. Chad, Monica, and Nicky read novels, and the girls made a special point of having them on days when they had three study halls. Nicky was an especially avid reader who routinely traded novels with Rachelle. By mid-November she'd read six books, and by the end of the year, she'd read more than the 16 novels she'd read during her eighth-grade year. She read two V.C. Andrews novels while reading three assigned chapters each night of *David Copperfield*. She explained that it relaxed her.

Toward the end of the year, when the high school instituted a weekly 25-minute reading break, Chad, Ginny, Monica, and Nicky made sure to have their novels with them. John read magazines or thumbed through his textbooks. Most everyone liked the break; Ginny said it was a lot better than listening to the teachers. Nicky noticed that some of the teachers didn't read with the class the way they were supposed to, but she said she didn't care as long as they didn't bother her when she was reading.

Since Meadowbrook students hadn't encountered basal readers, literature anthologies were a new genre for them. Ginny was struck by the page format. To her, each column on the two-columned pages seemed like a separate page, which made her feel like she was reading four pages before she could turn one. Additionally, since text lines were short, her eyes couldn't go as fast as they did when she read a novel. "I want to read fast, but my eyes won't go that fast." She twice fell asleep on the first selection and blamed it on the story's being boring.

Chad's English class read many of the stories aloud in class so that Mrs. Evert could be certain that students read them. Individually and most often during class, they wrote out the answers to questions that accompanied each selection. There was a lot of seatwork, but Chad liked it because it meant he didn't have much homework. After they read a number of stories, they had tests—mostly on literal information about characters' names and pieces of plot. They didn't read everything in the anthology but read *That Was Then, This is Now* by S. E. Hinton, *Johnny Tremain* by Esther Forbes, and an adaptation of *Romeo and Juliet*. They read the novels and the play silently and aloud, almost always in class, completing study guides and taking quizzes on vocabulary and content as they went.

Chad liked the reading, especially *Romeo and Juliet*, and he understood why Mrs. Evert assigned questions. "Some people don't read at all. And to have those stories and answer the questions, she'll know that they read the story." He couldn't say what he learned from answering the questions, though. He thought they were easy, but he had a hard time with the content and vocabulary tests. (He scored 40% on a 20-word Edgar Allan Poe vocabulary matching test: *trepidancy, perusal, educe, dissever, concision, pestilent*. Evert had given students photocopied lists of the words on Wednesday and dictated their definitions to the class. The next day, Evert read aloud "The Pit and The Pendulum." Chad failed the vocabulary quiz the following day.) He was often the last one to turn in his tests, and, as usual, he had difficulty recalling factual information. English was Chad's first-period class, and a poor test grade had the power to depress him all day. He thought the reason they read stories and novels was to make kids like reading, but he already liked reading.

From the beginning Mr. Frost's students knew that reading in English would not be fun. When Frost distributed anthologies to students in late October, one of the students in Ginny's and John's level-2 class asked if they were going to read any "real books." (Frost didn't answer the question, but time did. They read nearly everything in the anthology and nothing outside it.)

Although levels 1 and 2 had different anthologies, the routine was the same for "covering" *all* stories. Students silently read the stories and wrote definitions for vocabulary lists Frost provided. The following day, before any discussion, they took a quiz. After taking and checking the quiz, they went over the vocabulary. Then students wrote out answers to the comprehension questions that accompanied each story. The next day they discussed the story by orally answering those questions as well as Frost's supplementary questions—sometimes reading answers directly from their papers. At the end of each unit of reading, there was a comprehensive vocabulary test on one day and a comprehension test on the next. Students had to be able to spell all vocabulary words and characters' names correctly, as well as define any literary terms that Frost had "given" them.

When Monica's and Nicky's class read *David Copperfield*, the only selection that wasn't in their level-1 anthologies, they had quizzes every day that primarily asked for locations and characters' names. After they exchanged papers and checked the daily quizzes, Frost asked them questions about plot and subplots: "Has he learned any discipline as a child or a man? Has she done him a service by spoiling him? What was the somewhat of a good thing he did back in Salem House? Does anyone know why Littimer is there? What does Emily have to do with the funeral furnisher?" (The day Frost asked these particular questions, among dozens of others, Monica drew a map for Rachelle so she could find Jan's housekey. She sat directly in front of Frost's podium and said later that she wasn't afraid of him.) Only a handful of students volunteered answers. Monica, Nicky, and Sharon seldom did.

Students in both levels learned that reading stories didn't always correlate with quiz scores. Those who hadn't done the reading sometimes scored better than those who had. Literal questions were typical of the level-2 quizzes Ginny and John took: "Both of the young men share a common interest. It is the sport of _____. What time of year did this story happen? Does this contest end the friendship of the two main characters?" Level-1 quizzes for Monica, Nicky, and Sharon were publisher-written multiple-choice tests that required students to make "judgments and interpretations." Students could use their books, but given that there was no discussion prior to the quizzes, students often missed questions—even when they'd read carefully. Paul, the boy who sat behind Monica and who often did well despite having only skimmed chapters or stories, said that sometimes it was a matter of common sense and the way the questions were worded. Nicky said that sometimes she got ideas from the reading that confused her on the tests. Both Monica and Nicky said that reading ahead in *David Copperfield* made the quizzes more confusing.

Level-2 students also had a "Reading Handbook" section at the end of their anthologies that contained exercises on reading skills such as inference, skimming, figurative language, and sentence meaning. They completed these exercises and took tests on skills, separate from the reading in the rest of the text. Ginny explained that they did them when Mr. Frost didn't want to teach. Checking the exercises sometimes took 2 days, during which time students wrote notes, dozed off, or stared into space. Students also took publisher pre- and posttests on these sections on successive days, with no intervening exercises or instruction. At one point, Monica's and Nicky's class took an equally unconnected comprehension test that featured paragraphs and multiple-choice questions. They later commented that they had no idea why Mr. Frost might have given it to them.

When Frost gave the level-1 students the publisher's multiple-choice quizzes with each anthology story, he believed that the experience would teach students to think. On the day he distributed anthologies to students and after they'd left the room, he explained, "This is when it gets tough. It gets tough because these kids can't think, and I'm going to make them think." He said they went through life not thinking, that they were lazy, and that he was going to make them justify their answers, push them to do what they didn't want to do. "This is where it gets tough," he repeated several times. The students did think, but perhaps not in the way Frost intended. Nicky explained it: "We have to read and know what to pick out, so that on tests we know what we need to know."

One time Frost told the level-1 class, "Some of you don't belong in college prep, and some of you may realize that you don't belong here. . . . There are no morons here, no imbeciles . . . most of you can do the work here. . . . Don't expect any sympathy from me. Some of you will have to decide if you want to belong in level-1 or not." Monica figured he said those things to make them try harder, and to a degree it worked among students who were accustomed to doing well in school. She explained, "I was determined to prove that he couldn't get away with thinking he was so wonderful. I swear, he purposely tried to intimidate. I think he loved to make fun of people and make them feel stupid. And I didn't want him to do that to me." So Nicky and Monica concentrated on learning what was tested. They and the others learned to reduce school reading to things such as vocabulary, comprehension questions, and quizzes, or what the girls sometimes called "all that stuff"—activities that had little to do with the reading students did outside class.

Vocabulary Everywhere

It was science class, and Mr. Wright called on Chad. "What are ions? Define it in your own words." Chad couldn't do it and searched through his notes until he came up with "charged particles." Chad defined one term with another. It was in his notes, notes that he'd copied from the textbook. He answered the question, but he understood neither term.

"Vocabulary is in wellness, in business, English, science—everywhere but math and phys. ed.," Ginny complained one day after school when she was feeling down about her grades. Monica, Nicky, and John, who had different math teachers from one another and from Chad and Ginny, said that math terms were important in their classes. Whatever it was called—math terms, vocab., literary terms, or vocabulary—it was everywhere. If students wanted to understand the material that was being presented in any class, they needed to know the vocabulary and the concepts represented by the those particular vocabularies. The problem was access. Without concrete examples or experiences, much of the conceptual material was difficult to grasp, and without real understanding of the concepts, it was hard to remember the vocabulary—not only for tests but as a foundation for future work.

Some classes were particularly vocabulary/concept laden. Certainly science was concept-rich, but so were classes such as introduction to business and foundation art. Ginny had a particularly difficult time with art because it was mostly book work, and the text was loaded with unfamiliar terms and concepts. Even familiar words such as *sighting*, *scale*, and *exaggeration* had art-specific meanings. Each of the art textbooks' chapters was preceded by a list of terms ("Words to Learn") that needed to be mastered in the process of working through the chapter. Chapters built on chapters, and if students didn't keep up, they were lost. Ginny and her classmates, without the benefit of hands-on experience, had to deal with much of the vocabulary in the abstract, and dealing with it meant reproducing it on publisher-written tests. "When you make one part of the work dominant over the other, you add _____." Questions were not multiple-choice or matching tasks but fill-in-the-blank. Recognition wasn't enough. Short of memorization, real understanding of terminology was necessary to answer the questions correctly.

Ginny explained that she was not a good memorizer, and since the text was dense with concepts, she was lost even with the help of illustrations of artwork in the text. Under the heading of *repetition*, the term was defined in the textbook as: "Rhythm results from repetition. Motif and pattern are used frequently to talk about repetition in art." *Motif*, *modular*, and *pattern* were then defined in the next 125 words. Pattern was defined in terms of repetition, just as repetition was defined in terms of pattern. Terms were defined via terms that in turn needed definition. And since much of the instruction took place via worksheets—more words on paper—Ginny and many of her classmates could only struggle. By December, near the end of the course, Ginny scored a 5% on a chapter test that was mostly on art terms.

With each chapter in introduction to business came vocabulary words, "Adding to Your Business Vocabulary." Students looked for highlighted terms in their textbooks such as *communism*, *competition*, and *profit motive* and then matched them to one-sentence definitions that were part of the vocabulary exercises. Then they used the terms/definitions to fill in study guides, worksheets, and tests. "The rivalry among businesses to sell their goods and services to buyers: *competition*." Students wrote or heard the sentence-long definitions so many times that they eventually sunk in, providing them with the exact definitions for tests.

John didn't need to hear definitions more than a few times before they began to reverberate, at least well enough that with minimal effort he could pass tests. The concentration on vocabulary, however, was a challenge to Chad, who needed more than verbal reinforcement for understanding and retention. He explained that he just had to sit down and memorize the vocabulary; he didn't understand much of it. Since he couldn't memorize everything, he did poorly on tests.

Content-specific terminology made sense to students when they needed it. Those who complained of grammar in English dealt with it daily in Spanish. Parts of speech became important for ordering within sentences or for agreement between subject and verb or nouns and adjectives. Mrs. Larimer used grammatical terms to get at the intricacies of how Spanish was put together; students began to talk as she did. "First person plural, present tense" had meaning to students who were trying to decide which ending to attach to verb stems. Monica, Nicky, and the others didn't talk *about* the terminology; they used it. The vocabulary lists that accompanied each chapter in the Spanish textbook were more a matter of translation than of concept development. Yet, while students were required to use new vocabulary in speech and writing, they were not tested on individual words. Larimer asked students to do what the text didn't do—group vocabulary by parts of speech, use, or subject matter. In this way, students dealt with units of meaning that could be interchanged in sentences, a huge concept that students learned by manipulating components—not through explanation of something like transformational grammar.

Similarly, there were math teachers who used terminology to explicate procedures; the terms provided a common language, a kind of shorthand for explaining and understanding mathematical operations. The terms' value lay in their use, not simply in their acquisition. When Nicky wrote *trinomial square* or *reflexive property* in her notes, she not only knew what they meant but could manipulate numbers to reflect her understanding of them.

On the other hand, when Chad did "Building Science Vocabulary" from his science textbook, he did nothing more than an exercise. At the end of each chapter was a list of 10 terms. Each list of terms was accompanied by a list of 10 definitions. The task was to match each lettered term with a numbered definition. If Chad wasn't sure of a term, he looked back to the text for a boldfaced entry. He then wrote both the term and the definition into his notes. The list of terms found its way into questions, worksheets, and publisher-made study guides. As in business class, Chad needed to learn the definitions to pass tests. If he could repeat the definition of *oxidation number* as "the number of electrons an atom gains, loses, or shares in bonding," he got the right answer. His physical science class didn't do labs and there were few teacher demonstrations. Vocabulary wasn't necessary to operation but rather as an end in itself—something to get right on the test at the end of the chapter.

Teachers assigned vocabulary so that students could understand the required reading, and yet teachers admitted that most students rarely read the textbooks. Unless vocabulary was integral to what students actually did in class, it was for them an exercise in fulfilling homework requirements. When assigned as seatwork, it kept students busy. Ultimately, it became material on which students could easily be tested.

Needing to Talk

"Wellness. That was one of the few classes that seemed like Meadowbrook," Chad said in hindsight the summer following his freshman year. He was referring to how they sometimes sat in groups and worked on projects together. At Meadowbrook he'd become accustomed to talking and working with peers. He missed both whole-group and small-group discussions. "In high school, you don't do many discussions, not half as many as in junior high [referring to Meadowbrook]. You just don't get that in high school."

Class time was filled with seatwork, teacher explanations, checking homework, and taking and checking tests and quizzes. Teachers initiated and did most of the talking. Students usually needed to gain permission before saying anything. With the exception of one time in a wellness class and a few times in Spanish class when students rearranged their desks in circles and horseshoes, students sat in rows for whole-group instruction, which made discussion difficult. Small-group work, although common in a few classes, didn't exist in most. There weren't many opportunities for student talk—except in response to teachers' questions.

Direct as usual, Monica said, "I only learn when we're talking about things." She meant that she needed more than teachers' lectures and seatwork. She needed discussion. Sometimes she got it in science, a class she shared with Nicky and Jan. (The nine Meadowbrook freshmen had five different science teachers among them.) More often, she had chances to work with peers in Spanish. Mrs. Larimer was forever asking them to get partners or form groups. "That's how I learned. Spanish became more interesting. It was harder, but it was interesting. So I liked it."

Early on Nicky realized that the only place she received credit for class participation was in Spanish. She tried hard to volunteer answers, even when she felt nervous about it. Not garrulous or particularly outgoing by nature, she made a point of getting around the room to choose different partners for activities because she thought Mrs. Larimer expected it. In other classes, she spent period after period without volunteering answers. Or, if she thought the teacher would call on her, she volunteered early for a question she was sure about and then sat quietly for the rest of the period. Nicky understood that sitting in rows made real discussion difficult. She also thought that listening played a key role in talking:

> When you're in a line [rows], you can only talk to the person beside you, in front of you, and behind you. You can't talk to everybody. If you're in a circle, you can all say stuff. . . . It's easier to talk in a circle because then everybody listens—instead of groups or lines or something. It helps people listen and you can hear everybody else because you're all like facing each other.

Checking quizzes, tests, homework, or seatwork could set the occasion for limited discussion. Specifically, it was wrong answers that precipitated discussion—or at least another answer and possible clarification by the teacher. Students with wrong answers sometimes initiated the liveliest talk in defense of their errors, even though they seldom won their points. Even then, the dialogue was between teacher and student (not among students) until either the teacher put an end to it or another student suggested that the peer "give it up." In the case of multiple-choice homework and tests, students sometimes answered in letters—A, D, C—supplying full answers only when the first responses were wrong. "Going over" multiple-choice tests that had already been teacher-corrected was more or less an exercise in checking teacher accuracy. It also kept nonresponding students quiet and filled class time.

Students appreciated teachers who engaged in casual talk. Mr. Roux, their business teacher, joked around with students as he checked off their homework in his rank book; he smiled ruefully when someone gave a silly answer or teased students when they tried to get out of doing their homework. Students were often allowed to talk quietly with one another as they did seatwork. Chad's English classmates were also allowed to sometimes chat with one another as they did seatwork. Monica, Nicky, and their friends talked while they worked in their science class. Nicky explained, "It wasn't always fun, but what made it fun is that we could talk." When it was allowed, informal peer talk made teacher talk, worksheets, and textbook questions tolerable.

Students noticed certain teachers' tendencies to talk too much and played it, as they saw it, to their advantage. The idea was to get the teacher "off" on any subject except the work at hand, in effect reversing the usual roles of question-asker and question-answerer and putting the students, at least for awhile, in control. Ginny's level-2 science class operated by worksheets, supplementary worksheets, and questions at the ends of textbook chapters. (Ginny transferred out of the class and into a lower level midyear.) Except for Fridays, when students brought in current events, they did nothing but fill out or check worksheets, complete or check chapter questions, or take tests. Every day Mr. Francis sat behind his science bench and read questions from the textbook or worksheets. More often than not, his first words were something like, "Okay. Worksheet 2-2." Baiting the teacher in such circumstances became an especially appealing diversion. One day in the middle of questions such as, "What's a conclusion? What's a scientific law?" Francis starting talking, for reasons that escaped everyone, about *Star Trek*. Ginny's friend, Jerry, saw it as the opening he needed, and when Francis had exhausted the *Star Trek* subject, Jerry asked, "Have you seen the movie *The Fly?*" When it became apparent that Francis had taken the bait, Jerry whispered. "We can keep him going forever."

As Francis talked and talked, Ginny finished the science homework she hadn't done the night before. Students in the back rows passed chips and pretzels around. Others wrote letters to friends. One of the benefits of teacher digression is that it didn't show up on publisher-made tests, so students didn't have to pay attention. Even so, topics such as euphemisms for *vomiting*, the Spanish Inquisition, and skateboarding were much more interesting to students than worksheet drawings of voltmeters, beakers, and Celsius thermometers—especially since students never used science equipment at any time during the course.

Chad's science class was far more regimented, but like Mr. Francis, Mr. Wright sometimes "went off" on stories about things like bee keeping and avalanches. Even though the students didn't get to say much, the stories were more interesting than his lectures, which could also be long. The closest thing to extended talking for students was round-robin reading, for which Wright gave instructions: "Read each word individually. Speak up. Sit up. Don't read into your desk tops. Use your channel seven [local TV station] voices." Silent seatwork—with no one talking—was the most common mode of operation, however. At those times only the sound of the wall clock synchronizing with others in the school midway through the period broke the silence of students at work.

Boredom: Sleeping and Other Diversions

Bored. Boring. Boredom. Students mentioned it often. In November, Ginny described what boring meant in science, "I already know the order. There's the sheets, do the questions, and then there's stuff at the end. Then take the quiz. It's boring . . . even the worksheets . . . if he changed his order a little bit and had us do some experiments or something. How long are we going to be doing this?" Over time, students became so bored in Ginny's science class that they began chatting with one another, oblivious to Francis's questioning. When he directed questions to students by name, they began answering with lines such as, "It beats me," "I don't know," and "I don't have that part done." Students read books and magazines, craftily passed food to one another, wrote and intricately folded letters to peers, overpowered the room with the scent of marking pens, and did homework for other classes. Some of the boys, especially those sitting around Ginny, poked and laughed and joked among themselves so much that Francis began giving after-school detentions. One of Ginny's friends, Valerie, said one day, "This class is so boring. That's why so many kids get detentions. All we do is listen to Mr. Francis talk and do worksheets." Students endured by actively attempting to liven things up or through more passive activities such as letter writing.

One of the best ways to escape boredom was to doze off. Students propped their chins in their hands and rested their eyes. Or they laid their heads down on their desks—sometimes clearing the desks of books and papers first—and dozed. There was a written rule against sleeping in study hall, but there were no whole-school rules about sleeping in classes. In January, John began taking regular naps in English class, and he and Nicky talked about it at lunch. John said that it didn't matter if he slept, that he didn't learn anything even when he was awake. "Besides," he told Nicky, "Mr. Frost doesn't count anything off for sleeping." By the fourth quarter, John laid his head down almost every day. He said he usually managed to sleep, if only for a few minutes.

John wasn't alone in his perceptions. One day in April the class was reading a play aloud from their anthologies—a break from the usual routine. Different students had roles, but as Frost interrupted the flow again and again to ask questions and make comments, students began resorting to personal diversions. Ginny checked her hair and face in the mirror of her eye shadow compact. She watched to see when Frost would be looking at someone else and then put brown makeup on her eyelids. John laid his head down on his open book. Four other boys in class had already done so. Traci, who sat in back of John and next to Ginny, ate a chocolate Easter rabbit. Her book wasn't open. Louie, who sat behind Ginny, did a word-find with his anthology closed and on the floor. Ginny put her purse away and then followed along with the readers. Traci put her head down, and then another girl put her head down. Of 19 students in the class that day, 7 slept or gave the appearance of sleeping. By the time Ginny read her lines, John was breathing deeply, his back rhythmically rising and falling. When the play and Frost's comments were finished, the class took out their vocabulary homework. John and most of the others sat up as Frost began calling on students for words: *evasive, undulant, ominous*. After John gave a definition, he laid his head back down.

Nicky and Monica also complained that English was boring, although unlike Ginny and John, they didn't fall asleep. Their class was somewhat more active, and Frost wasn't as strict with them as he was with the fourth-period (level-2) class about students making small comments to peers. Nicky and Monica also had more invested in being good students—or in appearing to be good students. (Once Nicky pretended to be following along with Frost on one story in the anthology when she was actually reading a nonassigned one—which she later pronounced as "really good.") Nicky told John that if she slept she'd be afraid of missing something that would be on a test. She did say, however, that all of her classes were boring, even Spanish sometimes. She liked going to school because of her friends but said, "I dread it class-wise. . . . I want to learn, but I want to learn in a fun way, not in a boring way."

Nicky couldn't remember having been bored at Meadowbrook, even though she guessed she probably might have been. She said the difference was that they got up and *did* things. Monica remembered being bored sometimes in the eighth grade—especially when they'd watched a movie about the Cuban missile crisis—but she said that it was a different kind of boring. The boredom at high school was because they did the same things every day. It was this "sameness" that wore Chad down in science: "Outlines and worksheets for every chapter. That's it. That's all Mr. Wright likes to do. . . . I don't know why he doesn't want to make it more exciting. Outlines, worksheets, outlines, worksheets." Unlike John, Chad wouldn't allow himself to sleep, even when he was tired. He admitted to daydreaming, what he called "going into a daze." He tried, though, not to let teachers know how bored he was; he said it wouldn't have been nice.

Beyond Boredom: Frustration

One morning Art sat in Ginny's and John's English class and said loudly enough for those around him to hear, "I have so much to learn, and I'm stuck here in this class." Students were in a powerless position to change the nature of their learning situations. Their complaints to one another may have helped them cope somewhat, but frustration remained. In hindsight, Monica explained about what she perceived to be an overemphasis on textbooks and poor teaching, "I think they [teachers at WHS] go strictly by a book and there's no exceptions. Like Mr. Frost. He stuck to those ways. He didn't care if we were learning anything or not. He just *says* he's teaching it. Well, he's not really teaching it."

Kids did want to learn, and they appreciated teachers who taught. Nicky, for instance, thought that Mrs. Britton was so good at explaining math that she took Monica, whose own teacher was unable to meet with her, to Mrs. Britton to get help. Ginny, who'd stopped working in her level-2 science class with Mr. Francis, started doing homework and paying attention when she moved to Mr. Fitzgerald's level-3 class. Every time they did something like working with compasses or experimenting with static electricity, she was glad she'd made the move to a class where the teacher taught, and she told others about it.

Students saw good teaching as an exception, however, and for the most part, they just tried to "get through" what they perceived to be uninspiring classes and teaching. Sometimes it wasn't easy—especially when they experienced worse than usual teaching. Ginny, Chad, Rachelle, and Carl complained long and hard about Mr. Perry's level-2 algebra class. "He yells at kids," they said. "And when you ask for help, he has to put you down first" (e.g., telling a girl from Whitmore, "They shouldn't have let you out of the eighth grade if you didn't know your multiplication tables"). It didn't help that he confirmed their feelings of frustration and boredom: "I'll be honest with you. Algebra is boring. If you have the courage to stay through to calculus, you'll find the same thing there. It's boring . . . and you have to do all this before you can do the applications."

During the course of the year, student behavior deteriorated. There were students who didn't pretend to listen to Perry's customary 10 minutes of instruction at the beginning of every period. Those same students talked and fooled around during the half-hour or so that Perry gave the class each day to do homework. Those who continued to try, like Ginny, Rachelle, and Chad, were frustrated by Perry's inability to control the class, as well as his apparent inability to teach in an informative and interesting way. Ginny reacted by giving Perry dirty looks when he yelled at students and popping her gum when he was standing near. "I like to do little things that bother him," she explained.

While students didn't ordinarily confront their teachers, an incident in Perry's class illustrates frustrations that normally lay under the surface. During a particularly difficult chapter on word problems, Perry told the students that their eighth-grade teachers had been unqualified to teach algebra, that the students were unprepared for his class. Ginny became angry. She'd loved Miss Arno and thought she was a good teacher. "Who does he think he is?" she wanted to know. "Mr. Perry is the one who isn't qualified!"

Fueled by her anger and irritated by Perry's ineffectual explanations for how to do the word problems, she confronted Perry directly, "A lot of time you just *say* how to do the problems. A lot of us can't write that fast. You should write it down on the board so we can understand it. . . . If you wrote down some of the directions on the board so that we could understand, maybe we'd do better."

Perry responded, "If I wrote down what's in the book, you'd understand it?" Ginny explained further, "So that you'd explain it in different ways." A boy who was very shy and rarely said anything to anyone, told Perry without raising his hand, "Yes. The book's explanation is really hard." Perry ignored the boy's comment and addressed Ginny. "You need to practice note taking," he said. Ginny closed her book and told him, "I already know how to take notes. Forget it!"

A student from Whitmore asked if Perry could give them some more problems so they could have another try at learning how to do them (before an upcoming test), and Perry responded that there weren't any more problems in the book. Ginny, accustomed to Miss Arno's responsive teaching, said loudly enough for others to hear. "Can't he make some up?" She shook her head in disgust. Later she complained to the guidance counselor about Perry, and Ginny's mother made an appointment to see Mr. Perry, but nothing was resolved. Ginny and the others spent the rest of the year alternating among feelings of boredom, frustration, resignation, and anger.

Most students weren't as forthright as Ginny, and most teachers offered less provocation than Perry. Students' frustrations were largely hidden under a cover of politeness and acquiescence. For instance, even though the students from Meadowbrook alternately despised, feared, and tolerated Frost—and didn't believe they were learning much—they didn't directly challenge him. They understood that it would make no difference, except perhaps to make things worse. As Chad explained about Mr. Perry's class, he'd just have to get through it and hope for something better the next year.

SUMMARY

In the beginning of the year, Ginny, John, Nicky, Chad, Monica, and their peers appeared to be "doing Meadowbrook" at WHS. Within a few weeks most of them began to realize that they weren't at Meadowbrook anymore and started reorienting their energies. They found out what they had to do and, for the most part, did it. Class work was nearly entirely textbook-driven, and there was little opportunity for the kinds of writing Meadowbrook students had come to expect in school. Reading consisted of "looking" for answers to textbook questions or finding vocabulary words. Vocabulary, which was easily tested, dominated instruction. Classes were often boring, and one student's lament—"I have so much to learn and I'm stuck here in this class"—summed up the frustrations of many. With few exceptions, students felt little connection to their teachers or to the work that was required of them. Peer friendships sustained them, and the Meadowbrook students became part of the flow. As Monica explained, "People come. People graduate."

CHAPTER 6

School Ethos and Adaptation

Ethos varies from one school to another. . . . These differences in ethos will have significant impact on the child.

Gerald Grant
*The World We Created
at Hamilton High*, 1988, p. 117

Except for the most memorable occurrences, students didn't focus on individual events for long. This was true in Meadowbrook as well as at Whitmore High. There was a flow to school life that swiftly consumed days; students often forgot by Thursday what had happened on Tuesday. But like a river that flows rapidly toward its mouth carrying vegetation and soil from further up its banks, in each of the schools students unconsciously collected and adjusted impressions as they went from one day to the next. When they spoke of their eighth-grade teachers as being caring, they had difficulty giving specific examples; they just "felt" cared for and so returned their teachers' affections. When they spoke of too many rules at the high school, they had difficulty naming specific rules or citing instances when rules had thwarted their intentions. They just "felt" controlled. Their sense of school life was an intermeshed compilation of experiences and observations that directed their attitudes, efforts, and actions.

ETHOS

Sarah Lawrence Lightfoot (1983) writes that ethos represents the "sustaining values" of institutions, that it is the whole of an institution's parts—represented by its people, structures, relationships, ideology, motivation, and goals as well as by more measurable indices such as attendance records or college acceptance rates. Gerald Grant (1988), studying five schools over the course of a year, found wide variation in school ethos, variation that directly affected students' attitudes and motivation—both positively and negatively.

134

As the descriptions in earlier chapters indicate, the ethos of Meadow-brook Community School was much different from that of Whitmore High School. When Ginny, John, Monica, Chad, Nicky, and their peers graduated from eighth grade and entered Whitmore High, they experienced a change in school culture that could not be described solely in terms of a new building, new teachers, and new friends. As John said the summer following his freshman year when comparing the two schools, "It's just like the opposite of Meadowbrook." He attempted to understand why the schools were so different. "Teachers, there [at WHS], say they care, but I've gone to them and they don't."

John was talking about an attitude, one that students perceived as non-caring, one that spread to students. At WHS "I don't care" became a refrain when students' tests and homework with disappointing grades were returned to them. Whether or not they "really" cared (and privately, most admitted that they did care), their words united them in what they perceived to be the pervasive attitude. On the other hand, when at Meadowbrook an occasional student murmured "I don't care," it found no company. In fact, it signaled teachers and peers that something was wrong. In both cases, perceptions of accepted standards influenced behaviors.

How to explain such differences? In part, the difference in ethos might be explained by students' backgrounds. Meadowbrook students were, in spite of some variation in background, a homogeneous group who for the most part had been together for 8 years. The school, important to the town (see Chapter 2), endowed students with a sense of importance. Education was the joint effort of everyone involved. Caring was endemic to the school community. At the high school, students came from five different towns, each bringing attitudes established in their individual elementary/middle schools. Freshman boys from Barton bragged about the fist fights they'd had the year before on the elementary school's outdoor basketball court. Students in the level-2 classes from Wayhill, a town with a transient population and widespread unemployment, told tales of eighth-grade suspensions and teachers who were relieved to pass them along to high school. Students from Whitmore's middle school had been ability-grouped throughout middle school, and many of the lower-placed students had learned the game of underachievement (Oakes, 1985). There was a higher percentage of students identified as "at-risk" at Whitmore High than there had been at Meadowbrook.

There are also important comparisons to be made regarding leadership. As Grant (1988) and Rutter, Maughan, Mortimore, Ouston, and Smith (1979) observe, school adults are responsible for actively working to build a strong positive ethos. In his retrospective study of Hamilton High, Grant learned that leadership, specifically that of the principal, is key, and he implied that shared vision is at the heart of a positive school ethos. "Leaders must have a vision and then make it live in the imagination of all members of the community" (1988, p. 187). This finding seems particularly salient when considering the leadership at Meadowbrook Community School and Whitmore High.

Bill Peterson and the teachers at Meadowbrook consciously revisited their school's philosophy when making decisions or planning programs and events. They sometimes complained that they had too many meetings and too much work, but again and again they worked together and individually in order to do what was "best for the kids." Peterson's initial vision was shared and developed through countless encounters with teachers and townspeople. Even when issues became difficult, there was a certain excitement of possibility at the school.

The adults at Whitmore High School had been working without a contract for 3 years. That, together with a recent and controversial administrative reorganization and deep budget cuts, made for a staff that was not only unhappy but divided into camps. Except for a monthly staff meeting, there were almost no meetings, even among administrators, and because of a job action related to the contract, most teachers were not at the school outside of regular teaching hours. The principal, Thomas Webster, assumed his position the year the teachers' contract was originally defeated by taxpayers. Much of his energy was spent dealing with budgets, policies, and day-to-day operations. Teachers understood that Webster was busy, and they didn't covet his job, but they didn't view him as a visionary leader either. They were grateful that he didn't get in the way of their teaching and appreciated his support when they asked for it. There was a sense that the school was "holding on," waiting for better times.

Student mix and adult influence played roles in the school ethos, as did community support, long-distance transportation for students, and school size. Meadowbrook Community School and Whitmore High also represented two levels of schooling. Secondary schools are often viewed as the last stop for students before they leave home to pursue jobs and/or further education. Many would argue that high school is a time to get down to business—no more messing around. A "business" orientation is far different from one of community, an idea that is explored by the nineteenth-century philosopher and sociologist, Ferdinand Tönnies.

Community and Society

Whitmore High School represents a model of schooling in its own right, and to think of WHS and schools like it only as "what they are not" limits understanding and discourages dialogue. Ferdinand Tönnies's (1887/1957) theory of *Gemeinschaft* (community) and *Gesellschaft* (society) provides a useful frame for analysis of students' experiences in schools that might easily be conceptualized as more *Gemeinschaft-like* (community-like) or more *Gesellschaft-like* (society-like) in nature. Essentially, students and adults at Meadowbrook Community School saw themselves as a big community with smaller classroom communities, and they operated on assumptions that fit that vision. In comparison, students and adults at Whitmore High School saw themselves as part of an orderly organization whose structure and policies formally guided behaviors.

Tönnies characterized community as a relationship in which people share understandings and work toward common goals. He differentiated specific kinds of community but noted that community of mind, a "unity of mind" represented by shared values and cooperation for common goals, is the most important and unifying kind of community. The "we" in community becomes the strength from which the individual "I" develops: "There is no individualism in history and culture, except as it emanates from *Gemeinschaft* and remains conditioned by it" (Tönnies, 1971, p. 5). The individual is born and nourished through community, just as the child is born and nourished through family.

Not a few educators and philosophers (e.g., Bloome, 1986; Dewey, 1916; Eisner, 1991b; Grant, 1981; Peterson, 1992) have drawn on the concepts of family/community in describing their visions of schooling. Nel Noddings (1992), for example, links family with school in order to make a point about emphasis in curriculum: "The school, like the family, is a multipurpose institution. It cannot concentrate only on academic goals any more than a family can restrict its responsibilities to, say, feeding and housing its children" (p. 63).

Sergiovanni (1994) writes that if we think of schools as communities rather than as formal organizations, it changes what we expect of them. A school that perceives itself as a community and acts in accordance with that perception will look very different from a school that operates as a formal organization. Contrasts would be found, for instance, among issues of authority and control, curriculum, social organization of classrooms, relationships among teachers and students, and desired outcomes. Whitmore High School operated more as a formal organization than as a community, and its ethos is illuminated by Tönnies's (1887/1957) notion of *Gesellschaft*:

> The Theory of *Gesellschaft* deals with the artificial construction of an aggregate of human beings which superficially resembles the *Gemeinschaft* in so far as the individuals live and dwell peacefully. However, in the *Gemeinschaft* they remain essentially united in spite of all separating factors, whereas in the *Gesellschaft* they are essentially separated in spite of all uniting factors. (pp. 64–65)

As institutions designed for "calculated intervention" in the learning process (Spindler & Spindler, 1987), it would seem that schools are not natu-

ral communities. Children's and contracted teachers' attendance is manda-
tory, length of day and year are regulated, participants disperse at the bell,
and children are divided by age and grade and are placed in separate rooms
where they may again be divided by perceived ability. Knowledge may be
treated as a commodity, something that can be conferred and then traded
for grades. Students themselves may be understood as commodities—the
product of schooling, tested periodically to assure quality. Yet some schools,
like some classrooms, are more communal than others. "Unity of mind"
would seem to overshadow the initial "artificial construction." Meadowbrook students often referred to the "family" atmosphere of their school.
"We're like brothers and sisters." "Mr. Carew is like a second father to me."
"It's like a big family kind of school."

Community and society are not opposites. As Tönnies (1971) clarified,
the concepts are more like the end points of a continuum: "I do not know of
any condition of culture or society in which elements of *Gemeinschaft* and
elements of *Gesellschaft* are not simultaneously present, that is, mixed"
(p. 10). Dewey (1916), a contemporary of Tönnies's, seemed particularly concerned that some might interpret the concepts of community and society nar-
rowly, "Such words as 'society' and 'community' are likely to be misleading,
for they have a tendency to make us think there is a single thing correspond-
ing to the single word" (pp. 20–21). However, if we think of community and
society as blended elements along a continuum, it's possible to explore the
complexity of ethos in terms of communal and societal relationships.

The Role of Relationship

Sustaining values, played out in daily school life (e.g., through pedagogy,
curriculum, and regulations), can impact students' attitudes as well as what
and how they learn (Grant, 1988; Newmann, 1992; Sergiovanni, 1994). If
students wanted to do well in their classes, they had to do what they thought
their teachers expected of them. This was true at Meadowbrook as well as
at Whitmore High. However, differences in student–teacher relationships,
along with students' perceptions of school/classroom practices, affected the
sincerity of students' efforts and attitudes. At Meadowbrook, teachers' expectations were outgrowths of values shared by the community. Although
community values were largely engineered by adults, students also shaped
and defined them through ongoing interaction. In this way, students' expectations often closely matched those of the teachers (e.g., the importance of
trying hard, helping others, being dependable, taking on challenging tasks).
Teachers, in turn, were expected to facilitate interesting and educative learning experiences in which, at least part of the time, students exercised choice
of process and/or product and had opportunities for working collaboratively.

Relationship was also key to fulfilling teacher expectations (see Phelan, Davidson, & Cao, 1992). Students knew and liked their teachers and didn't want to let them down, any more than they wanted to let one another down. Meeting teachers' expectations was enmeshed with intersecting responsibilities, difficulties, and joys of living within a community. When Meadowbrook's principal spoke to the eighth-graders about throwing stones on the playground, he appealed to their sense of community, shared understandings, and their relationship with him: "You've had a great year. . . . You know how to behave out there. . . . I'm asking you as a favor to me." When students worked to meet the school's and teachers' expectations, they received far more than external rewards of grades and promotion; they strengthened community and thus benefited themselves (see Peterson, 1992).

At the high school, meeting teachers' expectations was more akin to complying with a legal contract. The rewards and consequences were clearly spelled out in teachers' written/verbal criteria and in the school's handbook. The student who was absent no more than the allotted days, passed most of the tests, and came to class with a covered textbook, paper, a pen, and completed assignments had a good chance of passing. The student who didn't would fail. In either case, an individual's effort had little impact on the rest of the group. Only the Spanish teacher and the power and energy teacher offered credit for class participation. Meeting or not meeting teachers' expectations was an individual's affair.

The problem was that while students wanted good grades (or "good enough" grades), they varied in their individual motivation to do what they had to do in order to get them. Their relationships with teachers only occasionally helped build that motivation, and the work itself didn't help the situation (see Eccles et al., 1993). Meadowbrook students found most assignments lifeless and repetitive or, in their term, "boring." They followed along doing paperwork, not terribly interested in the subject matter or how it was being taught. They often commented that they had too many "facts" to learn and missed the talk and social interaction that had been a part of their former school learning.

Vygotsky (1934/1965) suggests that concept formation is "a function of the adolescent's total social and cultural growth, which affects not only the content but also the method of his thinking" (p. 59). Meadowbrook students were accustomed to class activities and informal talk to make meaning of "facts." Without that social interaction, without a sense of relationship to others, classes were not only boring, but course content remained as a collection of disembodied facts. With little help from supportive relationships, especially teacher–student relationships, and with academic tasks that were less than engaging, students had to find ways to make school meaningful. By examining the nature of adaptation and the nature of individual students' specific adaptations to Whitmore High, it's possible to better understand school ethos and its implications for student learning.

ADAPTIVE STRATEGIES

Nicky was a conscientious student and liked to read. Even though she'd never used a basal reader or a literature anthology, she was excited when, after 2 months of grammar and writing exercises, Frost assigned the first short story (and accompanying end-of-story questions). That night, with great gusto, she read her anthology and then answered each question carefully and fully—as if she were writing short essays. When Frost called on her the next day, she read a page-long answer. By the time she'd finished, one of the boys was teasing her about writing the great American novel. Frost told Nicky that she didn't need to write that much, that a few lines would do. He then called on another student for the next question, comparing the answer against the teacher's edition. Nicky was embarrassed by the incident and after that wrote shorter answers. And because she wrote according to classroom standards, the answers became authentic schoolwork for her, just as longer reflective writing had once seemed authentic. By spring, she'd forgotten that she'd initially answered as if she were still in the eighth grade. She adapted.

To varying degrees, the Meadowbrook students did adapt to the expectations and climate of Whitmore High. That doesn't mean that they divorced themselves from their Meadowbrook heritage; nor does it mean that they simply "adopted" new practices. Adaptation, after all, is not only an "adding to" prior beliefs but also an interactive process of adjustment to new conditions, one in which people draw on deep-seated values in light of new options and constraints (Schram, 1994). The Meadowbrook students drew on communal understandings, but they also employed individual adaptive strategies that reflected differences in personality, temperament, and interests. For instance, Nicky and Monica shared common beliefs developed through in-school and out-of-school interaction with one another, with their peers, and with adults, but they often reacted very differently to situations. Monica was quick to anger, while Nicky was content to see how things played out before passing judgment or taking action. During fieldwork I came to appreciate the differences in students' personalities as I ferreted out the common beliefs of the group. I expected that each of the students would adapt somewhat differently to the high school culture, and I anticipated a variety of strategies.

Spindler and Spindler (1989, 1991, 1994) provide a frame for categorizing the Meadowbrook students' adaptive strategies. Based on their work among the Menominee and later with minority students in mainstream schools, they suggest that in instances of cultural conflict, especially when that conflict has potential for causing instrumental failure, people respond in certain predictable ways. They define instrumental competence as the ability to identify which activities are linked to which goals (acquiring possessions, recognition, power, status, and satisfaction) and successful engagement in those requisite activities. In schools, instrumental competence might be conceived of as academic achievement—passing. (Instrumental competence at Whitmore High included such indices as grades, friends, levels for classes, and staying out of trouble.) Failure involves a breakdown in understanding or an inability to fulfill the necessary tasks.

Instrumental competence is also situational and dependent on context. A student might do well at a job but have great difficulty following school rules. If I apply this understanding to the Meadowbrook students' transition, it would follow that, depending on atmosphere, practices, and content, students could mentally withdraw from one class but make a different adaptation in another class. Ginny could write letters to friends in science but attempt to "keep up" in business class. I would also argue that instrumental competence is relative to the individual. A grade of C in any class was a good grade for Ginny, but it would have meant failure to Monica. C's might not have reflected John's ability, but given his effort, he was satisfied with them. In other words, students didn't have to fail absolutely in order to experience a measure of instrumental failure.

Confidence about the ability to get work done, or what the Spindlers refer to as self-efficacy, is linked to this instrumental competence. Success breeds success. Spindler and Spindler (1989, 1991) have found that people predictably respond to threatened self-efficacy by reaffirmation, withdrawal, constructive marginality, biculturalism, or assimilation. Students' most commonly respond to actual failure and damaged self-efficacy through compensatory reaffirmation and exclusion of threatening elements or through withdrawal that is more self-destructive in nature.

"Reaffirmation" is a return to the values of the native culture. The Meadowbrook students' morning "circle" in the crowded lobby might serve as an example of reaffirmation. "Withdrawal" is doing nothing, what is referred to as a transitional state. Withdrawal indicates identification with neither culture. "Constructive marginality" is similar to withdrawal in that people identify strongly with neither culture, but rather than doing nothing, they adapt by building a personal culture that allows them to succeed while keeping a "wry view" of any cultural conflict. "Biculturalism" is an adaptation in which people are fully competent in either culture. The more different the cultures are, the more difficult bicultural adaptation is. I think of "assimilation" as jumping in with both feet, what Spindler and Spindler refer to as becoming more proficient in the new culture than those native to it.

The Meadowbrook students' experience of cultural conflict was definitely less extreme than that of the Menominees upon entering the mainstream culture or even of minority students upon entering mainstream schools, yet relative to individuals and circumstances, students experienced anxiety, confusion, and fear or failure. Using the Spindlers' categories to describe how students adapted to the perceived cultural demands of the high school gives meaning to those adaptations and sheds light on what the students valued.

Individual Students' Adaptations

Nicky's prior "school reading" had consisted of novels, nonfiction, and poetry of her choice. While she read, she watched for things she might write about in weekly dialogue journal letters to her teacher. But as she explained, she read as much as she did because she liked to read, not because she wanted to remember names or specific facts and details.

At the high school, she enjoyed much of the assigned English reading, but she had to learn that the "school value" of reading lay in the successful completion of follow-up activities and tests. Once she understood this, she could redirect her energies and do what was necessary to succeed in the class. For instance, when reading nightly assignments of a condensed version of *David Copperfield*, she found satisfaction in trying to guess what questions Frost would ask in daily quizzes. Rather than reading solely for meaning or for enjoyable "pictures in her head," Nicky learned to note correct spellings of names, specific things that were said between characters, and details of plot that she might otherwise have deemed insignificant. "I knew he was going to ask that," she'd tell me with delight after class. While she didn't believe it was intrinsically important to be able to correctly spell characters' names or attribute specific dialogue to characters, she found a way to justify her efforts. Continuing to enjoy reading, she achieved a kind of bicultural adaptation.

Sometimes, though, she forgot herself—became involved in the novel and read beyond the assignment. That made quiz taking more difficult because she couldn't always remember what happened in which chapter. Similarly, when she became "caught up" in an anthology selection, she sometimes forgot to pay close attention to small details. Nicky's long habit of enjoying what she read sometimes interfered with the task of "English class reading" (see Purves, 1993).

Similarly, her habits of writing cost her percentage points when Frost assigned essays. There were only a few writing assignments during the year, and if there had been more, she might have figured out that writing short simple pieces would have reduced the odds of making errors. As it was, she tried to write interesting pieces as if she were still at Meadowbrook, and since Frost's grades were based solely on deductions for errors, "Meadowbrook ways" cost Nicky. She said she didn't care, and in that sense, reaffirmation of prior values softened the blow of lower grades. Saying that she didn't care might also have indicated that she had adapted to the situation through a form of "withdrawal."

Students felt conflicted when they could do nothing about the discrepancies they recognized between their Meadowbrook heritage and Whitmore practices. Monica said that the grammar exercises they did in English class were "stupid" and that they didn't have anything to do with writing. On the other hand, she said that her older sister hadn't had enough grammar—even at Whitmore High—and had nearly flunked college writing. Confused about the value of grammar, she was angry that the Meadowbrook teachers hadn't given them grammar exercises. She blamed them for the poor grades she received on the initial grammar quizzes and for the trouble she had figuring out exercises. She mistakenly perceived that she, Nicky, and Sharon were the only ones in her class who didn't know grammar. One day she turned to the boy who sat in back of her and said loud enough for Mr. Frost to hear, "We never did any of this stuff in Meadowbrook. We didn't even have English last year." Once she'd firmly laid the blame on Meadowbrook (even telling Frost that they hadn't "covered" subject–verb agreement in Meadowbrook), she started doing better with the exercises. By the end of the unit, she'd survived and could be more forgiving of Meadowbrook—even though she still wished that they'd done exercises in the eighth grade. In effect, she'd adapted through "assimilation," not so much by accepting the value of grammar instruction but by viewing the lack of it at Meadowbrook as a handicap. Interestingly, Sharon didn't see that the grammar unit was a big deal. She did what she had to do by identifying with neither "side"—a kind of "constructive marginality."

In the first days of school, Ginny behaved as if Whitmore expectations would be the same as Meadowbrook's had been. She tried hard, assumed that academic activities would be purposeful, and attempted to build relationships with teachers. In her level-2 science class boys called her a "schooler" because she tried to take class notes and had her worksheets finished on time. She attempted small talk with a number of her teachers and made a point of asking Mr. Frost how she could go about getting some of her poetry published (imagining that the high school had a facility for "publishing" student work).

Within 3 weeks, Ginny's enthusiasm was markedly dimmed. I wrote in my fieldnotes "What's happening to Ginny?" and spent a day with her going from class to class. Her level-2 classes relied heavily on in-class completion and checking of worksheets. The monotony wore Ginny down. (Phelan and colleagues [1992] found that high-achieving students "gritted their teeth" and went along with this kind of instruction, while lower-achieving students were more apt to withdraw and fail.) On September 21 she complained of teachers who didn't make classes interesting. She explained that she learned best through hands-on activities and by working in groups. Indeed, at Meadowbrook, Ginny had appeared to work more diligently when partnered with a friend or as part of a group. In the eighth grade she'd been able to integrate social aims with academic ones.

At the high school, her learning was book-centered, and as the content in her classes moved beyond the introductory chapters, she found the work-sheets more difficult to answer. Her teachers didn't question why she didn't turn in homework as they had at Meadowbrook, nor did they follow up on missing assignments. Ginny sensed that she was falling behind and kept telling herself that she'd try harder with the next chapter or with the next unit. Ginny later explained, "I had my times when I was really trying hard. But then it didn't matter how hard I tried. I still failed at it. So I think that's one of the reasons I kind of gave up." Like the others in her classes, she didn't read the chapters but used them as places to "find" answers to homework questions. Ginny called it busywork, and if something more important came up, she did it. She was unable to memorize lists of vocabulary; the terms were difficult because she didn't understand the concepts they represented. Tests became more and more discouraging.

Ginny adapted to the whole of high school through compensatory reaf-firmation and withdrawal from threatening elements. While her English teacher was assigning exercises and "stupid boring stories," Ginny wrote at home, chronicling family difficulties. "I just write everything down when I'm really confused and I'm all up tight about it and I'm really stressed about it." Sometimes she threw away what she wrote, and other times she let her mother read what she'd been thinking. She wrote poems and gave them to her mother and friends as presents. She kept a book in which she copied favorite poems—ones that she and her friends had written as well as a few by poets such as Shelley, Kilmer, and Sandburg. She said she wrote five or six letters a day to friends and received that many or more everyday. She shared magazines with friends and talked for hours on the telephone.

She said she sometimes felt "dumb" in school, the way she used to before she moved to Meadowbrook. She compensated for those bad feelings by making lots of friends, many of whom also had difficulty with schoolwork (what Cusick [1973] and Newmann [1981, 1989] explain as affiliation based on common alienation). When at the end of the year I asked her what she'd done that had made her feel most proud, she answered, "Realizing that I can be part of the crowd. So many people care about me." She'd generated caring relationships, and her awareness of that "caring" may have been an outgrowth of her experience at Meadowbrook.

John was a puzzle to me. He hadn't engaged with Meadowbrook values the way the others had. While there, he read very little and wrote even less during times specifically set aside for personal reading and writing. He did read and write for specific assignments, and he usually did his homework, even though his teachers said he didn't put much effort into it. John admitted to doing as little as possible. He said he was lazy. I suspected that a change of schools might spur him into more action. It didn't. In fact, he expended even less energy at the high school. The only times he really worked were when he thought he'd fail. In science he'd contracted to do a certain amount of work in order to earn a B. The night before the work was due, he took everything home (including books that weren't supposed to leave the classroom) and worked through the night filling in worksheets and answering textbook questions. With the exception of English, he took level-1 courses. For his sophomore year, he signed up for Spanish (scheduling gave him French, and he said it didn't make any difference) and level-1 English. His friends were mostly in level-1 classes, and it was important to him to stay with that crowd.

John's adaptive strategy seemed to be one of "constructive marginality," a viable adaptation in which he avoided feelings of conflict. Perhaps it was just "school" that distanced him, no matter the ethos or sense of community. He seemed unattached—somehow above it all. He worked more in Meadowbrook because teachers and peers kept pulling him into their activity. Mrs. Taylor had routinely set him up in groups with girls. Mr. Carew had positioned him in an array of social configurations that forced him to function in a variety of group roles. Nicky partnered with him whenever possible because she knew she could make him work. Jaci had great patience with his reluctant participation. Working individually in high school, he found it easier to do nothing or "just enough to get by." He did like sports (soccer, basketball, baseball) and said he "worked his butt off" when he was on the field. He also cared about his Meadowbrook peers, especially his girlfriend, Jan. When they broke up in late winter, John devoted more energy to engineering a reunion than he'd expended throughout 2 years of class work.

Chad had a harder time than the others differentiating between the Meadowbrook and Whitmore cultures. It's impossible to determine how much his learning disability (a delay in auditory processing) may have contributed to his lack of perception, but Chad often framed high school occurrences entirely within Meadowbrook understandings. Before the teacher arrived for first-period English, he sometimes sat at her desk or stood behind the podium—something that would have been common at Meadowbrook but was definitely unusual at the high school. He had no conception of writing used as punishment, so when a teacher assigned a written summary of an article because the class hadn't done its homework, Chad didn't "get it." After class he said he'd enjoyed the assignment, and when I explained that the assignment had been a punishment, he didn't believe me until he asked another student. He often made more of worksheets and study guides than he needed to, writing small and fitting as much as he could onto the lines.

Promptness, which had not been an issue at Meadowbrook, was very important at Whitmore. Especially at first, but intermittently throughout the year, Chad had a hard time getting to homeroom and classes on time. Chad hated detentions, and when he asked if I thought he was "bad" for getting them, he signaled cultural confusion. Detentions would have been "bad" at Meadowbrook; they'd have signaled a breakdown in understanding or relationship. At the high school, they were almost as common as worksheets, but Chad apparently still judged himself by Meadowbrook standards—even if the detentions were given for infractions that didn't exist at the elementary school.

Chad was, as Spindler and Spindler described the "native-oriented" Menominee, a "cultural survivor." He sometimes behaved as if he'd never left Meadowbrook. Unlike John, he felt strong cultural conflict; he was often confused, for instance, by flashes of insight that his math teacher didn't care what or whether he learned. He was puzzled when his science teacher collected and graded a word-find sheet that had nothing to do with what they were studying. He was troubled that students in his level-2 classes chose to do no work. Because he wanted to learn and because his reading comprehension tended to be slow, he ran out of time and lost credit for late and incomplete assignments.

Going with the Flow

Usually students just went along with things, whether or not they found practices in harmony with what they'd come to expect in elementary school. My observations of students' acquiescence were similar to what Patthey-Chavez (1993) found among Latino high school students:

> Students were apparently able to "take the good with the bad" in their interactions with the institution. They brought a unique resignation to the situation that seemed remarkably mature to me: while they preferred to disengage from problematic situations rather than change or challenge them, at the same time they took advantage of those opportunities they found to be of genuine value. (p. 49)

Often students found little to gain in resisting the differences they encountered. Besides, they liked some of the changes (e.g., the chance to learn

Spanish and keyboarding—things that had been unavailable in Meadow-brook). Still, I was surprised by how easily they adapted to new ways: sitting in rows, answering textbook questions, filling in blanks, using a "seven-step writing process" to compose paragraphs, or working in silence for entire periods. These were not only new experiences for students but ones that they and their eighth-grade teachers had sometimes cited when comparing themselves to other schools. Although surprising to me, students' reactions were similar to ones summarized by Newkirk (1991a) in a review of the literature that high school students were generally content, if not happy, in English classes that emphasized repetitive coverage of facts and skills. Over and over again, I was struck by the quiet passivity of students as they attended to the next chapter, the next set of questions, or the next teacher explanation—an observation that is in keeping with Goodlad's (1983, 1984) findings of dominant classroom behaviors being written work, listening, and preparing assignments.

Students even seemed relieved by the precise assignments (worksheets, textbook questions, chapter outlines). Unlike the frequent long-term assignments of Meadowbrook, homework at the high school usually came one day at a time. It was easier to know when a worksheet was finished than whether a project proposal was complete. There seemed to be an underlying assumption at the school that learning was neat, orderly, and contained in separate textbooks. (This is not a unique observation. See, for example, Apple, 1983; Barnes, Britton, & Torbe, 1990; Cusick, 1973; McNeil, 1988.) Students like Nicky found satisfaction in piling up completed assignments, even when the work itself was boring or perceived as busywork. Monica, referring to what she called the "format" of tests and homework, commented that high school was easier than she'd expected it to be but that having to learn "more facts" also made it harder (glimpses of Freire's [1993] "banking" concept). They didn't have to make any decisions, just do what they were told.

In general, albeit with varying amounts of grumbling, students acquiesced to academic and social constraints. I suspect, however, that students would have reacted quite differently if their teachers at Meadowbrook had one day changed their curriculum to incorporate practices dominant in the high school culture (even though students did dutifully study various parts of speech, take midterms and finals, and outline some textbook chapters in "preparation" for high school). Based on how they reacted to Carew's bogus rules (see the section in Chapter 3, "Controlling Their Own Behaviors"), students probably would have complained directly to their teachers, questioned procedure, arranged to work through their student council, and asked for a hearing with Mr. Peterson. But the high school wasn't Meadowbrook, and students had to adapt in order to get along.

"Play the Game"

Game playing was another adaptive strategy that supported students' ability to "go along" with school and maintain a sense of what mattered to them. I suspect that by making a game from the disparity they felt, they reduced inner conflict and were able to preserve deep-seated beliefs about themselves as learners. This is not to suggest that the students were always consciously aware of contradictions between how they thought classes should run and how the classes actually operated. Nor is it to suggest that play had to be a conscious act.

The term *game playing* is a familiar one. Popularized and defined by Berne (1964) as a series of ulterior transactions resulting in a payoff, the term is now part of our everyday vernacular. When we refer to game playing, we assume that there may be meaning in personal interaction that lies beyond or outside of what is immediately evident—a notion that when rooted in cultural analysis is at the heart of ethnography, or, as Geertz (1976) so eloquently states it, "figur[ing] out what the devil they think they are up to" (p. 224). The concept of game playing in educational settings is not new, and reference to it in the literature is common. Atkin, Patrick, and Kennedy (1989) refer to "schooling games" and describe ones that students invent (e.g., ways to get around attendance policies) as well as classroom games that involve students' compliance with teacher-stated rules (e.g., bringing pencils and paper to class, taking notes, and turning in homework). Fillion (1990) refers to unstated "rules" that organize "the classroom game" (e.g., that students must keep their answers to a minimum and may not evaluate their teachers' statements). Purves (1993) explores what he calls "the very serious rules" in the "game of school literature" (e.g., that the purpose of reading school literature is to pass tests).

At issue here is how game playing might help students deal with the differences between what they value and what they are asked to do. When do the games become important, and what do students know of the rules? What do the players reveal about themselves and their environment in the course of play? In the following anecdote, the teacher refers directly to "the game," in effect giving explicit recognition to something that is almost always played without verbal acknowledgment. The students are able to play this game but also fashion a variant of it. Control is at the heart of both games, however, and control games were played again and again in almost all the students' classes.

One 10th period in October, the students in Mr. Frost's level-1 English class had been checking a series of "Fact or Opinion" homework exercises from their writing textbook and were bored. Ben had drawn a picture on the back of Ryan's close-shaved head, Paul was sneakily doing his homework as they checked it, and Sarah was taking a nap when they began an exercise of identifying facts that could be deduced from observing a photograph in their textbook. There were no blanks to be filled in as in the previous exercises, and the students became a bit silly with the freedom that the photograph provided. Several began baiting Frost with opinions rather than the facts he was seeking. They argued with him about whether an item was a kerosene heater or a popcorn popper. Monica and Nicky laughed with the others but didn't offer any answers; they rarely volunteered in English class. Ryan started raising his hand for every answer, and with few other volunteers, Frost called on him frequently. Still, Ryan interrupted others to offer additional answers like, "The guy's got a sweater on." After a few minutes of this, Frost turned to Ryan and said evenly, "Play the game," apparently meaning that Ryan needed to raise his hand or otherwise be quiet. Immediately, Ben raised his hand and responded before Frost called on him. "*I* am [playing the game]!" he teased. About everyone except Frost laughed, including Monica and Nicky. Before things got out of hand, Frost distributed worksheet #70, "Pronouns and Antecedents." The students began filling in blanks with pronouns.

The game to which Frost had referred was "the good student game," his game and his rules. The students had engaged in a variation, a light game of "Who's got the upper hand?" Control shifted several times and ultimately became the province of worksheet #70. Students understood that they could get away with sleeping, head-drawing, and doing homework as long as they were quiet about it and didn't interfere with the checking of homework. Frost managed the class by referring to shared understandings of class-appropriate behavior (explicitly stated as rules at the beginning of the year) and by judiciously managing material. Interestingly, when Frost mentioned "the game," everyone appeared to know what he was talking about, even though "the game" had never before been mentioned. When Ben raised his hand to say that he was playing "the game," his peers' laughter showed that they "got it." He should have waited for Frost to call on him, but Frost had implied that Ryan wasn't playing the game because he failed to raise his hand. On a technicality, Ben got away with speaking before being called on, while at the same time making the point that it didn't matter what he said—as long as he raised his hand.

The game took place in an atmosphere of disengagement (Newmann, Wehlage, & Lamborn, 1992). Students felt connected to neither the teacher nor the material. They discounted Frost's game by trivializing his rules. They also devalued the content of the exercises by giving silly answers that technically satisfied requirements. As with some of the others in the room, Nicky and Monica were only sideline participants, yet they joined in the spirit of the more active students. They had complained for several days about the textbook unit ("pointless" and "boring to do and boring to check") and had made faces with others in the class when they finished one exercise to go onto the next. They admired the way the boys handled Frost and appreciated the brief respite from routine. When the class settled down with the worksheet, they demonstrated their understanding of how far they could go without getting into trouble. These were level-1 students who expected to do well in school. They could play Frost's game as well as their own.

The games that students played in some level-2 classes revealed a similar sense of disengagement, but students were more likely to risk their grades or getting into trouble for their behaviors. (WHS teachers admitted to exerting more control over the lower-level classes—a practice that Oakes [1985] documented.) Covering textbooks (or not covering textbooks) was, at times, the subject of major game playing. Mrs. Anderson sent students to the discipline office for not having books covered. Others, like Mr. Frost, collected them until students brought covers. For 2 days in a row, Dave took an uncovered book to wellness. He'd taken and failed the class with the same teacher the year before and knew that the second day without the cover meant going to the discipline office. And yet he persisted. Why? He told me that he just liked to "get her"—that he knew it made her mad. Being sent to the detention office got him out of class for the day. It didn't mean detention, just a day out of class. To Dave, it was a welcome break. Similarly, confiscated books in Mr. Frost's class meant that students couldn't do their homework. They collected zeros in Frost's rank book, but they had a classroom sanctioned excuse. It was legitimate play given school rules, and those who engaged in it showed that they didn't particularly value class time or class exercises.

Interestingly, students in level-1 classes were more apt to "borrow" covers from other books, leave uncovered books in their lockers, or hide uncovered books in their bags than their peers in level-2 classes. Monica explained that it was better to get scolded for forgetting a book than to forfeit it, miss class, or lose credit for homework. It would seem that, in general, students in the level-2 classes felt they had less to lose than the level-1 students. It also appeared that teachers were more alert to uncovered books in level-2 classes than they were in level-1 classes. Teachers told students that covers preserved books and saved taxpayers' money, but control seemed the real issue. The number of uncovered textbooks and students' casual comments (e.g., "I wondered if she'd notice") would indicate that at least some of the students saw it as a game of control.

Students also played individual games. As mentioned in Chapter 5, Ginny chose not to sign in at the office when she returned from being absent. She saw it as a win–win game. If the secretaries wanted her to sign in, they'd have to call her name on the intercom between classes. Ginny didn't mind having her name announced; she said she kind of liked it. If she then went to the office, she had an excuse for being late to her next class (about the only legitimate excuse for being late). If for some reason the secretaries didn't call her name, she didn't have to bother with signing in at all. Since there was no punishment for not signing in, Ginny could, as she explained it, "cause them a little trouble" and risk nothing. Apart from the fun Ginny experienced by not signing in, she made "the school" call her by name and deal with her individually.

John played a game of producing "just enough" work to assure passing grades. It was as if he experienced a certain exhilaration from figuring his percentages and turning in just enough work to get him over the mark he needed. Teachers who routinely posted percentage grades or who encouraged him to keep averages assisted him in his game.

Nicky and Monica were more likely to play teachers' games. Monica didn't like the way her science teacher gave textbook tests but didn't follow the textbook in his lectures. She also didn't like the requirements he established for science notebooks. She complained to him after school, told him how she was used to paying attention to what her science teacher said in class. She told him that keeping a notebook "his way" didn't make sense to her. After receiving several poor grades, she announced to Jan in Spanish, "I'm just going to do what he says. It's not worth fighting him. He'll never understand." As far as she was concerned, it was the teacher's game. If she was going to get a decent grade, she'd have to play by his rules. Public capitulation and continued complaints (part of the game) allowed her to think what she wanted to think while she did what she had to do.

Chad tried to do what teachers wanted, but I don't think he saw it as a game. His sincere nature and Meadowbrook-colored glasses didn't allow him to see the situation as others did. Somewhat like Ginny, he believed that teachers would give him good grades if they knew he was trying—even if he didn't do well on tests. When that didn't happen, he blamed himself rather than the situation. School life was too serious to be a game. Perhaps this was why he couldn't understand why some of the students in his classes seemingly chose to fail. Those students played games that Chad couldn't comprehend.

Games functioned in a number of ways. Depending on the game, the situation, and the student, they offered diversion, a sense of control, a degree of autonomy, and a means of putting teachers' and students' expectations in perspective. They could also spell trouble for players (e.g., when students chose not to play teachers' games or when students' games were incompatible with those of the school). In order to engage successfully in games, students needed a sense of the culture, an ability to see things as they were, and an appreciation of unstated rules as well as those that were stated.

The Meadowbrook students' ability to adapt to the high school culture, whether demonstrated by reaffirmation, withdrawal, constructive marginality, biculturalism, assimilation, or game playing, was crucial to their emotional and social well-being. However, their educational well-being was also at stake, and the students' ability to adapt to the high school culture meant a suspension of various developing social and cognitive abilities.

CHAPTER 7

Diminished Literacy Demands

Literacy is not monolithic; rather, it depends on the community for its definition. How students use reading and writing, what they use reading and writing for, how reading and writing are defined, how students interpret written texts, depend on the community and can differ across communities.

David Bloome
"Building Literacy and the
Classroom Community," 1986, p. 72

Most of the schoolwork that students did in the ninth grade was fundamentally different from the work they did in the eighth grade. However, while students did have quick flashes of insight or general feelings of disappointment or disillusionment during their first year of high school, they didn't realize the extent to which the actual work had differed until the summer after they completed ninth grade, when they sat down with me individually to compare papers from both years. Reading through eighth-grade science reports, Ginny was amazed: "I look at it now, and like wow! We did so much stuff [in the eighth grade]!" Comparing projects from seventh and eighth grades to the worksheets they did in high school, Nicky explained that even though they had more homework at MCS, it hadn't seemed so bad because she'd liked it. "You felt like you accomplished something. And what you did made you feel good."

WHAT THEY COULD DO AND WHAT THEY WERE ASKED TO DO

When students graduated from Meadowbrook Community School, they were able to write in a variety of genres: poetry, nonfiction, fiction, several types of journals, summaries, reflections, essays, content reports, lab reports, class notes, answers to prompts and test questions, proposals, progress reports of individual or group work, evaluations of their own performance and the performance of others, opinion pieces, arguments, interpretations, outlines, announcements, letters, descriptions of process, surveys, musical lyrics, plays, and instructions. They understood that writing processes varied with genre, purpose, and audience. They could confer with one another about writing, knew the difference between revision and editing, had various ways for coming up with ideas or getting "unstuck," could evaluate what they'd written, and understood that writing served various purposes (e.g., to learn information, sort out feelings, or entertain).

They could do independent research involving multiple methods of inquiry: interviews, library searches, surveys, and arranging by phone or letter to get further information. They had read a variety of texts including fiction, nonfiction, poetry, maps/charts, reports, periodicals, atlases, encyclopedias, instructions, plays, one another's writing, and textbooks. They understood that purpose affected how they might choose to read (e.g., scanning, reading for detail, or reading for a sense of the piece). They could represent understandings in a variety of fashions: written reports, poetry, drawings, skits, videotapes, simulations, oral reports, songs, debate, and class/small-group discussions. They could conduct science experiments, work in groups to accomplish tasks, assume a variety of group roles, set personal/group goals, teach others, and talk about current events. They felt comfortable integrating subject areas.

This is not to say that all students were equally competent in all areas. Some students were inherently more capable than others. Motivation varied among students and changed with subject areas. Indeed, some students like John felt distinctly uncomfortable with writing fiction or reading long books and only occasionally found satisfaction in writing factual reports. Some worked better in groups than others, and some preferred to work individually—at least some of the time. Some students were more creative than others. Chad loved getting up in front of the whole group, while Monica preferred to stay seated. Some always met deadlines, while others needed prompting. Nicky took better class notes than John but couldn't spell as well as Monica. Ginny wrote a lot of poetry but read less than Nicky. If given a choice about projects, some always drew instead of writing, just as others usually wrote instead of acting out skits or designing objects. Students had individual strengths, interests, and degrees of confidence, but what seemed particularly salient was that students were willing to try almost anything. If they didn't think they could do it on their own, they found a friend who could help. Sometimes the "doing" mattered more than the outcome.

When students entered Whitmore High School, they discovered a narrower band of literacy expectations than they'd previously experienced. They were required to "read" textbooks in order to write outlines, complete study guides and exercises, answer textbook questions, and study for quizzes and tests. For the most part, the students adapted to these expectations and did what was asked of them, but the work they did masked what they *could do*. In the ongoing completion of textbook (or similarly controlling teacher-devised) activities, Meadowbrook students had little occasion for engaging in exploration, synthesis, and reflection—ways of learning that were more familiar to them. They needed to adapt to elements of the high school culture in order to build and maintain feelings of self-esteem and self-efficacy. They needed to do what their teachers asked in order to get desired grades and earn credits toward graduation. But adaptation was a two-edged sword; it meant neglect, if not suspension, of developing abilities—ones that had been nurtured throughout prior years of schooling.

STUDENTS' ANALYSIS

Shortly after the conclusion of their freshmen year, Monica, John, Ginny, Chad, and Nicky met with me individually in day-long sessions to compare the work they'd done at Meadowbrook to the work they'd done at Whitmore. With papers from both years piled high before them, they had no trouble identifying that they'd done mostly worksheets and book questions in high school and papers and projects in the eighth grade—but they initially had difficulty making further comparisons. How could they compare one year's work to the next? It was so different.

Nicky tried for a comparison between easy and hard. "Sometimes it was easier to do projects rather than worksheets, but then sometimes it was the other way around. Some of the worksheets are like hard. You don't know what *they* want, or you can't *find* it." *They* referred to the unknown, unseen textbook writers. *They* hadn't been in class, and *they* didn't know what Nicky had discussed or previously "covered." Nicky had to guess what *they* might have been thinking when *they* wrote the question. And then, she had to *find* the answer somewhere in the text. She knew the answers "had to be there somewhere." The length of blank spaces on worksheets or the number of blank lines offered clues as to what might be right. Sometimes, though, she wrote in an answer for one question and had to switch it to another blank.

Nicky read some of the tests she'd taken and what she'd had to learn. She thought some of the teachers at the high school had made it hard for her to learn: "They expect you to learn it just from a book, and they expect you to memorize everything. But it's not that easy. You have to do stuff." For Nicky, "doing stuff" meant projects, simulations, getting out of her seat, and doing her own research. "Out of every class [in high school], I remember Spanish the most." Nicky was talking about retention of content, and Spanish had been her most active class, one in which she had worked with a partner or in small groups, one in which they had done projects and skits. She'd learned Spanish by using it in a variety of contexts.

Monica also tried to compare work by how difficult it was. Memorizing "facts" had been hard in high school, but when she reread some of the "reflections" (short reflective essays) she'd written in response to activities in eighth-grade humanities, she said, "Sometimes when we only had to write a paragraph, I'd end up writing two pages. I hated writing them, though, but I liked doing it, too. This doesn't make any sense, but before I would do it, I wouldn't want to do it, but once I got started, I wanted to keep at it. It was hard to start." Reading her reflections about Gandhi and then about the Cuban missile crisis, she seemed pleased and commented, "I sound so sure of myself when I read this, 'War is a senseless way to end international disputes . . .' When I read these [reflections], I remember everything that we did then. Some day I'm going to put them all together." Through writing, Monica had internalized what her class had studied. The artifact of that thinking was still valuable to her.

A few minutes later she was describing how they hadn't done much writing in high school. "The only thing we wrote for science this year was the element report." The report had to be 500 words long, and it counted for a test grade. At the beginning of the year, she'd written a seven-page summary of articles from *Scientific American*, writing that was reminiscent of some of the writing she'd done at Meadowbrook. She earned 10 extra-credit points (about a tenth of what the element report counted) and after that decided that extra credit didn't help her grade much. She did only one extra-credit reading after that. Paging through the pile of papers, she looked somewhat surprised and said, "Actually, we probably had the most [frequent] writing in Spanish." She'd expected to do more writing in high school English, and given what they'd done in ninth grade, she didn't expect much in the coming year: "And next year we're not doing much writing either, are we? We're doing like rhythm and stuff. The little symbols and breaking words up. He told us we were going to be doing that, and I'm like, 'Oh boy.'"

Chad compared the worksheets they had in eighth-grade science to the ones they had in ninth-grade science. "We had worksheets in both classes. Mr. Wright's [ninth grade] were on the book. Mrs. Taylor's [eighth grade] were on things we did in class. So I liked her worksheets better. His just weren't very exciting. He didn't do any experiments, you know. We just did things from the book that we never really tried." Chad differentiated between the process of "looking up" answers for study guide worksheets and using worksheets to guide or explain experimentation. In the first instance, he didn't really need to understand what he wrote down. He just had to find sentences in the text that were almost like the ones on the sheet. In the second instance, he needed to understand what had happened in the experiment and get it down in writing.

All of the students, including John, noticed that they'd taken a lot more class notes in the eighth grade than in high school. Ginny was particularly impressed, because although she'd begun ninth grade taking class notes, the notes became less thorough and more irregular as the year progressed. Looking back at the eighth-grade notes, she resolved, "Next year I'm going to take good notes like these. Jeez. These are good. I guess I do have that ability." She'd had to take notes in the eighth grade because they didn't usually use textbooks, and the teacher didn't give them a lot of worksheets. She'd depended on her notes for writing assignments and tests; they'd had an authentic purpose. Sadly, during her ninth-grade year, she'd forgotten that she'd ever been good at note taking.

In comparing papers from both grades, students rediscovered projects from Meadowbrook that reminded them of good times. Monica, for instance, recalled, "I loved doing all those mock trials and things. We had to get our own evidence and act them out and everything. Write our own questions and everything. And how to prove our points. We had like both sides, and then there'd be a judge. So we'd have to prove our points, but we didn't know what was going to happen. One time I was a lawyer . . ." None of the students could remember doing such "fun" things in high school.

The students' analysis of their work in the two schools is telling. They made clear distinctions between work that was meaningful to them and work that wasn't. Completing worksheets most often meant finding answers that were essentially "planted" in textbooks. There was no mystery as to whether answers would be there; it was more a matter of finding out exactly where they were and how they'd be worded. Sometimes sentences in study guide worksheets and textbooks were identical; sometimes students had to infer the information. But it was there, and that understanding made the task very different from something like doing research for writing papers. Students said that "finding answers" for worksheets helped them memorize information, but they knew that it didn't really help them learn. To learn, they also needed to "do stuff" (which meant that they had to use reading, writing, and talk in a variety of ways and for a variety of purposes). None of the students complained about using textbooks; they complained about not doing anything else. Writing had significance as a study tool, as a way to think, and, importantly, students found satisfaction in doing it and looking back on it. When they reviewed both years' work, they were a bit disappointed. As Monica said, "I really don't think we did much in ninth grade for some reason." In November or in March, Monica might not have felt that way. Apart from John, the students had worked hard. It's just that when they compared one year to the next, it seemed to them that they'd accomplished a whole lot more in eighth grade.

What students may not have appreciated was the important role that school and classroom community played in their perceptions of meaningful and "fun" work (Myers, 1992). At Meadowbrook, social relationships could transform what might have been "boring" assignments (analyzing song lyrics or writing lab reports) into engaging activities. As Myers points out, students' perceptions of "authentic" schoolwork vary, depending on the context in which it is done. Students may be happy and willing to do routine work if they feel that doing so makes them members of what Myers calls an "achievement club," or, in the case of Meadowbrook, part of the community. The community's expectations no doubt shaped, at least in part, students' perceptions of the work they did. This is not to diminish their analysis of the work itself (there were obvious comparisons to be made between study guides and reflective essays), but it does recognize that social contexts may have rendered the work at Meadowbrook more meaningful to them—both at the time they actually did it and during their analysis of it. The same notions of context can be applied to their ninth-grade work.

IN KEEPING WITH SCHOOL CULTURE

Given the operational philosophies of the two schools, it's not surprising that students' school artifacts (and their feelings about them) would be so different. Meadowbrook Community School operated on the assumptions that learning is social in nature (Vygotsky, 1978), that order is established through social cooperation and community life (Dewey, 1900, 1902/1990), and that knowledge is developed and experience made meaningful through purposeful direct interaction with subject matter (Dewey, 1938). It was believed that students not only learn to read, write, and talk through mediated reading, writing, and talking (e.g., Cazden, 1988; Dyson, 1983; Graves, 1983; Moffett, 1983; Smith, 1985), but that reading, writing, and talk (also art, music, and movement) are means of learning about the world and the self—an integration of process and product across subject areas (e.g., Cazden, 1992; Goodman, Hood, & Goodman, 1991; Harste, 1989). Community underlined and supported these assumptions.

Whitmore High School operated as a rational-bureaucratic organization (see Bryk, Lee, & Smith, 1990) typical of traditional comprehensive high schools and characterized by

> a functional division of adult labor into specialized tasks; defined teaching roles by subject matter and types of students; an emphasis on social interactions that are rule-governed, affectively neutral, and with limited individual discretion; and a form of authority that is attached to the role within the organization rather than to the person. (p. 137)

This characterization is in keeping with aspects of Tönnies's description of *Gesellschaft* and helps contextualize some of the assumptions under which Whitmore High School appeared to operate—such as an understanding that learning is individual, that order is established through regulation, and that language and learning can be segmented for delivery to students. It was believed that students learn content and develop skills by completing teacher- and commercially prepared instructional materials (see Dole & Osborn, 1991; Nespor, 1991; Shannon, 1989a) and that students' reading, writing, and talk are somewhat extraneous to that process (see Applebee, 1984; Barnes et al., 1990; Richardson, Fisk, & Okun, 1988). These assumptions were hardly unique to Whitmore High School (see Boyer, 1983; Cusick, 1973; Goodlad, 1984; Newmann, 1992; Shanker, 1990) and were consistent with the conceptualization of school as a rational-bureaucratic organization.

It's important to understand that the students' work in both schools was a reflection of school culture—as well as the larger culture's expectations for both elementary and high schools (Cuban, 1993; Sarason, 1982)—not just a result of individual teachers' preferences and practices. Assumptions about what constituted learning, and how that learning should occur in each of the schools, affected what teachers asked students to do and what, in turn, students expected themselves to do. Certain practices were particular to each of the schools.

At Meadowbrook, for instance, overlapping student voices most often signified students at work and the teacher at work among them (see Cambourne & Turbill, 1987). Seemingly similar behavior in a Whitmore High classroom would not only have been unusual but might have signified that work was finished for the period or that a substitute teacher was at the helm. Just as too much silence would have been suspect at Meadowbrook, too much overlapping talk would have raised suspicion that a class was out of control at Whitmore. Chad noticed a difference among students' behaviors. When his eighth-grade teacher, Mrs. Taylor, went too many days without hands-on experiments, students complained. Yet, as Chad explained, if the students in his ninth-grade science class had been given the freedom he'd experienced in eighth grade, they'd have "burned the place down."

Even physical aspects of culture that students and teachers take for granted can have an effect on behaviors (Eisner, 1991a). Consider room arrangement and standard classroom materials. Ginny explained that high school teachers put students' desks in rows so that students couldn't get away with anything (talking). Nicky said that rows made it harder for students to listen to one another (during teacher-led discussions), that she had to see someone's face in order really to listen. The seating arrangement was a subtle clue that student talk, whether formal or informal, was not a priority. The arrangement, in effect, dissuaded such communication. Because high school desks were mostly "armed" and not rectangular, students couldn't make "tables" (shared work spaces) by pushing them together. Not only did the type and arrangement of students' desks suggest nothing but individual work, but it made group work and associated collaborative projects physically awkward. Desks in rows were the norm at the high school, just as clustered seating was the norm at the elementary school. Practically speaking, room arrangements influenced the range of activities that could take place in them.

Classroom materials, by their type and by their dearth or abundance, also signaled the nature of classroom activities. What did it say, for example, if the only materials available to students in an English class were their own textbooks and a set of dictionaries? When students wrote in Meadowbrook, they not only had easy access to the library but immediate access to classroom resources such as encyclopedias, atlases, and magazines—as well as computers, white-out, and a variety of paper. In a narrow sense, the presence or absence of writing amenities not only demonstrated the value placed on writing but, along with seating arrangements, ease of collaboration, and a host of other variables, influenced the scope of writing that could take place in classrooms. No matter the subject area or topic being addressed, various cultural aspects influenced what and how students learned. It is true that teachers' personal beliefs about instruction and their individual teaching styles also affected students' learning, but it should be remembered that teachers' practices and expectations were also shaped by—and were generally in keeping with—those of the larger school culture.

TEACHERS' INTENTIONS

Teachers at the high school didn't set out to straight-jacket students' literacy development. Even those who relied most heavily on commercially prepared materials or those who most restricted students' classroom behaviors said they wanted more from their students than rote learning and right answers.

When during an interview I asked Mr. Frost why he assigned short stories and poems to his students, he told me that he wanted students "to appre-- ciate a piece of good writing . . . and to see how one kind of writing compares to other kinds of writing." He also said that long short stories and novels gave students more opportunities to relate to characters and situations. Yet, he explained, in order to make certain that students did the work (reading and comprehension questions), he quizzed them on each selection. "If I didn't give quizzes, there's probably a large percentage of kids [in each class] who would not do the work. And the percentage who wouldn't do the work is probably larger than it was 15 years ago [noticeably less attention to homework assignments]." He gave literal "little fact questions" because he said that it would take him forever to correct essay questions. Students could correct "quick things" in class. When I asked if perhaps there was too much emphasis on grades, he responded, "I grew up with this way of grading. I don't know how else to grade kids. This is the way it's done. And I personally feel comfortable with it."

While Frost wanted students to appreciate "good" literature, he believed that most kids wouldn't read unless quizzes loomed. He felt he needed to control behavior through quizzes, which put instruction at cross-purposes with his goal. The homework questions, and the quizzes that accompanied each story, trivialized a larger appreciation of the literature. The time spent taking and checking quizzes consumed significant portions of class time. Did it matter, for instance, how many people attended the game in which Casey struck out? Perhaps more to the point was the degree to which students needed to understand baseball in order to appreciate "Casey at the Bat." Or, given a concern that students identify with characters, did any of the students relate to Casey's experience? Instead, they checked their "Casey" vocabulary homework. Frost did what was comfortable for him and seemed to indicate that he taught in the manner he himself had been taught. As he said, "This is the way it's done."

He'd always used textbooks and indicated that he taught less grammar than he once did because the school bought new books that had fewer formal exercises. He saw no reason to assign readings outside the anthology (except for a novel such as *David Copperfield* for level-1 students).

> I've seen what I consider an improvement in textbooks over the last 10 to 15 years because they're a lot more interesting and a lot more comfortable. And I think, again, we have homogeneous grouping here, so I think they [the publishers] gear better to the levels than they used to. And I think there's a good variety of writing in them. The questions in them are a lot more thoughtful—even at the level 2 and level 3—than they used to be.

Good questions, books geared to various ability levels, and interesting stories. Actually the kids didn't mind the stories. They thought the accompanying book work was boring and that the quizzes and tests hurt their grades, but it was Monica who identified the problem of working exclusively from the text. There was no linkage between reading and writing:

> He'd tell us about foreshadowing and get into all those things, and we didn't do anything about it. We'd just read things, but we wouldn't have a chance to write, except for once he made us write about something [in response to an end-of-story writing prompt]—and he

gave us a certain amount of time and you had to pass it in right then. And I can't write like that.

Frost was seeking students' appreciation of literature and Monica was looking for connections that would make both reading and writing more meaningful, but the rugged pace of comprehension questions, in-class checking of questions, vocabulary/terms lists, in-class checking of definitions, quizzes, in-class checking of quizzes, plus "discussion" based on Frost's oral questions—repeated with each story—made both goals hard to reach. The tasks associated with the reading took more time than the reading itself.

Chad's English teacher, Miss Evert, who had begun her teaching career at Whitmore 3 years earlier, explained that the primary goal of an English teacher, at least with freshmen, was to get students organized. (Chad's class was filled with students who appeared to be unmotivated about school in general—a difficult class.) She explained that she also wanted students to understand literature and enjoy reading. She said that having textbooks organized students, even if it meant just having to remember to bring them to class everyday. She explained that students needed to learn to write, whether they liked it or not, if only to fill out job applications and write résumés. Writing, she said, organized thought and could help students learn.

As the other English teachers did, she used anthologies in her classes, explaining, "We're very textbook-oriented here." (See Menke & Davey, 1994, for a discussion of teachers' views on textbooks.) Even though she supplemented the text with several novels (and accompanying study questions) and skipped many of the textbook exercises, she felt somewhat uneasy about what she was teaching: "I'm teaching the same things I learned in high school and that people 20 years before me learned in high school and there's something wrong with that."

Evert was a published writer, and although she occasionally mentioned to students that she wrote fiction and poetry, she didn't bring that writing to school or encourage students to write more than the occasional structured or exercise-type assignment for which she provided little instructional support. She felt limited by the scope of materials available to her, and even though she explained that students were "regurgitating stuff back" at her, she relied on the materials the school provided. Chad's notebook was a compilation of comprehension questions, vocabulary lists, several short pieces of writing, grammar worksheets, and quizzes and tests. It was neatly organized. In spite of Evert's personal literacy interests, materials and the need to keep unmotivated students "busy" dominated the class.

Individual teachers in other freshman content areas talked about goals they had for students, which included critical thinking, reading and writing skills, and the ability to synthesize material. Still, they relied mostly on texts, and class time was spent completing and checking supplementary materials (see Smith & Feathers, 1983, for discussion of students' reading of textbooks). Mr. Brinkley, Nicky's and Monica's science teacher, spoke of raising students' confidence and self-determination. He wanted them to be willing to do projects for themselves as opposed to doing them for someone else. He didn't think the school met the needs of individual students—that it wasn't set up to do that. He said that grades didn't necessarily reward persistence, imagination, or the ability to put things together. He did a lot of talking in class and didn't strictly limit the talk to science. He told stories to dramatize scientific principles. He wanted students to challenge him, ask him questions. Occasionally, he arranged for students to work in groups to experiment or solve problems. He offered extra credit for written summaries of outside reading, and he once assigned research papers on elements and required that students present them orally to the class.

Still, it was the book and accompanying questions and worksheets that determined how and what students studied. He compared the textbook to a skeleton on which everything else was hung:

> There may be a thousand things you could have done that's not in your textbook, but the book defines what you cover and it gives a solid, tangible item to put your finger on and say, "This I will go to. This I will cover. This I will know. This I will be tested on. This I will have a midterm on. This I will have a final on."

So it was important that his students be able to read each chapter, outline the contents, and answer the end-of-section questions in a "complete manner." (Brinkley spent after-school hours going over student work.) The tests were publisher-written, and if students wanted good grades, they paid attention to what was in the text. Nicky and Monica complained that Mr. Brinkley's discussion was confusing because he didn't say things the way the book did. Test questions would be worded like the book, so that's what they studied. They didn't take class notes as they did in eighth grade. Brinkley explained about tests, the textbook, and the dilemmas he faced:

> Should they be tested on more than the skeleton? Yeah. Theoretically. They should be asked to think at a higher level than just notes and facts. But the system is such that it does not encourage that kind of thing. *The game* [emphasis added] doesn't call for it. You can be an eminent success without using very much of your brain. What you have to be able to do is play within the rules of the game. And the system is set up so that it does not encourage you, the instructor, to do the extra. You can get along just fine and survive just fine, and

everybody is just absolutely happy by doing this. Let's read the book and answer the questions.

And that has been a bone of contention, I think, with anyone who is a conscientious teacher, forever. So what happens? You go as far as you can, trying to keep your work load down to a point where you can survive. There are two types of teachers. There's the humanist, and then the nonhumanist. The humanist will put a lot of themselves into it. They'll do a lot of the extras. The kids will see, they'll feel, they'll know what the flesh and the blood and the skin and the senses are, all around. They'll go on field trips. They'll do activities. They'll know with their hands. I have found few of these people [humanists] who survive. The other person doesn't [do a lot of extras] but they survive.

Now, in between these two extremes, how much can you do and survive? And that is the question which I ask myself every day. I ask myself with each class. Have I had success? Yeah. But every day I go in there, I say, "I could do more." But the question is, "When I do more, what is the price I extract from myself?" And the price must be compensated for, somehow, because you're taking it out.

Brinkley was talking about a system, a kind of rational-bureaucratic system where "education-by-the-book" made sense. It made instruction very orderly. The book not only defined curriculum and established goals but also provided a behavioral framework for students. Certainly, creative use of textbooks was possible, and teachers could personalize instruction to fit their teaching styles and their students. However, as Brinkley pointed out, there wasn't much incentive in the system to go far beyond the text: "You can go along just fine and survive just fine." No one was pushing anyone by example or mandate to do anything else. The more inspired teachers kept their exploits and plans to themselves.

Teachers lacked strong leadership and a collective vision of what "might be" for students. Individually, they had instructional goals and priorities that would have broadened students' opportunities for literacy development and learning, but for most, those goals were masked—just as students' interests and abilities were masked—by a numbing adherence to a system-sanctioned "textbook orientation" (see Shannon [1989a, 1989b] for discussion of reification). As the more successful students did, they did their work; they got along.

Brinkley, as well as other teachers, told me that my regular presence in class made him look at his teaching from another perspective. Brinkley hadn't had another adult in regular attendance since he'd student-taught 16 years earlier. By contrast, teachers at Meadowbook always seemed to have other adults around: specialists, teaching interns, volunteers, visitors, and instructional aides—adults who could appreciate their efforts and encourage new ideas. Teachers at Meadowbrook sometimes complained of being over-whelmed and tired, but they drew needed energy not just from the children they taught but from the adults in the school community.

Research indicates (see McLaughlin & Talbert, 1990) that both indi-vidual attributes and settings affect how teachers teach and that effective-ness is highly dependent on how teachers think and feel about what they do. Sometimes I wondered how teachers at the high school would have responded if they'd been plucked from their classrooms and dropped into schools where caring and supportive relationships might have provided the "compensation" that Brinkley seemed to need.

PREPARED?

When Monica, John, Ginny, Chad, and Nicky were in the eighth grade, there was increasing publicity about whether or not Meadowbrook Community School graduates were prepared for high school. The controversy, mostly centering on grammar, had been brewing for a number of years but gained impetus when, at the urging of grammar advocates, the school board decided to survey graduates about their preparedness for high school. Although only 30 of about 300 students returned surveys that were mailed to them (com-plaining among other things, that there had been too few tests and quizzes at Meadowbrook and that there hadn't been enough grammar instruction), there were newspaper articles and letters to the editor, along with a petition and a public hearing on curriculum. There was a small group of parents who wanted a return to the "basics" (see the section in Chapter 2, "Controversy").

Throughout the debate, no one really defined what was meant by gram-mar, nor did there seem to be any reason to do so. When one of the speakers at the public hearing referred to "a decent old-fashioned English curriculum where you're teaching them nouns and verbs and predicates," she was talk-ing about traditional school grammar (Hartwell, 1985; Woods, 1985), a prescriptive grammar (Warner, 1993). She and others were talking about the kind of exercises found in *Warriner's English Grammar*, the kind of instruc-tion they remembered having in school; writing instruction was no substitu-tion. It was, as Woods (1985) points out, a matter of cultural values:

> It's a paradox: even though we rationalize the teaching of school grammar as a means of training the mind, or as a corrective for language skills, we are capable of arguing, often passionately, against its replacement by other kinds of skills training—like sentence combining, or composition writing—because we sense that grammar study is in fact a cultural necessity, that leaving it out would be in some way "wrong." (p. 2)

School grammar instruction persists even though researchers question its effectiveness (see Hartwell, 1985; Hillocks & Smith, 1991; Weaver, 1979). Each of the five high schools that Meadowbrook students attended offered varying amounts of traditional instruction (as reported by students). Those parents who were concerned that their children were leaving Meadowbrook unprepared for the rigors of high school grammar instruction, however, didn't question the value of the instruction itself or consider that grammar taught didn't necessarily mean grammar learned. It wasn't something they needed to think about; they just "felt" it was important.

In fact, the eighth-grade students' cumulative language arts folders contained evidence that students had been exposed to traditional grammar—at least in terms of defining parts of speech, usage (e.g., *then/than, witch/which, your/you're*), punctuation, and capitalization. Except for naming parts of speech, both their seventh-grade midterm and final exams included assessment of these items, separately and in the context of letter writing and essays. In the eighth grade students periodically reviewed parts of speech, elements such as possessives, and various uses of punctuation. Sometimes the review was connected to the writing they were doing, and at other times it was out of that context—such as when students wrote sentences to demonstrate their understandings of adjectives. They also found errors in "correctable sentences" Carew wrote on the board during whole-group sessions. And all their writing was returned to them with checks in the margins, indicating that students needed to correct usage/grammar errors. However, students did not complete textbook exercise or grammar worksheets.

Interestingly, when students reviewed their elementary papers following the completion of ninth grade, they either didn't remember doing the grammar (especially in seventh grade, despite concentrated study), remembered that they had grammar but couldn't remember what they'd learned, or didn't think what they'd learned was relevant to the demands of ninth grade. Research (see Hartwell, 1985; Warner, 1993) confirms this tendency to not retain instruction, but the fact that Meadowbrook students didn't remember having had much grammar instruction seems significant in terms of their own feelings about preparation, especially given the controversy that swirled around them. It's impossible to know how much the controversy added to students' insecurity about high school grammar or how that insecurity affected their performance.

Could there have been more grammar instruction in seventh and eighth grades? Certainly. Could that instruction have been formatted to more closely resemble worksheets and grammar book exercises? Without a doubt. Would that instruction have fit Meadowbrook teachers' understandings of how students learn language? No. As it was, teachers made compromises. Politically, they needed to show that they were addressing grammar (most often usage) in their classes. Before humanities was initiated, the seventh- and eighth-grade English teacher had decided she had no choice but to conduct grammar lessons, whether or not she could make them relevant to the writing students were doing.

Ironically, the controversy about preparation for high school grammar instruction was out of proportion to the amount of time students actually dealt with it (at least at Whitmore). If Meadowbrook teachers had devoted significantly more time to grammar instruction, slighting other areas of instruction, it would have meant a disproportionate preparatory emphasis—given only 2 months of grammar instruction in the ninth grade. Had Meadowbrook teachers decided to approach grammar instruction more intensively in the context of students' writing (see Noguchi, 1991; Vavra, 1993), it might have helped composition, but it would not have addressed the preparation issue because students didn't need to write much in high school.

All in all, the controversy boiled down to a great hullabaloo about very little—except that it made students nervous about high school English. It also should be noted that grammar instruction may have been particularly intimidating since it occurred at the beginning of the year—when students were most vulnerable. The restrictive tone of the grammar instruction (seatwork and right/wrong answers) set the pattern for classroom management—a rather daunting one given the students' school backgrounds. Warner's (1993) description is apt: "No noisy group work, no writer's block, no messy discussions about a piece of literature. Students keep cranking out the worksheets, scores add up in the gradebook, and life in the classroom is orderly and predictable" (p. 79). Achieving order and ultimately control over students through grammar curriculum (McNeil, 1983) appeared to perpetuate cultural values as much as the "doing" of grammar.

Apart from grammar, students felt well prepared for high school. Monica explained,

> Meadowbrook helped me to be organized, and half the students who go there [Whitmore High School] aren't organized or anything. And they don't know how to take notes. They don't know how to write essays. They don't know how to do reports as well. There are things like that—that everyone from Meadowbrook can do so much better.

When I reminded Monica that they hadn't been asked to do many of those things, she answered, "Yeah. But when they did, we were good at it."

Unfortunately, through heavy reliance on standardized textbook and worksheet assignments, the preparation Monica talked about lay mostly fallow. When talking about the differences in backgrounds that students brought to the high school from their elementary schools, Frost explained,

"I think that by the time the Meadowbrook kids get through here, they're probably indistinguishable from anyone else, just as the Wayhill kids are." If that's true, the shame lies in what's lost in the process. Monica, Chad, Ginny, John, Nicky, and their Meadowbrook peers were prepared for more than what Whitmore asked of them, and it would seem that Monica was onto something when she said, "I think we were more prepared for Whitmore High than it was prepared for us."

CHAPTER 8

Learning from the Particular

We never educate directly, but indirectly by means of the environment. Whether we permit chance environments to do the work, or whether we design environments for the purpose makes a great difference.

John Dewey
Democracy and Education, 1916, p. 19

The eventual breakup of the Meadowbrook students' morning circle in the high school lobby might serve as a metaphor for the transition students made between *Gemeinschaft-* and *Gesellschaft-*oriented schools. More than a convenient way to stand in the crowded lobby, the circle represented the students' understandings of "how to be" together, what Dewey (1916) describes as "the symbol of the collective life of mankind in general" (p. 58). When the circle gradually began to weaken in late February and early March, I was again reminded that the collective life students had known at Meadowbrook Community School was incongruous with that of the high school culture. The kinds of students they'd been, the things they'd learned, the literate processes they'd practiced—all were bound up in a collective school life that, in large part, no longer existed for them.

GENERALIZING

No two schools are exactly alike. Each has unique qualities that are shaped by elements such as supporting communities, leadership, individual personalities, demographics, and sociopolitical contexts. What, then, can be learned by studying students' lives in two particular schools? What generalizations can be made? What meaning can be abstracted from the concrete? Peacock (1986) suggests that "readers must decode the description in order to grasp for themselves the underlying values, then juxtapose these implicitly abstracted patterns to illuminate their own experience, as well as that which they imagine to have been lived by the natives" (pp. 83–84).

169

The literature (e.g., Barnes et al., 1990; Boyer, 1983; Goodlad, 1984; McNeil, 1988; Newmann, 1992; Wagner, 1994) indicates that Whitmore High School is not altogether dissimilar from other high schools. Evidence of what Eisner (1988) refers to as "structured fragmentation" is compelling among studies of high schools. The 40 eighth-grade students from Meadowbrook went to five different high schools, and in informal chats, some of those students described situations and practices that fit with those of Whitmore.

Meadowbrook Community School, however, seems to be somewhat less typical of elementary and middle schools, especially in its communal nature. However, in recent years, there's been a movement toward more affectively oriented middle schools and a restructuring of junior high schools (e.g., Carnegie Council on Adolescent Development, 1989; George, Stevenson, Thomason, & Beane, 1992; Jackson & Hornbeck, 1989). Educators such as Bloome (1986), Grant (1981), Peterson (1992), and Sergiovanni (1994) have called for a reconceptualization of schools and classrooms as communities. The adults at Meadowbrook would deny that they have goals and practices "all figured out," but given stories of successful schools (e.g., Horenstein, 1993; Sergiovanni, 1994; Wood, 1992), it would appear that the school is at least headed in the direction that many educators are currently advocating.

Ginny, Chad, John, Monica, Nicky, and their peers remind us that students are people with beliefs, perceptions, feelings, insights, and histories— as well as futures. It's not hard to imagine that there are students like them in every school. Their stories should make us uncomfortable, if not angry. Why, some might ask, did these kids from Meadowbrook choose this particular high school? Why did they stay? Why weren't there complaints, if not public outcry? The answers are complicated, bound up in tradition and cultural expectations. What do we, as a society, expect from schools? Do we expect different things from elementary schools than we do from high schools? If we do, why? Questions spawn questions. The closer we look, the more angles we take, the more complicated it becomes.

By interacting with and closely observing adolescents in their transition from one school to another and by studying the culture of each school from a broader perspective, I've learned that adults' philosophies and values (whether examined or unexamined) directly affect students' learning and, more specifically, their development as literate beings. If we view schools as agents of cultural transmission that instill beliefs about *what* knowledge is and *which* skills are important, as well as viewing them as institutions that teach (or dispense) that knowledge and those skills, then the whole notion of education shows itself to be enormously complex. Yet if the students in this study and their transition between two schools highlight multiple differences in school cultures, it also appears that many, if not most, of those differences can be connected to how the schools organized and saw themselves. At issue is the concept of community—a complex concept in itself. I now reflect on community more closely, specifically in terms of the inter-relatedness of three components: interpersonal relationships, control, and structure.

RELATIONSHIP, CONTROL, AND STRUCTURE

It was no accident that "community" was Meadowbrook Community School's middle name. When the new school was built, the town wanted to emphasize the communal nature of the school, that it should be a place where everyone in the community could meet for social and educational purposes. "Community" also referred to the school community—all the people who lived, worked, and played together there. The school was a community of classroom communities, not unlike a neighborhood with families nestled within it. Teachers cared about one another and provided models of caring as they nurtured classroom communities. Caring relationships sustained daily school life. Shared relationships made school fun, lent it meaning, and pro-pelled it beyond the simple "doing" of work. Going to school could be fun because social interaction, as evidenced by collaboration, group decisions, and peer assistance, was integral to motivations and processes of learning.

There didn't have to be a lot of rules because people knew what they were supposed to do, and their motivation for doing what was right didn't depend on threats of punishments or extrinsic rewards. It depended more on a desire to fit within the community, to maintain relationships that were integral to it. This is not to say that teachers lacked intellectual or moral authority or that they did not take students to task for misconduct or inap-propriate behavior. But their authority, as Grant (1988) suggests, was "legiti-mated by the group." Common sense prevailed, and respect and empathy were fostered even in the early grades. Students were expected to think of others in their behavior. In a discussion about the differences among extrin-sic gain, intrinsic worth, and moral ties, Sergiovanni (1994) describes the power of caring relationships found in communities:

> Moral ties emerge from the duties we accept and the obligations we feel toward others and toward our work that result from commitments to shared values and beliefs. Moral involvement also comes from within. And, since moral ties are more grounded in cultural norms than psychological gratification, they are likely to be stronger than extrinsic or intrinsic ties. (p. 55)

The adults in the school drew on these moral ties to help students develop understandings of what was appropriate in various situations. For instance, the lunchroom, as stated in the school handbook, was "a place where good human relations can be developed" and in which students were expected to practice "good manners." Students needed a degree of freedom within which to make decisions—whether it was in the lunchroom, on the playground, or in the classroom during reading and writing times. Vygotsky's (1978) concept of the "zone of proximal development" is most often thought of in terms of classroom instruction and learning, but the teachers at Meadowbrook recognized that social, emotional, and cognitive development was ongoing across contexts—not just in the classroom. Adults gave students support in terms of general guidelines and provided more specific direction only when students needed additional help. Had the rules been too restrictive or all-encompassing, they wouldn't have allowed space for students to develop a sense of responsibility to themselves and others.

Caring relationships were central to the teaching and learning of content and skills. Students believed that their teachers wanted them to learn and would spend extra time and energy helping them do so. Students' feelings of being "cared for" came as much from their perception that their teachers tried to make learning interesting as it did from social and emotional interaction. Social, emotional, and academic growth were bound together. Noddings (1986) writes, "To suppose, for example, that attention to affective needs necessarily implies less time for arithmetic is simply a mistake. Such tasks can be accomplished simultaneously, but the one is undertaken in light of the other" (p. 499). When students wrote in school, they did so in the company of others, taking time to listen to one another, trusting that someone, in turn, would respond to their work. In the process, they simultaneously practiced and manipulated writing strategies, used spoken and written language to develop and refine ideas, and further developed social skills such as collaboration and problem solving. And, as they drew on community to support writing, they strengthened it with their actions.

Community and caring relationships among teachers and students force a rethinking of how schools and classrooms are structured. Eisner (1988) describes an ecology of the school in which dimensions such as intentions, structure, curriculum, pedagogy, and evaluation cannot be separated: "Given a critical mass, what one does in one place influences what happens in another" (p. 29). Caring relationships influence and are influenced by how long and for what purposes teachers and students will remain together, how classroom learning will be organized, how seating will be arranged, whether or in what way students will be tested, how students will be grouped, and how days will be structured. It was concern for caring relationships that served as the impetus for magnets and humanities, but it wasn't incidental that these new programs also served to help integrate subject matter and provide authentic contexts for literacy development. Those who planned the programs understood not only the connectedness of the elements but also the dynamic nature of their interaction.

If relationship, issues of control, and structure were integral to one another at Meadowbrook, they were equally interdependent at the high school, but in a *Gesellschaft*-type school, the outcome looked very different. When in the spring of her freshman year, Nicky, who had loved going to school in Meadowbrook, told me that she dreaded going to high school—that the only good part was her friends—she seemed to indicate that she'd separated peer relationships from the "doing of school." Teacher–student relationships were almost nonexistent. While Nicky was luckier than some of her peers and had several teachers who established rapport with students, there was little time to get to know teachers—or for them to know students.

The same students who the year before had praised their teachers as caring, complained that their high school teachers didn't care what they learned. Similarly, adolescents in Ahola-Sidaway's study (1988) missed their caring elementary teachers after they moved to a departmentalized seventh grade. In Phelan and colleagues' (1992) 2-year study of 54 high school students' perspectives on school and learning, they found a recurring theme of students' "tremendous" value for caring teachers. The high-achieving students in the study defined caring teachers as those who provided careful academic assistance, while low-achieving students equated caring with teachers' personality traits such as humor and the ability to listen. Caring teachers were especially important to low-achieving students (such as Ginny), who reported that they lacked incentive to do schoolwork when they felt their teachers didn't care what they did.

The Meadowbrook students hadn't expected to have the close personal relationships with high school teachers that they'd enjoyed with their eighth-grade teachers. For one thing, they'd known their eighth-grade teachers for at least 2 years and in a variety of circumstances (e.g., town/school gatherings, magnets, community projects) and they'd spent significant amounts of time with their teachers (e.g., those in the Music and Media Magnet and Mr. Carew's homeroom spent about 3 hours with him each day). There were both time and opportunity for relationships to grow. Noddings (1984) asks why teachers and students can't stay together for 3 or more years and why teachers can't teach more than one subject in order to extend contact between teachers and students. Through the extended humanities time and magnets, the Meadowbrook teachers were consciously aiming to extend meaningful time between adults and students.

Whitmore High School wasn't structured for such caring interaction. Meadowbrook freshmen didn't usually see their teachers outside 50-minute instructional blocks, and even during classes, the business of covering material was usually primary. Eisner (1988) writes about structure in high schools:

The existing secondary school structure not only separates teacher from teacher and divides what is taught into small units with virtually impenetrable boundaries, but it also exacerbates the anonymity of students. . . . In short, our students often have limited contact with caring adults who know them well. (p. 28)

As freshmen, students were set adrift. They no longer had the individual support of caring adults, and they were often separated from their friends.

Given this state, it was surprising that Meadowbrook students seemed initially to take for granted teachers who made obvious attempts at rapport, even as they began to complain about others whom they described as "just doing a job" (teachers who didn't go out of their way to make learning fun or interesting). I wondered if students had become so accustomed to caring teachers that caring overtures seemed unremarkable—even in the high school setting. Trying to figure out what was going on in those early weeks, I asked Monica, Nicky, and Jan if Mrs. Larimer, their Spanish teacher, reminded them of any of the teachers they'd ever had. She didn't, but the girls said that she taught like an elementary teacher, meaning that she gave them a lot of encouragement, that she changed the pitch of her voice when she talked, and that she did fun things (various groupings and activities) with the class. They didn't describe her as caring, however, and when I asked why not, they said they didn't know her well enough. It had been hard to get to know her in a fast-paced class with no opportunity for out-of-class contact. It wasn't until winter carnival in February that Nicky was able to have a somewhat prolonged conversation with her. After that, she and the other girls started feeling closer to her. The system wasn't set up for caring teachers.

Nicky's and Jan's algebra teacher, Mrs. Britton, was the cheerleading coach, which meant that she spent time with the girls after school. She also invited them to her house several times when they couldn't arrange rides home and back to school again before basketball games. So, when Nicky saw that Monica was having trouble with math, she made sure to introduce Monica to her algebra teacher, because she knew that Mrs. Britton wanted students to do well in math and that she wouldn't mind staying after school to help someone. She knew Mrs. Britton cared about them. Out-of-class contact allowed students to interact with their teachers as people. The problem was that it didn't happen often, and the overall ethos of the school colored how students reacted to friendly teachers. In Meadowbrook, caring was pervasive; at Whitmore, it was isolated. Without a supporting community, caring could seem "weird."

Without a strong sense of community and with schoolwork that students considered boring, it was only natural that issues of control dominated behaviors. School adults became responsible for controlling students, which, in turn, made caring relationships more difficult. Whether that control was established by the threat or promise of grades, by a heavy reliance on a depersonalized textbook-based curriculum (McNeil, 1988), or by stated rules and consistently meted out consequences, students had little choice but to do what they were supposed to or, as the handbook stated on the first page, "accept the consequences." Without some leeway for decision making, students had less responsibility than they'd known in elementary school. In effect, the external control undermined academic motivation and resulted in a kind of reluctant compliance among students such as Nicky and Monica and a strong measure of alienation for students like Ginny. It wasn't that students wanted chaos—far from it (see Phelan et al., 1992, for a discussion of high school students' perspectives on school issues, including others' disruptive behaviors)—but they needed some room to make decisions for themselves. Kohn (1993) explains:

> The structural and attitudinal barriers erected by educators often seem impregnable, with the result that students continue to feel powerless and, to that extent, burned out. For decades, prescriptions have been offered to enhance student motivation and achievement. But these ideas are unlikely to make much difference so long as students are controlled and silenced. (p. 19)

Control, relationship, and structure (among a host of other elements including curriculum) are thus entwined. Change in one area would affect others. It would seem that those who desire to make positive changes in schools should first identify important elements of school culture and then study how those elements impact one another. Sarason (1990) posits that the first step is to "flush out" the web of power relationships that inform and control the behaviors of everyone.

CULTURAL CHANGE

Cultures by nature are resistant to change. Yet when we think of the Meadowbrook students as freshmen at Whitmore High School, when we think of their social development (e.g., as collaborators and planners), and when we think of their diminished opportunities to read, write, and talk in meaningful contexts, how can we be comfortable with the status quo? It would seem that change is in order, but are we as a society willing to shift, as this study might suggest, the emphasis of a traditional high school and traditional curriculum from one of externally controlled behaviors to one in which behaviors are intrinsically managed through communal understandings?

Real change, as Sarason (1982, 1990) suggests, is not the result of tinkering with policies and programs. Putting computers in all classrooms, scheduling longer instructional periods, moving classroom furniture, silencing bells, assigning trade books for English class, setting up writing workshops—innovative as they might seem—are sadly superficial actions unless they're connected to an overall vision of what a school might be. A few years before this study began, for example, Whitmore High School established a writing center so that students, using computers, could work on writing assignments from various classes with help from teachers who staffed these periods in lieu of other duties. After an initial flurry of activity, the center quieted down and was ultimately moved to the tutoring center, where it went largely unused. Whitmore lacked a unifying vision, and like plants with underdeveloped root systems, innovative programs and ideas were short-lived. As a result, tradition prevailed, and the school tended to resemble high schools of previous generations.

In his discussion of school change, Wagner (1994) suggests that schools need to have clear academic goals and *articulated* core values and need to foster collaboration among students, faculty, parents, and community members. Whitmore High School had none of this. The notion of academic goals appeared to be limited to acquisition of credits toward graduation. Core values were not articulated and by default centered on issues of order and control. Collaboration, even among teachers, was close to nonexistent.

Where to begin? Whose goals? Whose values? Whose vision? Where does leadership fit? Grant (1988) noted that school ethos shifts as leadership changes. Leadership does make a difference. But what kind of leadership? That which models itself on industry and top-down decision making? Or leadership forged through facilitating connections among people? Certainly the latter, as evidenced by Bill Peterson at Meadowbrook, would make sense in terms of fostering collaboration, articulating core values, and establishing clear academic goals. Once again, the focus becomes one of relationship, finding ways to draw on all those who have interest in schools: residents, school board members, teachers, administrators, students, and parents. The Meadowbrook experience would indicate that *time* for listening, reflection, and consensus building is a crucial ingredient to building those relationships—within schools as well as between the school and the larger community.

Fostering collaboration, establishing academic goals, and articulating core values are Herculean tasks, and what's more, the process would seem to be never-ending. More than a dozen years into the task, the constituents of Meadowbrook still argue, for instance, about the value of grammar instruction and how students might best be prepared for high school. Tradition and layers of culture influence which values and what goals will drive school operation. This may be particularly true at the secondary level. In a historical analysis of education and the role of high schools, Cohen and Neufeld (1981) suggest that elementary schools once carried the responsibility of "preparation for adulthood." As high school attendance became universal, this burden eased for elementary schools and they could become more child-centered: "More relaxed schooling became possible at the elementary level as long as the market-oriented competition was maintained in the high schools" (p. 77). It appears that people expect different things from high schools than they do elementary schools.

When Nancy Wilcox from Meadowbrook said, "I have no problem with creativity in the first, second, or third grades, but after that, they [students] need to settle into learning something," she was voicing an honest concern that "real life" was coming up and that students needed to be ready. Her invocation at a public meeting—"I want to see our children get an education to compete in high school and in the world. We want textbooks. We want testing. We want classroom learning and homework"—strikes at the core of many people's beliefs. School ought to be hard; it doesn't matter if kids like it. We got through it, and so can our children. Perhaps there is no public outcry about Whitmore High School and schools like it because deep down, our society still values what goes on there. But how did these values translate to the Meadowbrook students' everyday school life? Grammar exercises; study guides that propelled students and teachers through textbooks; paragraph-writing exercises; questions whose answers could "be found" in the book; memorization of lists, facts, and definitions; silent seatwork; multiple-choice, matching, true/false, short answer tests—all of it the work of assembly lines. It wasn't fun, but it wasn't meant to be.

Geertz (1973) writes, "Cultural analysis is intrinsically incomplete. And worse than that, the more deeply it goes the less complete it is. It's a strange science whose most telling assertions are its most tremulously based" (p. 29). This study details a dramatic change in learning and literacy development as the result of students' transition between two very different schools. That much is clear. Getting at the dynamics of school culture, even in two particular schools, especially in terms of exploring change, seems particularly "tremulous." Earlier I drew on Tönnies's theory of *Gemeinschaft* and *Gesellschaft* in order to make comparisons, especially about the types of relationship in both schools and to analyze the nature of school community. Here, I've sketched the interdependent nature of three aspects of that community: relationship, control, and structure in order to briefly highlight the complexity of school ethos and culture. Tremulous, indeed—I've only alluded to possible areas where change might begin, while at the same time, I've questioned whether we, as a society, want to think of high schools as communities.

And so, we're left with the kids. Line them up. Distribute the worksheets. The difference between this study and other high school studies is that we know that Nicky, Chad, Monica, Ginny, and John were capable of doing far more than they were asked and that literacy development—at least in high school—was stalled. The students were once, however, part of a very different learning community, one that valued reading, writing, talk, and listening. What if teachers at the high school had asked students how they preferred to learn; what if they'd asked them if they had any opinions, for instance, about how writing could be integrated throughout the curriculum? In seeking avenues for school change, Sarason (1990) compares students in schools to workers in factories and wonders why, like managers seeking worker input, we don't ask students what they know:

> We often act as though students are the products of school, when, in fact, kids must be the workers in order to learn. They must want to come to school, and they must be willing to work, even when no one is hanging over them. If we can't achieve this, no kind of school reform, however ambitious, will improve student learning and public education. So it's hard to explain why we don't routinely ask kids . . . about how to improve schools. (p. 113)

Throughout this study, I listened to what students had to say about their literacy and learning. Occasionally they'd tell me that they wished some of their high school teachers would teach the way their Meadowbrook teachers had. When I prodded for specifics, they came up with things like "fun" ways to learn and respect for kids. To them, it didn't matter if their answers were somewhat vague; they knew that nothing would change based on their opinions. The Meadowbrook students were few in number, and while my presence may have emboldened them somewhat or perhaps made them more aware of the contrasts between schools, the students were usually reluctant (with the exception of Ginny and sometimes Monica) to make suggestions to teachers. Relationships between adults and students are, after all, unequal by nature and appeared to be especially so at the high school.

What if students were expected to engage in dialogue with their teachers about values and expectations? What if students, as Shannon (1989b) puts it, "insisted that they be treated as active learners by everyone? . . . What if they demanded that all their learning environments be coherent, authentic, sensible, and purposeful" (pp. 631–632)? Similarly, Ahola-Sidaway (1986, 1988), in reflecting on Canadian students' transition from sixth grade to high school, questioned whether students could be encouraged to challenge the authority of their teachers.

In the eighth grade, students felt that they had voice and choice. They routinely offered suggestions for projects or configurations for working together. They were able to choose some areas of study and could negotiate assignments. In the high school, they did what they were told to do, and their voices were quieted. What if these students, who appeared to be so confident in the eighth grade, had felt empowered to make demands on the high school? What if they'd had avenues through which they could have explored and defined their expectations for literacy development and formal schooling? Is it possible that they could have been active participants in changing school culture—making it more *Gemeinschaft*-like? Perhaps our attention should be directed toward enabling students to better understand and articulate their learning processes (see Oldfather, 1992, 1993), while at the same time we structure ways that their voices can be heard.

Still, we have the account that's told in these pages. It only seems logical that cultural change must be preceded, at least in part, by an understanding of what now exists. Ginny, John, Nicky, Chad, Monica, Jan, Carl, Sharon, Rachelle, and their friends, by allowing their story to be told, have helped us do that. Their perspective is immediate to their experience, undiluted by time and further enculturation. Their story and that of their two schools should do more than simply give us pause.

I can't help wondering what will happen to the Meadowbrook students as they continue to make their way through school and then enter adult life. How will they, as adults, influence and react to the schools in their communities? What understandings of learning and literacy will they share with their own children? Will they someday watch as their children leave a Meadowbrook Community School to attend a Whitmore High School?

References

Ahola-Sidaway, J. A. (1986). *Student transition from elementary school to high school*. Unpublished doctoral dissertation, McGill University, Montreal.

Ahola-Sidaway, J. A. (1988, April). *From Gemeinschaft to Gesellschaft: A case study of student transition from elementary school to high school*. Paper presented at the meeting of the American Educational Research Association, New Orleans, LA. (ERIC Document Reproduction Service No. ED 297 450)

Apple, M. W. (1983). Curricular form and the logic of technical control. In M. W. Apple & L. Weis (Eds.), *Ideology and practice in schooling* (pp. 143–165). Philadelphia: Temple University Press.

Applebee, A. N. (1984). Writing and reasoning. *Review of Educational Research, 54*(4), 577–596.

Atkin, J. M. , Patrick, C. L., & Kennedy, D. (1989). *Inside schools: A collaborative view*. Washington, DC: Falmer.

Barnes, D., Britton, J., & Torbe, M. (1990). *Language, the learner and the school* (4th ed.). Portsmouth, NH: Heinemann.

Berne, E. (1964). *Games people play*. New York: Grove.

Bloome, D. (1986). Building literacy and the classroom community. *Theory into Practice, 25*(2), 71–76.

Boyer, E. L. (1983). *High school: A report on secondary education in America*. New York: Harper & Row.

Brown, R. G. (1991). *Schools of thought: How the politics of literacy shape thinking in the classroom*. San Francisco: Jossey-Bass.

Bryk, A. S., Lee, V. E., & Smith, J. B. (1990). High school organization and its effects on teachers and students: An interpretive summary of the research. In W. H. Clune & J. F. Witte (Eds.), *Choice and control in American education: Vol. 1. The theory of choice and control in education* (pp. 135–226). New York: Falmer.

Cambourne, B., & Turbill, J. (1987). *Coping with chaos*. Rozelle, Australia: Primary English Teaching Association.

Carnegie Council on Adolescent Development. (1989). *Turning points: Preparing youth for the 21st century*. New York: Carnegie Corporation.

Cazden, C. B. (1988). *Classroom discourse: The language of teaching and learning*. Portsmouth, NH: Heinemann.

Cazden, C. B. (1992). *Whole language plus: Essays on literacy in the United States and New Zealand*. New York: Teachers College Press.

Chang, H. (1992). *Adolescent life and ethos: An ethnography of a U.S. high school*. Washington, DC: Falmer.

Cohen, D. K., & Neufeld, B. (1981). How schools change: Lessons from three communities. *Daedalus, 110*(3), 69–89.

Cook-Gumperz, J. (1986). Introduction: The social construction of literacy. In J. Cook-Gumperz (Ed.), *The social construction of literacy* (pp. 1–15). New York: Cambridge University Press.

Corsaro, W. A. (1981). Entering the child's world: Research strategies for field entry and data collection in a preschool setting. In J. L. Green & C. Wallat (Eds.), *Ethnography and language in educational settings: Advances in discourse processes* (pp. 117–146). Norwood, NJ: Ablex.

Cuban, L. (1993). *How teachers taught: Constancy and change in American classrooms 1880–1990* (2nd ed.). New York: Teachers College Press.

Cusick, P. A. (1973). *Inside high school: The student's world.* New York: Holt, Rinehart & Winston.

Dewey, J. (1916). *Democracy and education.* New York: Free Press.

Dewey, J. (1938). *Experience and education.* New York: Collier.

Dewey, J. (1990). *The school and society & The child and the curriculum.* Chicago: University of Chicago Press. (Original works published 1900 and 1902)

Dole, J. A., & Osborn, J. (1991). The selection and use of language arts textbooks. In J. Flood, J. M. Jensen, D. Lapp, & J. R. Squire (Eds.), *Handbook of research on teaching the English language arts* (pp. 521–525). New York: Macmillan.

Dyson, A. H. (1983). The role of oral language in early writing processes. *Research in the Teaching of English, 17*(1), 1–30.

Eccles, J. S., Midgley, C., Wigfield, A., Buchanan, C. M., Reuman, D., Flanagan, C., & MacIver, D. (1993). Development during adolescence: The impact of stage–environment fit on young adolescents' experiences in schools and in families. *American Psychologist, 48*(2), 90–101.

Edelsky, C. (1991). *With literacy and justice for all: Rethinking the social in language and education.* New York: Falmer.

Eisner, E. W. (1988). The ecology of school improvement. *Educational Leadership, 45*(5), 24–29.

Eisner, E. W. (1991a). *The enlightened eye: Qualitative inquiry and the enhancement of education practice.* New York: Macmillan.

Eisner, E. W. (1991b). What really counts in schools. *Educational Leadership, 48*(5), 10–17.

Erickson, F. (1982). Taught cognitive learning in its immediate environments: A neglected topic in the anthropology of education. *Anthropology and Education Quarterly, 13*(2), 149–180.

Erickson, F. (1984). What makes school ethnography "ethnographic"? *Anthropology and Education Quarterly, 15*(1), 51–66.

Erickson, F. (1988). School literacy, reasoning, and civility: An anthropologist's perspective. In E. R. Kintgen, B. M. Kroll, & M. Rose (Eds.), *Perspectives on literacy* (pp. 205–226). Carbondale: Southern Illinois University Press.

Fillion, B. (1990). Language across the curriculum: Examining the place of language in our schools. In T. Newkirk (Ed.), *To compose: Teaching writing in high school and college* (2nd ed.; pp. 235–250). Portsmouth, NH: Heinemann.

Fine, G. A. (1987). *With the boys: Little League baseball and preadolescent culture*. Chicago: University of Chicago Press.

Fine, G. A., & Sandstrom, K. L. (1988). *Knowing children: Participant observation with minors*. Newbury Park, CA: Sage.

Freire, P. (1993). *Pedagogy of the oppressed* (2nd ed.). New York: Continuum.

Geertz, C. (1973). *The interpretation of cultures*. New York: Best Books.

Geertz, C. (1976). "From the native's point of view": On the nature of anthropological understanding. In K. H. Basso & H. Selby (Eds.), *Meaning in anthropology* (pp. 221–237). Albuquerque: University of New Mexico Press.

George, P. S., Stevenson, C., Thomason, J., & Beane, J. (1992). *The middle school—and beyond*. Alexandria, VA: Association for Supervision and Curriculum Development.

Glassner, B. (1976). Kid society. *Urban Education, 11*(1), 5–22.

Gold, R. L. (1969). Roles in sociological field observations. In G. J. McCall & J. L. Simmons (Eds.), *Issues in participant observation* (pp. 30–38). Reading, MA: Addison-Wesley.

Goodenough, W. H. (1981). *Culture, language, and society*. Menlo Park, CA: Benjamin/Cummings.

Goodlad, J. I. (1983). What some schools and classrooms teach. *Educational Leadership, 40*(7), 8–19.

Goodlad, J. I. (1984). *A place called school: Prospects for the future*. New York: McGraw-Hill.

Goodman, Y. M., Hood, W. J., & Goodman, K. S. (1991). *Organizing for whole language*. Portsmouth, NH: Heinemann.

Grant, G. (1981). The character of education and the education of character. *Daedalus, 110*(3), 135–149.

Grant, G. (1988). *The world we created at Hamilton High*. Cambridge, MA: Harvard University Press.

Graves, D. H. (1983). *Writing: Teachers and children at work*. Portsmouth, NH: Heinemann.

Hansen, J. F. (1979). *Sociocultural perspectives on human learning: Foundations of educational anthropology*. New York: Prentice-Hall. (Reissued by Waveland Press, 1990)

Harste, J. C. (1989). The future of whole language. *The Elementary School Journal, 90*(2), 243–249.

Hartwell, P. (1985). Grammar, grammars, and the teaching of grammar. *College English, 47*(2), 105–127.

Heath, S. B. (1983). *Ways with words: Language, life and work in communities and classrooms*. New York: Cambridge University Press.

Herskovits, M. J. (1948). *Man and his works: The science of cultural anthropology*. New York: Knopf.

Hillocks, G., Jr., & Smith, M. W. (1991). Grammar and usage. In J. Flood, J. M. Jensen, D. Lapp, & J.R. Squire (Eds.), *Handbook of research on teaching the English language arts* (pp. 591–603). New York: Macmillan.

Horenstein, M. A. (1993). *Twelve schools that succeed*. Bloomington, IN: Phi Delta Kappa Educational Foundation.

Jackson, A. W., & Hornbeck, D. W. (1989). Educating young adolescents: Why we must restructure middle grade schools. *American Psychologist, 44*(5), 831–836.

Kohn, A. (1993). Choices for children: Why and how to let students decide. *Phi Delta Kappan, 75*(1), 8–20.

Lightfoot, S. L. (1983). *The good high school: Portraits of character and culture.* New York: Basic Books.

Mandell, N. (1988). The least-adult role in studying children. *Journal of Contemporary Ethnography, 16*, 433–467.

Manning, P., & Matthews, S. (1992, January). *Dilemmas of classroom research: Preliminary findings of an ethnographic study in an inner-city intermediate school.* Paper presented at the meeting of Qualitative Research in Education Conference, Athens, GA.

McLaughlin, M. W., & Talbert, J. E. (1990). The contexts in question: The secondary school workplace. In M. W. McLaughlin, J. E. Talbert, & N. Bascia (Eds.), *The contexts of teaching in secondary schools: Teachers' realities* (pp. 1–14). New York: Teachers College Press.

McNeil, L. M. (1983). Defensive teaching and classroom control. In M. W. Apple & L. Weis (Eds.), *Ideology and practice in schooling* (pp. 114–142). Philadelphia: Temple University Press.

McNeil, L. M. (1988). *Contradictions of control: School structure and school knowledge.* New York: Routledge.

Menke, D., & Davey, B. (1994). Teachers' views of textbooks and text reading instruction: Experience matters. *Journal of Reading, 37*(6), 464–470.

Moffett, J. (1983). *Teaching the universe of discourse.* Portsmouth, NH: Boynton/Cook.

Myers, J. (1992). The social contexts of school and personal literacy. *Reading Research Quarterly, 27*(4), 297–333.

Nespor, J. (1991). The construction of school knowledge: A case study. In C. Mitchell & K. Weiler (Eds.), *Rewriting literacy: Culture and the discourse of the other* (pp. 169–188). New York: Bergin & Garvey.

Newkirk, T. (1991a). The high school years. In J. Flood, J. M. Jensen, D. Lapp, & J.R. Squire (Eds.), *Handbook of research on teaching the English language arts* (pp. 331–342). New York: Macmillan.

Newkirk, T. (1991b). The middle class and the problem of pleasure. In N. Atwell (Ed.), *Workshop 3: The politics of process* (pp. 63–72). Portsmouth, NH: Heinemann.

Newmann, F. M. (1981). Reducing student alienation in high schools: Implications of theory. *Harvard Educational Review, 54*(4), 546–564.

Newmann, F. M. (1989). Reducing student alienation in high schools: Implications of theory. In L. Weis, E. Farrar, & H. G. Petrie (Eds.), *Dropouts from school: Issues, dilemmas, and solutions* (pp. 153–177). Albany: State University of New York Press.

Newmann, F. M. (Ed.). (1992). *Student engagement and achievement in American secondary schools.* New York: Teachers College Press.

Newmann, F. M., Wehlage, G. G., & Lamborn, S. D. (1992). The significance and sources of student engagement. In F. M. Newmann (Ed.), *Student engage-*

ment and achievement in American secondary schools (pp. 11–39). New York: Teachers College Press.

Noddings, N. (1984). *Caring: A feminine approach to ethics and moral education.* Berkeley: University of California Press.

Noddings, N. (1986). Fidelity in teaching, teacher education, and research for teaching. *Harvard Educational Review, 56*(4), 496–510.

Noddings, N. (1992). *The challenge to care in schools: An alternative approach to education.* New York: Teachers College Press.

Noguchi, R. R. (1991). *Grammar and the teaching of writing: Limits and possibilities.* Urbana, IL: National Council of Teachers of English.

Oakes, J. (1985). *Keeping track: How schools structure inequality.* New Haven, CT: Yale University Press.

Oldfather, P. (1992, December). *Sharing the ownership of knowing: A constructivist concept of motivation for literacy learning.* Paper presented at the meeting of the National Reading Conference, San Antonio, TX. (ERIC Document Reproduction Service No. ED 352 610)

Oldfather, P. (1993). What students say about motivating experiences in a whole language classroom. *The Reading Teacher, 46*(8), 672–681.

Patthey-Chavez, G. G. (1993). High school as an arena for cultural conflict and acculturation for Latino Angelinos. *Anthropology and Education Quarterly, 24*(1), 33–60.

Peacock, J. L. (1986). *The anthropological lens: Harsh light, soft focus.* New York: Cambridge University Press.

Peterson, R. (1992). *Life in a crowded place: Making a learning community.* Portsmouth, NH: Heinemann.

Phelan, P., Davidson, A. L., & Cao, H. T. (1992). Speaking up: Students' perspectives on school. *Phi Delta Kappan, 73*(9), 695–704.

Purves, A. C. (1993). Toward a reevaluation of reader response and school literature. *Language Arts, 70*(5), 348–361.

Richardson, R. C., Fisk, E. C., & Okun, M. A. (1988). Reading and writing requirements. In E. R. Kintgen, B. M. Kroll, & M. Rose (Eds.), *Perspectives on literacy* (pp. 254–260). Carbondale: Southern Illinois University Press.

Robinson, J. L. (1988). The social context of literacy. In E. R. Kintgen, B. M. Kroll, & M. Rose (Eds.), *Perspectives on literacy* (pp. 243–253). Carbondale: Southern Illinois University Press.

Rutter, M., Maughan, B., Mortimore, P., Ouston, J., with Smith, A. (1979). *Fifteen thousand hours: Secondary schools and their effects on children.* Cambridge, MA: Harvard University Press.

Sarason, S. B. (1982). *The culture of the school and the problem of change* (2nd ed.). Boston: Allyn & Bacon.

Sarason, S. B. (1990). *The predictable failure of educational reform: Can we change course before it's too late?* San Francisco: Jossey-Bass.

Schram, T. (1994). Players along the margin: Diversity and adaptation in a lower track classroom. In G. Spindler & L. Spindler (Eds.), *Pathways to cultural awareness: Cultural therapy with teachers and students* (pp. 61–91). Newbury Park, CA: Corwin.

Scribner, S. (1988). Literacy in three metaphors. In E. R. Kintgen, B. M. Kroll, & M. Rose (Eds.), *Perspectives on literacy* (pp. 71–81). Carbondale: Southern Illinois University Press.

Scribner, S., & Cole, M. (1988). Unpackaging literacy. In E. R. Kintgen, B. M. Kroll, & M. Rose (Eds.), *Perspectives on literacy* (pp. 57–70). Carbondale: Southern Illinois University Press.

Sergiovanni, T. J. (1994). *Building community in schools*. San Francisco: Jossey-Bass.

Shanker, A. (1990). The end of the traditional model of schooling—and a proposal for using incentives to restructure our public schools. *Phi Delta Kappan, 71*(5), 345–357.

Shannon, P. (1989a). *Broken promises: Reading instruction in twentieth-century America*. New York: Bergin & Garvey.

Shannon, P. (1989b). The struggle for control of literacy lessons. *Language Arts, 66*(6), 625–634.

Smith, F. (1985). *Reading without nonsense* (2nd ed.). New York: Teachers College Press.

Smith, F. R., & Feathers, K. M. (1983). The role of reading in content classrooms: Assumption vs. reality. *Journal of Reading, 27*, 262–667.

Spindler, G. (1963). The transmission of American culture. In G. D. Spindler (Ed.), *Education and culture: Anthropological approaches* (pp. 148–172). New York: Holt, Rinehart & Winston.

Spindler, G. (1982). *Doing the ethnography of schooling: Educational anthropology in action*. Prospect Heights, IL: Waveland.

Spindler, G., & Spindler, L. (1987). Ethnography: An anthropological view. In G. D. Spindler (Ed.), *Education and cultural process: Anthropological approaches* (2nd ed.; pp. 151–156). Prospect Heights, IL: Waveland.

Spindler, G., & Spindler, L. (1989). Instrumental competence, self-efficacy, linguistic minorities, and cultural therapy: A preliminary attempt at integration. *Anthropology and Education Quarterly, 20*(1), 36–50.

Spindler, G., & Spindler, L. (1991, October). *The processes of culture and person: Multicultural classrooms and cultural therapy*. Paper presented at the Cultural Diversity Working Conference, Stanford University, Palo Alto, CA.

Spindler, G., & Spindler, L. (1992). Cultural process and ethnography: An anthropological perspective. In M. D. LeCompte, W. L. Millroy, & J. Preissle (Eds.), *The handbook of qualitative research in education* (pp. 53–92). San Diego: Academic Press.

Spindler, G., & Spindler, L. (1994). What is cultural therapy? In G. Spindler & L. Spindler (Eds.), *Pathways to cultural therapy: Cultural therapy with teachers and students* (pp. 1–33). Newbury Park, CA: Corwin.

Szwed, J. F. (1988). The ethnography of literacy. In E. R. Kintgen, B. M. Kroll, & M. Rose (Eds.), *Perspectives on literacy* (pp. 303–311). Carbondale: Southern Illinois University Press.

Tönnies, F. (1957). *Community and society* (C. P. Loomis, Ed. & Trans.). East Lansing, MI: Michigan State University Press. (Original work published 1887)

Tönnies, F. (1971). *On sociology: Pure, applied, and empirical: Selected writings* (W. J. Cahnman & R. Heberle, Eds.). Chicago: University of Chicago Press.

Trueba, H. T., Rodriguez, C., Zou, Y., & Cintrón, J. (1993). *Healing multicultural America: Mexican immigrants rise to power in rural California.* Washington, DC: Falmer.

Vavra, E. (1993). Welcome to the shoe store? *English Journal, 82*(5), 81–84.

Vygotsky, L. S. (1965). *Thought and language* (E. Hanfmann & G. Vakar, Trans.). Cambridge, MA: MIT Press. (Original work published 1934)

Vygotsky, L. S. (1978). *Mind in society: The development of higher psychological processes* (M. Cole, V. John-Steiner, S. Scribner, & E. Souberman, Eds.). Cambridge, MA: Harvard University Press.

Wagner, T. (1994). *How schools change: Lessons from three communities.* Boston: Beacon Press.

Warner, A. L. (1993). If the shoe no longer fits, wear it anyway? *English Journal, 82*(5), 76–80.

Wax, R. H. (1979). Gender and age in fieldwork and fieldwork education: No good thing is done by any man alone. *Social Problems, 26,* 509–522.

Weaver, C. (1979). *Grammar for teachers: Perspectives and definitions.* Urbana, IL: National Council of Teachers of English.

Wolcott, H. (1994). *Transforming qualitative data: Description, analysis, and interpretation.* Newbury Park, CA: Sage.

Wood, G. H. (1992). *Schools that work: America's most innovative public education programs.* New York: Dutton.

Woods, W. F. (1985, March). *The cultural tradition of nineteenth-century "traditional" grammar teaching.* Paper presented at the meeting of the Conference on College Composition and Communication, Minneapolis, MN. (ERIC Document Reproduction Service No. ED 258 267)

Index

About the Author

M. Cyrene Wells is an assistant professor of education at the University of Maine at Machias. She received her Ph.D. in reading and writing instruction from the University of New Hampshire. As a teacher-researcher, she studied her seventh- and eighth-grade students' reading and writing processes and contributed articles to various journals and a chapter to *Workshop 2: Beyond the Basal* (Nancie Atwell, Ed., Heinemann, 1990). She has worked in public schools with practicing teachers to develop curriculum and explore teaching practices and is currently working with prospective teachers to explore ways they might best facilitate students' literacy development. Cyrene and her husband, Jim, are parents to a son and daughter and enjoy coastal life in downeast Maine.